I0494253

Collaborative Clinical Supervision

Collaborative Clinical Supervision

Principles and Practices to Foster Development

Edward A. Johnson

BUSINESS EXPERT PRESS

Leader in applied, concise business books

Collaborative Clinical Supervision:
Principles and Practices to Foster Development

Copyright © Business Expert Press, LLC, 2026

Cover design by Edward A. Johnson

Interior design by Exeter Premedia Services Private Ltd., Chennai, India

All rights reserved. No part of this publication may be reproduced, stored in a retrieval system, or transmitted in any form or by any means—electronic, mechanical, photocopy, recording, or any other—except for brief quotations, not exceeding 400 words, without the prior permission of the publisher.

First published in 2026 by
Business Expert Press, LLC
222 East 46th Street, New York, NY 10017
www.businessexpertpress.com

ISBN-13: 978-1-63742-936-5 (paperback)
ISBN-13: 978-1-63742-937-2 (e-book)

Business Expert Press Healthcare Management Collection

First edition: 2026

10 9 8 7 6 5 4 3 2 1

EU SAFETY REPRESENTATIVE
Mare Nostrum Group B.V.
Doelen 72
4831 GR Breda
The Netherlands
gpsr@mare-nostrum.co.uk

Description

Collaborative Clinical Supervision: Principles and Practices to Foster Development provides new and practicing supervisors with best-practice guidance on how to supervise effectively by orienting supervision to three priorities:

• Attending to the supervisory relationship,
• Using experiential learning methods, and
• Implementing a clear, organized approach to supervision.

A primary theme is on developing a positive, trusting, and collaborative supervisory relationship as a "safe base" for promoting supervisee growth and navigating the inevitable tensions in supervision.

The author succinctly shares how to:

• Define supervision and review its effectiveness.
• Describe professional competencies and their development in supervision.
• Navigate the key phases of supervision collaboratively.

Collaborative Clinical Supervision: Principles and Practices to Foster Development incorporates current supervision research findings and includes sections on broaching cultural differences, working with supervisees who require accommodations, and approaching difficult conversations with supervisees. Each chapter concludes with questions for reflection to help supervisors integrate their own experiences of supervision with the guidance presented.

Written in an inviting conversational tone, the book draws on the author's experience to illustrate helpful ways to accomplish the goals of supervision and avoid pitfalls.

Contents

Preface

I am excited to share *Collaborative Clinical Supervision: Principles and Practices to Foster Development* with you, which updates and extends my earlier book, *Working Together in Clinical Supervision* (E. A. Johnson, 2017). The goal, then as now, is to provide a brief, practical guidebook to complement more comprehensive supervision textbooks. In it, the reader receives guidance on navigating psychotherapy supervision, and how to manage some of the problems that can emerge along the way with specific strategies. Students taking a course in supervision or those engaging in supervised supervision will find the book helpful as will more seasoned supervisors who wish to acquaint themselves with new skills and ideas to update their supervision practice.

I have adopted a personal voice in parts of this book that speaks to you directly from my thirty years of experience as a supervisor and teacher of clinical supervision in courses, practica, and workshops. The recommendations and supervisory experiences I have included illustrate widely agreed-upon principles, practices, and supervision research. The book includes the most recent findings and perspectives from the supervision literature and reflects the collective wisdom about how to practice supervision as gathered in best practice guidelines and ethical principles for supervision. Thanks to Scott Isenberg and Charlene Kronstedt of BEP for their support, and to Dhinesh and the team at Kriyadocs for their work to prepare the text for publication. I also wish to thank my writing group members Moira Somers, Mira Brancu, and David Kloak for their writerly wisdom and encouragement. For their helpful comments on an earlier draft of the book, I am deeply grateful to my colleagues Don Stewart, Marjory Phillips, and Jen Theule, and my student, Hope Hutchings. Finally, I am especially thankful for the support and feedback offered by my wife, Leslie Johnson, to whom I dedicate this book.

CHAPTER 1

Supervision's Importance, Purpose, and Impact

The foundational premise of this book is that developing and maintaining a positive supervisory relationship is the key to successful supervision. My overall aim is to provide usable guidance on how to build trust, safety, and openness in the supervisory relationship to facilitate achieving the three primary goals of supervision, namely, to educate and evaluate supervisees, ensure their clients' welfare, and help them cope with the emotional demands of clinical work. The book's six chapters are organized as follows. Chapter 1 defines supervision and summarizes the research on its efficacy. Chapter 2 describes what competencies are and how to promote competency development in supervisees. Chapter 3 discusses how to establish a positive working alliance at the outset of a new supervision relationship by clarifying the roles and responsibilities of supervisor and supervisee, collaboratively setting goals, acknowledging differences, and initiating an open, mutually respectful dialogue. Chapter 4 describes effective strategies for achieving the three goals of supervision at different stages of supervising a course of psychotherapy. Chapter 5 identifies common problems that can occur in supervision and how they can be addressed, including how to approach a difficult conversation. Chapter 6 discusses how to conclude supervision with fair and accurate evaluation procedures, gatekeeping when necessary, and procedures for overseeing client termination and the closure of client files.

A few words are necessary to establish the scope and context of what follows. This book describes individual, rather than triadic or group supervision, which has a more complex dynamic than I have space to address. My focus is on supervision in the context of a course of individual adult psychotherapy, though many of the principles and practices discussed are applicable to other forms of clinical work. No specific model of therapy is assumed; rather, the guidance is intended to be useful across diverse therapeutic and supervisory orientations. Also, while the primary audience for the book is professional psychology supervisors, much of the material will be relevant to supervisors in related professions of social work, psychiatry, occupational therapy, and nursing.

The Importance of Supervision: A Personal Anecdote

The value of supervision as a professional relationship was first brought home to me in a powerful way during my residency year, ironically by its absence. I was excited to begin that pivotal year of my professional development as a clinical psychologist. Having relocated to a new city and province, I was anxious to get oriented to the residency and to meet my first clinical supervisor, who would oversee my work on an acute inpatient mental health ward, my first such experience.

To my great surprise, however, I learned on day one that my supervisor was on holiday and would not be back for three weeks! The residency director's assurance that a temporary supervisor, who worked in a different part of the hospital, would be available for consultation in the interval felt anything but reassuring. A note of panic crept in: "What will I do? What am I supposed to do? How do I do it?"

Residency being new to me, I supposed that this must be how things are done. After an initial meeting with my temporary supervisor, who seemed equally uncertain about what to do with me, I decided to turn for more immediate guidance to the warm and welcoming clinician (a non-psychologist) who worked in the office next to mine. In the absence of other supervisory or collegial supports, I spent my lunchtime and breaks every day with my adopted mentor. So began my understanding of the ward.

Little did I realize—until my primary supervisor returned—how far my thinking about my role had drifted into this clinician's idiosyncratic perspective. To cope with an unfamiliar and complex multidisciplinary hospital system, in the absence of a solid orientation and the guidance of an involved and available supervisor within my profession, I sought direction from a well-meaning, but unintentionally misleading, source. More than that, the commencement of my supervision was now more complicated than it would normally have been. Upon his return, my supervisor needed to not only create a connection to me, but to wean me from the influence of his colleague. Fortunately, my supervisor was able to accomplish this task and help get me on track for what was ultimately an excellent training experience.

In hindsight, this episode illustrates several key elements of supervision. First, it underscores how grounding supervision is, especially at the outset of a new training experience. Without it, I felt lost and desperate for professional guidance to navigate my new environment. I also experienced a relational void. I missed having a trusted and concerned mentor looking out for my best interests who had a stake in my well-being. Clearly, what I needed at that juncture had as much to do with attachment processes as with professional oversight and guidance. The whole experience illustrates how supervision encompasses a multi-faceted relationship that touches not just on professional roles, but also on the personal and interpersonal spheres, the cognitive and emotional realms. Consequently, in this book, I provide guidance on how supervisors and supervisees can develop a positive working relationship that meets the diverse needs of all those affected by supervision: supervisee, supervisor, and their clients.

Once my supervision truly got underway, I observed how my supervisor skillfully integrated me into the work of the multidisciplinary team, mentored me regarding its dynamics, sheltered me from inter-professional conflicts, and capably advised me on my clinical work. Supervision plays an essential role in helping supervisees navigate within complex institutional and inter-professional environments. Having experienced, in quick succession, first the absence and then the helpful presence of effective supervision, I have no doubt about how much it can make a difference. Later in this chapter, I review evidence of supervision's impact.

Why then did I initially consider my colleague a reasonable substitute for my absent supervisor? In part, it was because I did not have a clear grasp of the scope and functions of the supervisor role and the purposes of supervision despite having received a good deal of it beforehand. This is less surprising when you consider supervision's complexity.

More Than Meets the Eye: Mapping the Complexity of Clinical Supervision

Supervision, especially when it is working well, appears deceptively simple. This is partly because, on the surface, it involves a familiar human relationship of teacher and student. Underneath this well-understood aspect, however, lies a complex web of roles and functions that are intricately interconnected. If not clarified, such complexity can create *role ambiguity* for supervisees that may leave them uncertain of their responsibilities, contribute to conflict in the supervisory relationship, and undermine supervisee engagement (Ladany and Friedlander 1995; Min and Kim 2024; Olk and Friedlander 1992). To reduce role ambiguity and the potential for conflict, supervisors and supervisees need to have a shared understanding of what supervision is and how it works. Supervisors can help accomplish this by developing a clear mental map of supervision and communicating this to their supervisees. As a result, both gain a sense of predictability, trust, and control in their work together. Our mental map of supervision begins with clarifying what supervision is.

Defining Supervision

Many people use the term supervision quite loosely to refer to what are in practice distinct professional relationships. So, let's begin by clarifying what supervision is not. Supervision is not *peer consultation*. In peer consultation, one practitioner consults another about a client, and receives advice or guidance that looks like supervision. What distinguishes it from supervision, however, is that the client is not the consultant's responsibility; they bear no legal or professional responsibility for the client's well-being, nor do they have any evaluative or gatekeeping responsibility for the consultee. As a result, the consultant's guidance is only advisory. In fact, the entire relationship is voluntary. Supervision is obligatory, however, because supervisees are not sufficiently competent, nor legally qualified, to practice independently. Consequently, the client is the supervisor's professional responsibility; supervisees assess and treat clients at the direction and discretion of the supervisor. That said, supervisors may at times choose to entrust supervisees with a high degree of autonomy, in effect enacting the role of a consultant, to promote the supervisee's sense of professional responsibility and agency toward the client.

Supervision is also not equivalent to *mentoring*. Mentoring and mentorship commonly refer to "excellent developmental relationships in academic settings" (W. B. Johnson and Griffin 2025, p. 19) in which a more experienced faculty member acts as a role model, guide, or teacher of a mentee (a student or less experienced professional) to facilitate their career development. Mentoring is not primarily focused on the supervisee's work with clients under the supervisor's care, nor is it obligatory or evaluative. Supervisors may at times adopt the role of mentor, such as when offering advice about training opportunities or career pathways, and this can be helpful in developing a trainee's sense of professional identity. Some caution, however, that if mentoring is undertaken uncritically, it can contribute to professional self-reproduction (Manathunga 2007).

Finally, supervision is not *therapy*, and supervisors must not provide therapy to supervisees. That said, supervisors should at times adopt the stance of a counselor to help supervisees work through their feelings and attitudes toward their clients (e.g., countertransference, vicarious trauma), both to enhance their effectiveness with them and to help prevent supervisee burnout (P. Martin et al. 2021).

Now, let's consider what supervision is and does. Supervision may be defined as the:

> formal provision, by approved supervisors, of a relationship-based education and training that is work-focused and which manages, supports, develops and evaluates the work of colleague/s....The main methods that supervisors use are corrective feedback on the supervisees' performance, teaching, and collaborative goal-setting. The objectives of supervision are "normative" (e.g., case management and quality control issues), "restorative" (e.g., encouraging emotional experiencing and processing, to aid coping and recovery), and "formative" (e.g., maintaining and facilitating the supervisees' competence, capability, and general effectiveness). (Milne 2007, as cited in Milne and Watkins 2014, p. 4.)

Let's unpack the main elements of this definition. The "formal provision by approved supervisors" means that supervision is an explicitly contracted arrangement—not *ad hoc*. It typically involves ongoing, regular meetings that span the duration of the training activity—not a one-off. It is sanctioned by one or more relevant organization(s), which might include a professional training program, licensing body, or an institution that approves the supervisor to supervise. I consider the training, skills, and experience necessary to supervise competently in Chapter 2.

Supervision is *relationship-based*. Milne (2007) observes that supervision is "confidential and highly collaborative, being founded on a learning alliance and featuring (e.g.,) participative decision making and shared agenda setting; and therapeutic interpersonal qualities, such as empathy and warmth" (p. 440). These relational elements distinguish supervision from other forms of learning, which can be impersonal (e.g., lectures) or independent (e.g., solitary study). The relational aspects of supervision are explored in Chapters 3–6.

Milne's definition specifies that supervision is *work focused*, having an applied focus on aiding a supervisee's work with their clients. It typically does this by addressing topics and material selected by the supervisee with the supervisor adding professional and ethical/regulatory knowledge and skills as needed. The focus on the trainee's clinical work also defines a useful boundary when considering whether the nature of the activity is supervisory or is crossing a boundary into another type of relationship (e.g., therapeutic, friendship, intimate, exploitative). I address the boundaries of the supervisory relationship in Chapters 3–6.

Finally, the phrase "manages, supports, develops and evaluates the work of colleague/s" speaks to how the supervisor achieves the normative, formative, and restorative functions of supervision (Proctor 1986). The normative function ensures clients receive services that meet professional standards (norms) and are not harmed. The formative function develops (forms) and evaluates the supervisee's competencies and ability to continue learning independently. The restorative function facilitates the supervisee's emotional processing of the challenging aspects of clinical work to restore effectiveness and reduce the likelihood of burnout. Although all three functions are essential to supervision, the normative and restorative functions often receive much less attention in supervision than the formative function (Bradley and Becker 2021). In Chapters 3 and 4, I discuss how to address all three functions in supervision.

Supervisor and Supervisee Roles and Responsibilities

The above definition is consistent with other writings in the supervision literature regarding the supervisor's role. Specifically, there is a clear consensus internationally that supervisors bear clinical, ethical, and legal responsibility for their supervisees' work (Thomas 2014) and that ensuring the welfare of the client is supervision's overriding purpose (Milne and Watkins 2014). Enhancing client welfare requires a collaborative effort between supervisor and supervisee that depends on both parties forming and maintaining a strong supervisory relationship in which the qualities of mutual respect, openness, commitment, and support are present. When supervisees feel a safe, trustworthy supervisory relationship is in place, supervisors can more effectively undertake the educational and evaluative components of their role. These teaching and feedback functions need to be tailored to the unique goals, needs, and requirements of each supervisee, including issues of culture and diversity (Beinart 2014; Mitchell and Butler 2021).

For their part, supervisees are responsible for following the guidance of their supervisors and for honestly and faithfully reporting to supervisors about their work with clients, raising any concerns for client welfare in a timely way. More generally, supervisees can enhance the supervisory relationship by being open to learning, demonstrating enthusiasm and commitment, adopting a proactive stance, working hard on their own development, and making a productive contribution to the clinical service (Falender and Shafranske 2012). Both supervisor and supervisee need to engage in the supervisory relationship and with the client(s) in a respectful and ethical manner.

Returning to the dilemma I faced when I began my residency, had I better understood just what supervision is fully meant to be, including the roles and responsibilities of supervisor and supervisee, I might have better appreciated that the other clinician could not possibly substitute for my absent supervisor. I also would have grasped that arranging proper supervision was not up to me, but rather was the responsibility of the residency.

Supervisory Complexity: Different for Supervisors and Supervisees

One further twist on the complexity of supervision is that it differs for supervisors and supervisees. For supervisors, complexity arises from the fact that supervision can simultaneously involve work with multiple supervisees, each of whom may be providing treatment to multiple clients, who are each likely dealing with multiple distinct issues. For each supervisee, the supervisor will need to consider the needs and well-being of each of their clients, as well as the supervisee's level of professional development, competencies, learning goals, and personal responses to clients. All these considerations must be kept in mind as the supervisor undertakes the tasks of monitoring, guiding, supporting, informing, and evaluating the supervisee's work. Becoming an effective supervisor will require you to develop efficient and effective strategies for taming this complexity. Chapters 3–5 describe essential methods that will facilitate your work as a supervisor.

From the supervisee's perspective, the complexity of supervision emerges over time as supervisees gain experience with different supervisors in different settings. Supervision, as delivered by one supervisor versus another, may be experienced as a very different enterprise. Each supervisor has a different therapeutic orientation, teaching style, personality, way of communicating, and set of expectations for their supervisees. As well, each practice setting has its own specific requirements. As a result, even advanced supervisees can feel like novices again when commencing with a new supervisor and setting. The challenge for supervisees in the face of this variability is to accept it as part of the learning experience (and to not rigidly expect consistency) and to focus on taking what is most useful from each supervisor and training experience to flexibly develop a coherent set of competencies that reflect their unique personality, strengths, and interests.

Understanding that each of your supervisees will approach your supervision in this manner will help you appreciate how they appraise your role and influence. On the one hand, it can be humbling to know that your supervision won't necessarily be the final word on how your supervisee learns to engage in professional practice. On the other hand, knowing this also takes some pressure off; you don't have to teach everything to your supervisee. A further challenge is that advanced trainees may sometimes have developed habits of thought and behavior from previous training experiences that may compete with the approach you are trying to teach. Encouraging them to be open to what you have to offer, while managing your own expectations of them, will help both of you avoid potential conflict and get the most from such a situation. Finally, it can be helpful for supervisors to address common factors (e.g., the therapeutic alliance, empathy, acceptance, and client preferences and feedback) that transcend specific therapy orientations as a frequent touch point in supervision to help supervisees integrate present with past and future training experiences.

Supervision Is Necessary—But Is It Effective? A Brief Overview of Supervision Research

Having defined what supervision is—and is not—this is a good time to ask a few fundamental questions: Why do we need supervision at all? What's the rationale for it? From a cost-benefit perspective, it is an expensive undertaking that consumes many hours of time from highly trained personnel. To illustrate, by the time the average clinical psychologist becomes licensed for independent practice in North America, they will have received well over 300 hours of supervision. Is all this supervision really necessary, and if so, is it effective?

The necessity of supervision follows from the fact that prior to becoming licensed for independent practice, psychologists-in-training and other mental health professional trainees are not yet competent to practice independently. By law, trainees are required to have their clinical work supervised by a licensed practitioner whose job is to protect the help-seeking public from possible harms by monitoring the work of trainees and developing their competence. But that still leaves unanswered whether supervision is effective in doing so.

Before we can answer that question, we must address another: Effective at what? Recall that supervision has three primary functions: normative (client welfare), formative (supervisee learning), and restorative (supervisee well-being). In the remainder of this chapter, I will summarize what we know about the impact of supervision on these three functions.

However, a word of caution is in order. The reader who is familiar with the voluminous psychotherapy outcome literature will be disappointed to discover that the literature on supervision outcomes is much more limited, both in number and quality (Watkins 2020b; Watkins et al. 2021).

One reason for this scarcity is that supervision effectiveness research is methodologically difficult. The difficulty arises from supervision's hierarchical, three-level structure, wherein each supervisor (level 1) typically oversees the work of multiple supervisees (level 2) who each see multiple clients (level 3). This nested structure creates dependencies within each lower level, which ideally should be accounted for in the research design and statistically controlled using multilevel modeling (Kahn 2011). That is, each supervisor's trainees share a common environment that is different from the environment experienced by the trainees of a different supervisor. Consequently, the trainees of one supervisor will tend to engage with their clients in ways that are more similar to each other than to the trainees of another supervisor. Likewise, the clients of a given trainee will experience therapy in ways that will be more similar to each other than to the experience of clients of other trainees. To control for these nested dependencies, multilevel modeling requires that sample sizes be sufficiently large to produce unbiased estimates of statistical parameters, ideally by increasing sample size at the highest level (i.e., at the supervisor level) (Maas and Hox 2005). Furthermore, the number of supervisors required is greater when the magnitude of between-supervisor effects is smaller (Schiefele et al. 2017). Thus, to have a large enough sample to reliably estimate supervisor effects on client outcomes, a researcher might need upward of 100 supervisors to each supervise 3 or more supervisees for a total of 300 supervisees, who each see 5 therapy clients for a total of 1,500 clients (Kahn 2011). Such a large undertaking is difficult to achieve as it would require a multisite collaboration with all the preparation and coordination across sites that entails (Watkins et al. 2021).

Another limitation on supervision research is that the strongest study design—the controlled trial—is simply not possible for studying supervision in the context of training. It would be unethical to deprive trainees (and their clients) of supervision to study its effects. This means that controlled trials of supervised versus unsupervised practitioners must be limited to qualified practitioners. Since qualified practitioners are presumably competent, the impact of supervision (relative to no supervision) on qualified practitioners is likely to underestimate what would be seen with unqualified trainees.

Despite these limitations, supervision research is essential for establishing supervision's validity and utility. Many of the findings described below help clarify what makes supervision successful. This information will be further developed and made actionable throughout this book.

Effects of Supervision on Clients: Normative Outcomes

The overriding purpose of supervision is to safeguard the well-being of the client, making client well-being arguably the *acid test* of supervision effectiveness (Ellis and Ladany 1997; Milne 2014). Despite this, relatively little research has been conducted on supervision's impact on client outcome, and what has been done often suffers from poor methodological quality (Watkins et al. 2021).

Only one study has used a controlled trial to examine the effects of psychotherapy supervision on client outcomes. Bambling et al. (2006) randomly assigned qualified master's-level therapists to supervision or no supervision conditions. Therapists in both conditions used a problem-solving therapy manual to guide treatment for depressed clients. All supervisors were trained to follow a common supervision manual. The results of the study showed that compared to the clients of unsupervised therapists, supervised therapists' clients reported stronger alliances with their therapists throughout treatment and greater symptom reduction at the end of treatment. They were also more likely to remain in treatment and to evaluate treatment favorably. The fact that supervision had a clear benefit to clients on a range of indicators is impressive, especially since the therapists were all qualified and used a common therapy manual. Nonetheless, this is but one study, and without replication and extension to other populations and approaches, we cannot draw any firm conclusions.

Another way to evaluate the impact of supervision on client outcomes is to use a correlational approach to estimate the magnitude of between-supervisor differences on client outcomes. Such research seeks to answer the question of whether some supervisors are more effective than others in promoting positive client outcomes and to estimate the size of such supervisor effects. Long before research on supervisor effects was carried out, Wampold and Holloway (1997) cautioned that supervisor effects would likely be small. They reasoned that any supervisor effect must first have an impact on supervisees, who, in turn, must transmit that effect to clients. Because supervisees will inevitably show variability (a) in their response to supervisors, and (b) in how they transmit supervisory influences on clients, supervisee variability will inevitably dilute any impact supervisors have on clients. Early studies found moderate-sized supervisor effects on clients' treatment outcomes (Callahan et al. 2009; Wrape et al. 2015). However, these studies had small sample sizes that precluded the use of multilevel modeling. Larger studies, which used multilevel modeling to control nesting effects, have found only small between-supervisor effects on client outcomes (Rousmaniere et al. 2016; Whipple et al. 2020).

Because supervision's impact is filtered through the quality of the supervisory relationship, it may be that the quality of the supervisory relationship carries more impact than the supervisor's personal qualities or style considered in isolation. A meta-analytic review of 12 studies found support for this hypothesis (Keum and Wang 2021). Specifically, the authors found that on average, supervision relationship process variables (as rated by supervisees) accounted for 6 percent of the variance in therapy outcomes (as rated by clients), which is a small but meaningful effect. Subsequently, two other studies have added support for this association. First, in a large study of novice therapists, DePue et al. (2022) found that the strength of the supervisory alliance as rated by therapists had a small but positive effect on client outcomes as rated by clients. Second, in a longitudinal study of novice Chinese counseling trainees, Li et al. (2022) found that the clients of supervisory dyads that exhibited a pattern of high, stable, and mildly increasing levels of supervisory alliance strength as reported by therapists (relative to the clients of supervisory dyads who exhibited more unstable alliance trajectories) reported greater symptom relief. Taken together, we can tentatively conclude that a positive supervisory relationship promotes positive client outcomes.

Finally, some have hypothesized that the quality of the supervisory relationship will have an influence on clients through its impact on the quality of the therapeutic alliance. The therapeutic alliance is the best predictor of client outcome and is a key consideration in all major therapy orientations (Flückiger et al. 2018). In their systematic review, Kühne et al. (2019) found evidence from several studies that supported a positive relationship between supervision and measures of the therapeutic alliance. In a subsequent study, DePue et al. (2022) also found support for this association, but only when the therapeutic alliance was rated by the therapist, not when rated by the client. This rater effect was also likely at work in a study by Teichman et al. (2023), which found large associations between supervisees' ratings of the supervisory relationship and their rating of supervision's impact on their client's outcome and the overall impact of therapy. Accordingly, these findings must be interpreted with caution.

Overall, what we can tentatively conclude is that, pending more and better-quality research, supervision has a small positive effect on client outcome. Thus, supervision is not only legally and ethically necessary, but good supervision also likely improves client welfare.

Effects of Supervision on Supervisees: Formative Outcomes

The majority of supervision research has examined its impact on supervisees' formative outcomes concerning supervisee learning and development. Overall, this body of research indicates that better supervision has a positive impact on enhancing supervisee confidence and skills. Reflecting this impact, qualified psychotherapists and psychologists-in-training alike rate supervision as a powerful influence on their psychotherapy practice (J. M. Cook et al. 2009; Liao et al. 2022; Lucock et al. 2006; Safran, Abreu et al. 2011).

In a meta-analysis of 27 studies, Park et al. (2019) found that more positive supervisory relationships, as rated by the supervisee, were highly associated with greater satisfaction with supervision. Breaking the supervisory working alliance down into its three main components revealed that a positive supervisory bond, as well as agreement on the goals and tasks of supervision, contributes to satisfaction with supervision. These findings suggest that when supervision is experienced as a safe, positive relationship, the educative learning opportunities reflected in the goals and tasks of supervision are more effective in promoting supervisee growth and development, as some have hypothesized (e.g., Ellis and Ladany 1997; Goodyear 2014).

A systematic review of 17 studies by Lohani and Sharma (2023) found positive impacts of supervision on supervisee self-efficacy. That is, better supervision promoted greater supervisee confidence in their therapeutic skills. The authors suggested that the use of goal setting allowed supervisees to build their confidence by working in a focused way in supervision on particular skills and to use supervisory support and feedback to further hone their development. A subsequent study of supervisee self-efficacy by Lo and Thompson (2025) found that the impact of supervisory educative methods such as reflective questioning, role modeling, and providing formative feedback on supervisees' development of professional self-efficacy was mediated by the extent to which supervisees perceived supervision as providing a *safe base*. Additionally, this study showed that the degree of supervisor commitment (e.g., enthusiasm for supervision) mediated the impact of educative methods on supervisees' self-efficacy and rapport-building abilities. That is, the quality of the supervision relationship served to filter the impact of educative activities on supervisee skill development. These findings are supported and extended in a recent study showing that higher supervisee' ratings of supervisor competence predicted higher levels of supervisee professional competence (Davis-Wright et al. 2025).

A study by Bambling and King (2014) shed light on how supervisors' interpersonal skills and the quality of the supervisory alliance each contribute to supervisee learning. Their study of 40 supervisors and 50 supervisees found that the strength of the supervisory alliance strongly predicted supervisee learning. The study also found that supervisors' self-rated interpersonal skills predicted the quality of the supervisory alliance as rated by supervisees. In particular, three specific interpersonal skills were associated with stronger supervisory alliances, namely emotional sensitivity, social expressivity, and social control. The authors suggest that supervisors who are emotionally sensitive are likely to pick up on subtle nonverbal cues from their supervisees, to decode the feelings underlying them, and respond to them in supervision. Supervisors with social expressivity skills are verbally fluent and able to initiate conversations and elicit supervisee engagement as a way of promoting exploration and growth.

Social control refers to the ability to present oneself in a tactful, socially adept, and confident manner. Supervisors with this ability can responsively adjust their style to work with different supervisees while maintaining the ability to provide structure and direction in supervision.

Taken together, the findings underscore the value of building a strong supervisory relationship and using effective interpersonal teaching methods for promoting supervisee development.

Effects of Supervision on Supervisees: Restorative Outcomes

Counseling distressed persons, although often rewarding, also brings with it many stressors that can make it emotionally demanding, even overwhelming at times. Therapists report high levels of stress from working with clients who are acutely or chronically suicidal or depressed (Van der Hallen 2023), verbally or physically aggressive (van Leeuwen and Harte 2017), or traumatized (Pirelli et al. 2020). The fact that counseling is a sedentary, seated activity means that over time it can result in deconditioning and the loss of vigor necessary for full mental engagement (Panahi and Tremblay 2018). Finally, clinicians are regularly exposed, through their work with computers and smartphones, to the internet and social networks. Potential consequences of excess time spent on the internet and social networks may impact well-being (Huang 2022; Small et al. 2020) and productivity (Duke and Montag 2017).

The difficulties described above collectively contribute to high levels of burnout among clinicians from a variety of mental health disciplines (Aguglia et al. 2020; Råbu et al. 2016), including those who practice counseling or therapy (Westwood et al. 2017), with younger therapists reporting higher levels of burnout (Van Hoy and Rzeszutek 2022). Burnout also affects therapists in training (Hunt et al. 2025; Kaeding et al. 2017) who report emotional burdens and heightened stress of clinical training from the outset of their training (Ruiz et al. 2019; Tiet et al. 2024) at levels comparable to those reported by working clinicians (Warlick et al. 2025). Burnout clearly affects the personal well-being of the clinician. However, it can also erode clinicians' therapeutic effectiveness, as well as their ethics and professionalism, with potentially serious impacts on their clients' well-being (Simionato et al. 2019; Yang and Hayes 2020).

Research has shown that clinical supervision can play a useful role in reducing the prevalence of burnout in therapists. In a study of 298 qualified psychological therapists in the United Kingdom, higher quality supervision, as reflected in feelings of trust, safety, and openness toward the supervisor and supervision, was associated with lower levels of disengagement, a component of burnout involving feelings of disinterest, disconnection, or dislike toward one's work (J. Johnson et al. 2020). Also, receiving more frequent supervision is associated with lower levels of burnout (Forshammar Geisler et al. 2025; P. Martin et al. 2021; Westwood et al. 2017) and higher levels of well-being (Van Hoy and Rzeszutek 2022).

Chapter Summary

Supervision is a complex, multifaceted activity that functions to ensure the well-being of clients through the collaborative efforts of supervisor and supervisee. It involves normative (client welfare), formative (supervisee learning), and restorative (supervisee well-being) functions and is likely beneficial to clients and supervisees, although more research is needed to further support and understand how this occurs. Supervisor and supervisee play complementary roles in this process. While supervisors are responsible for guiding and overseeing the course of treatment and developing and evaluating supervisee competencies, supervisees are active collaborators in the process as they deliver treatment, report on therapy processes and outcomes, set goals, process their experience, and engage in new learning.

Questions for Review and Reflection

1. Reflecting on your own experience of receiving or providing supervision, to what extent do you agree with the statement in the text that "supervision encompasses a multifaceted relationship that touches not just on professional roles, but also on the personal, and interpersonal spheres, the cognitive and the emotional realms"?
2. When considering the multiple roles and functions of clinical supervision, many people are struck by its complexity. What aspects of supervision's complexity are more salient to you now?

3. Supervision is a *relationship-based* form of education and training. How is this different from non-relationship-based forms of education such as solitary learning? What in your experience makes for a positive supervisory relationship?

4. Thus far, supervision has been shown to have only a modest impact on client outcomes. How do you explain this finding?

5. Supervision has been shown to have positive impacts on supervisees' learning. What in your experience of supervision has helped make it a good learning experience?

6. Supervision can play a restorative role that can help supervisees avoid burnout by helping them process their emotional reactions to clients. Have you experienced restorative supervision? If so, was it helpful?

CHAPTER 2

Supervision's Foundations: Competency, Collaboration, and Effectiveness

Now that you know what your supervisory role and responsibilities are, this chapter examines the competencies needed for you to fulfill them, as well as the competencies that you will be seeking to develop in your supervisees. First, however, the chapter begins with some background on why competencies, as an explicit model for approaching professional education, came to replace the apprenticeship—an implicit model. This is followed by a discussion of the nature of competence, competencies and capability. This sets the stage for understanding what functional and foundational competencies are and how they develop through supervised training and practice.

The Apprenticeship Model

Supervision has been described as the most impactful element in the professional education and training of mental health professionals, its *signature pedagogy* (Bernard and Goodyear 2019; Shulman 2005). Supervision is influential in part because of its structure as an apprenticeship in which supervisor and supervisee share an intimate working relationship where the supervisee learns by doing and by observing the supervisor. The supervisor looms large for supervisees because their clinical experience and expertise make their guidance authoritative, their feedback is at times intensely personal, and their evaluative/gatekeeping role invests them with great power. Thankfully, supervision's immense influence is usually experienced very positively by supervisees (Orlinsky and Rønnestad 2005). At its best, the supervisor's impact is transformative (Watkins 2020a).

As I discuss further in Chapter 5, supervision can also be ineffective (Ladany et al. 2013), unhelpful (Chircop Coleiro et al. 2023), inadequate, and even harmful (Ellis et al. 2014, 2017). The effects of unhelpful supervision can be to create negative thoughts, fear of criticism, and psychological withdrawal from supervision. Harmful supervision can undermine supervisee confidence and self-esteem, increase self-doubt, anxiety, and feelings of helplessness (Chircop Coleiro et al. 2023; McNamara et al. 2017).

The profound impact of a supervisor, whether positive or negative, can persist for long periods when it is internalized in the form of a supervisor representation as an enduring mental image. This image can include sensory traces (e.g., visualizing the supervisor's face, hearing their voice), cognitions (e.g., memories of attitudes, strategies, or guidance), and affective influences (e.g., calming, encouraging, criticizing). Supervisees report that such supervisor representations influence their practice as therapists (Geller et al. 2010; Knox et al. 2014; Watkins 2018). It seems likely that supervisory representations will also have an enduring effect on the attitudes, beliefs, and habits that you hold about supervision. Unprocessed, these impacts have the potential to unconsciously influence how you approach your work as a supervisor. To help you process your supervisory experiences, I invite you to engage in the following exercise as a starting point for your development as a supervisor. The intention behind this reflection exercise is to ensure that the impact of supervisory modeling you have experienced becomes more than an uncritical basis for imitation and instead becomes one of critical evaluation and thoughtful uptake of desired behaviors or principles.

Exercise: Reflect on Positive and Negative Models of Supervision

Recognizing that supervisory relationships are complex and may include both helpful and unhelpful elements, and that even good, well-intentioned supervisors may unwittingly engage in harmful supervisory acts (Ammirati and Kaslow 2017), this exercise asks you to identify helpful and unhelpful or harmful actions or approaches you have encountered from previous supervisors. Think of two to four supervisors for this exercise. Starting with the first supervisor, take a few minutes to recollect your experience and write down your answers to the following questions (using the summary table below) about the positive or helpful impacts they had on your professional development:

- What did this supervisor do that was most helpful or effective?
  - How did these experiences make you feel at the time?
  - What lasting impact did they have?
- How did your supervisor bring about the helpful result?
  - Was it through teaching techniques like modeling, Socratic questioning, or feedback, or professional self-disclosure?
  - Or was it through personal qualities of warmth and kindness, or attentiveness and interest?
  - Or perhaps was it by cultivating a positive, safe, trusting supervisory relationship?
- Which of your supervisor's skills, attitudes, or knowledge would you like to emulate in your work as a supervisor?
- What would you choose to do differently from your supervisor?

Now consider the same questions concerning any unhelpful or harmful supervision experiences that occurred during your work with this same supervisor. Once you have answered these questions for each supervisor, carefully review what you have written and consider:

- What stands out to you about what makes supervision helpful or unhelpful?
- What general principles are involved, and what conclusions can you draw?
- How will you seek to embody the helpful qualities or principles you identified as helpful in your own work as a supervisor?
- How will you avoid exhibiting the unhelpful or harmful qualities?

(Continued)

Reflection activity summary

	Supervisor 1	Supervisor 2	Supervisor 3	Supervisor 4
Helpful/positive actions/ strategies				
Impact				
How accomplished?				
Aspects to emulate? Unhelpful/harmful actions/ strategies				
Impact				
How accomplished?				
Aspects to avoid?				
Conclusion(s)				

Limitations of the Apprenticeship Model

Prior to this century and the proliferation of courses, books, and workshops on supervision, most supervisors were not explicitly trained in supervision but rather expected to acquire the necessary skills through osmosis, simply from having been supervised. To call this apprenticeship approach to training supervisors a model is generous, insofar as it implies there was a plan or forethought involved. In fact, however, the apprenticeship method of supervisor training was simply an expedient based on the hope that mere exposure to different styles of supervision would somehow prepare one to supervise, an idea Falender and Shafranske (2023) rightly label a myth. As a result, ill-prepared beginning supervisors often felt like impostors, burdened by self-doubt even as they felt obligated to ease their supervisee's self-doubts (Thériault and Gazzola 2018).

Like most psychologists of my generation, I received no instruction during graduate school or residency on how to conduct supervision (E. A. Johnson and Stewart 2000; Thériault and Gazzola 2019). Thus, when given my first opportunity to conduct supervision (which, in retrospect, was actually peer consultation), I felt completely unprepared. During my residency, the outpatient interdisciplinary team I was on would observe a team member conduct an intake interview with a new patient through a two-way mirror. After about 45 minutes, the interviewer would pause the interview and join the observing team to discuss the patient's diagnosis, conceptualization, and whether treatment should be offered. The director of the clinic, my supervisor, supervised these team discussions and directly questioned the interviewer. One day, following the pause in the interview, the director said to me as the interviewer made her way back to the observation room, "Ed, why don't you supervise today?". Even now, I can still recall feeling stunned, unprepared, and intimidated at the thought of supervising a colleague from a different discipline who had 25 years of clinical experience. After some frenzied internal scrambling to come up with a plan, I somehow got through that experience.

Likely, my supervisor assumed that, having experienced and observed his supervision of myself and others, I would have implicitly absorbed how to do it. The idea that serving as an apprentice to a practitioner prepares one to not only be a practitioner, but also a mentor and supervisor to future learners, is rooted in the concept of observational learning (also known as modeling) as a vicarious form of learning (Bandura 1997). While modeling can promote competency for relatively simple skills, its value is much more limited for learning a complex network of knowledge and skills such as those involved in supervision. Without explicit training in supervision, modeling and experience are insufficient for supervisor development (Pelling 2021; Worthington 1987).

Perhaps most importantly, modeling does not provide an explicit, comprehensive map of supervision. To learn how to be an effective supervisor, you need to know not only what the roles and functions of supervision are, as discussed in Chapter 1, but also understand the supervisory competencies you need to fulfill these requirements, and how to exercise them. In short, you need a mental model of what supervisors do and the skills to do it effectively. A big part of what you'll do as a supervisor is help develop your supervisees' competencies. Let us begin by understanding what competencies are.

Competence, Competencies, and Capability

Competence is the coordination and application of competencies. If that sounds circular, keep reading. By the end of this section, you should have a clearer understanding of how these two concepts are distinct but intertwined. Understanding these terms will yield a more detailed grasp of what it is we are trying to cultivate in supervision.

During the past few decades, recognition of the need for greater accountability in health care education and protection of the public led to a paradigm shift in professional training toward the development of competence. Competence may be defined as the intentional coordination and flexible application of professional knowledge, skills, attitudes, values, reasoning, reflection, judgment, and emotion in the practice of one's profession (Barnett et al. 2007; Epstein and Hundert 2002). Competence, as the demonstrable outcome of professional education and training, is increasingly valued and emphasized across health care professions including medicine (Carraccio et al. 2002; Hamza et al. 2023) and professional psychology, including by the American Psychological Association (APA) (APA Commission on Accreditation 2015) and the Canadian Psychological Association (CPA) (2023a) (Falender and Shafranske 2021).

Prior to the *competencies revolution*, standards for professional education exclusively focused on educational inputs as markers of professional readiness, such as number of practicum hours completed, years of study, or possession of a graduate degree. The assumption was that requiring all trainees to complete a consistent set of inputs would guarantee a consistent result of professional readiness. This uniform approach ignored the fact that trainees' learning needs differ and respond to educational inputs differently. That is, if graduating competent practitioners is the primary aim of professional education, this requires a fundamental reconceptualization of the purposes and methods of training and supervision (Gonsalvez and Calvert 2014).

Fundamentally, competence is the ability to carry out tasks and roles to an expected standard (Eraut and du Boulay 2000). This definition emphasizes how competence reflects the ability to meet the requirements of external, societally defined expectations of professionals. Competence can also be conceptualized as the possession of internalized qualities (or competencies), typically including relevant knowledge, skills, and attitudes that competent professionals possess, which permit the application of knowledge and skills to achieve expected standards of practice (International Standards Organisation 2012). According to Epstein and Hundert's (2002) influential definition, competence functions to address cognitive, integrative, and relational/communicative tasks in a humane, judicious fashion that reflects an appropriate background of professional, scientific, and moral development. Further, they note that: "Competence depends on habits of mind, including attentiveness, critical curiosity, self-awareness, and presence. Professional competence is developmental, impermanent and context dependent" (p. 227). Clearly, competence is more than technical proficiency in executing a particular skill. Rather, competent practice is nuanced, holistic, and responsive.

Competence depends on having mastered many smaller, more specific competencies and being able to flexibly integrate and apply them in a logical way to meet the requirements of given clinical circumstances. Competencies are the components that are integrated in competent performance and include knowledge, attitudes, skills, and values (Kaslow et al. 2009; Ridley et al. 2011). Within each health profession, there is broad agreement on the nature of the competencies required for professional practice as prescribed by various educational and regulatory bodies. For instance, the professional competencies identified within the accreditation standards for the American (APA 2015) and Canadian Psychological Associations (CPA 2023a) have a good deal of overlap (e.g., both specify supervision, intervention, assessment, as well as individual and cultural diversity as competency domains). However, such organizations also may enumerate slightly different sets of competencies. For instance, CPA uniquely identifies Indigenous interculturalism as a distinct competency area. Similarly, regulatory bodies within each jurisdiction (i.e., state or province) specify their own required competencies. Accordingly, it is imperative that supervisors be familiar with the specific competencies that they are expected to train and supervise for both educational and regulatory purposes.

Within each broad competency domain, such as intervention or supervision, many more specific competencies exist within it that have a hierarchical structure that can be likened to a mountain. At the top of a mountain is a high-level, more abstract domain, which is increasingly specified further down the mountain at lower levels with increasing concreteness. For instance, underlying the general intervention competency are various mid-level competencies such as intake interviewing. Intake interviewing requires mastery of still more specific lower-level competencies, including knowing how to greet the client, review the limits of confidentiality, obtain consent for the interview, and open the interview.

Similar competency mountains can be constructed for each functional competency domain, such as assessment, consultation, and supervision.

Continuing the mountain metaphor, the entire set of functional competencies can be likened to a mountain range where each competency domain represents a specific mountain within the range. Within a mountain range, each individual mountain is most distinct from the others at the peak. Beneath each peak, an ever-widening base eventually merges with those of adjacent mountains into a common underlying base for the range as a whole. Similarly, each functional competency is most distinct from the others when considered in its most condensed, abstract form, stripped of detail or context, typically identified only by a simple word or phrase such as intervention or assessment. As one descends from this abstract peak, the description of the underlying specific competencies that make up the general competency grows increasingly more specific, concrete, and detailed. At the lowest level of greatest specificity, many of these more specific skills also belong to other competency areas, much as each mountain merges into the next at the base. The entire set of global competencies expected of competent practitioners (e.g., as enumerated by accrediting, regulatory, or educational bodies) is akin to the whole mountain range.

Mapping Functional and Foundational Competencies With the Competencies Cube

Clearly, there are many competencies. To help organize our thinking about them, it is useful to distinguish functional from foundational competencies. I develop that distinction in this section and consider how the two types of competencies relate to one another and develop over the course of training. I conclude by considering how professionals develop capability by exercising their competencies in new contexts.

Functional competencies describe *what* a practitioner does (e.g., intervention), whereas *foundational* competencies describe *how* practitioners exercise functional competencies (e.g., ethically and as informed by evidence). For instance, in its accreditation standards, CPA (2023a) recognizes eight functional competencies (e.g., assessment, intervention, supervision) and eight foundational competencies (e.g., individual, social, and cultural diversity; professionalism). Each mental health profession has its own distinct set of functional and foundational competencies. Nonetheless, there is enough overlap among competencies, especially foundational competencies, to allow for mutual understanding, clear communication, and collaboration on shared goals across professions to facilitate interprofessional collaboration.

Functional and foundational competencies intersect with one another and develop over time. This idea has been captured in the image of a *competencies cube* (Rodolfa et al. 2005). The competencies cube provides a visual metaphor of how foundational and functional competencies relate to one another and to various stages of professional development as displayed on the three faces of a cube that meet at a corner. On one face of the cube, six functional competency domains are represented as separate segments cutting through the cube face, namely: assessment, intervention, consultation, research, supervision, and administration. On a second face, six foundational competencies are similarly presented as separate segments: reflective practice, scientific knowledge, relationships, ethical and legal standards, diversity, and interdisciplinary systems. Together, the intersection of these two cube faces represents the idea that each foundational competency informs each functional competency.

The third face of the competencies cube portrays the various stages of professional development in succession as separate segments that cut through the cube. This is intended to illustrate the idea that for each of the 36 functional—foundational competency pairings, a supervisee may be functioning at a different level of professional development. For instance, if two supervisees have similar amounts of training and supervision but differ in the type and focus of their training and supervised experience (e.g., assessment versus intervention), their stage of professional development within those domains will be quite different.

In practice, professional development is incremental and gradual. However, when considered from a bird's eye view, we can recognize distinct stages or levels of professional development. Drawing from Hubert and Stuart Dreyfus's work on expertise development (Dreyfus 2004), five distinct stages of competency development can be distinguished (novice, beginner, intermediate, advanced, and proficient). The *Novice Stage* includes those who possess neither foundational nor functional knowledge or skill (e.g., someone who has just entered a professional psychology training program). Training programs typically begin by teaching novices foundational knowledge in classroom settings related to theories, principles, facts, professional attitudes, and values, as necessary preparation for acquiring functional competencies in their work with clients. Competence at the novice level requires mastery of conceptual/ theoretical knowledge as well as preliminary functional skill development from practicing clinical skills with non-client volunteers. Competence is assessed through evaluations of academic work reflected in course grades, though attention must also be given to the quality of interpersonal functioning as observed in interactions with faculty, peers, and staff. Learners in the *Beginner Stage* have sufficient foundational knowledge to safely commence applied learning (i.e., fieldwork or practica) through exercising functional competencies with easier clients under close supervision. Two crucial competencies at this level and beyond are the ability to form safe and effective working relationships with a diverse range of clients and the ability to accept feedback and learn from supervision. Those at the *Intermediate Learner Stage* have demonstrated sufficient competence to be entrusted to work with new, and possibly more challenging, client populations, or with greater autonomy under supervision (e.g., at external sites). Those at the *Advanced Learner Stage* are ready for an extended training opportunity (e.g., a year-long psychology residency) with a broad range of clients and different supervisors. Success at this level typically leads to the final level of development as a supervisee, namely *Proficient*, when supervisees are ready to be assessed for independent practice through pursuing licensure following graduation.

Professionals, through their commitment to continuing competence, seek to maintain and enhance their competencies through pursuing opportunities for life-long learning. Indeed, by applying their competencies in novel circumstances and evolving contexts, such as the many adaptations required during the COVID-19 pandemic, practitioners develop greater *capability* (Kaslow et al. 2022; Lester 2014). Furthermore, by honing their skills through deliberate practice, peer-consultation, and continuing education they may attain even greater levels of skill as to become expert (Ericsson 2018; Rousmaniere et al. 2017).

Supervisory Competencies

A cube model can also be used to depict the realm of supervision as reflected in its functional tasks, foundational parameters, and developmental considerations (e.g., Bernard and Goodyear 2019, p. 17). One face of the cube represents functional supervisory tasks. Following the previous chapter's definition of supervision, the supervisor's tasks include: organizing supervision (Chapters 3, 4, and 6), facilitating supervisee development (Chapter 4), facilitating supervisee emotion regulation and self-care (i.e., supervision's restorative function, Chapter 4), ensuring client welfare (throughout), and evaluating supervisee performance and gatekeeping (Chapters 5 and 6).

The second face of the cube represents the foundational considerations that inform how supervisors undertake each task. The central parameters are interpersonal relationships (e.g., the working alliance in supervision, Chapters 3 and 5), ethical/legal/regulatory considerations, multicultural and diversity issues, self-reflection, and professionalism. Other parameters include considerations related to scientific knowledge; interdisciplinary, institutional, and societal systems; and administration. Many of these foundational considerations apply to both the conduct of supervision (e.g., the supervisory working alliance) and to the conduct of the clinical services being supervised (e.g., the therapeutic alliance). The fact that these considerations apply at two levels creates an opportunity for supervisors to model the interpersonal attitudes and skills that they intend to teach.

The third face of the cube represents the developing supervisor's progress through various developmental stages. According to prominent supervisor development models, the initial, novice supervisor stage is the most difficult and can elicit feelings of shock and disorientation upon assuming the supervisory role (Watkins 2012). Beginning from a position of vulnerability, the novice supervisor feels unprepared and confused by the complexity and ambiguity of their role. A major challenge is to shift from the clinician's mindset with its focus on the client to a supervisory mindset where the focus is on helping the supervisee find their way without losing sight of responsibility for the client and one's evaluative role. Novice supervisors lack a clear sense of supervisory identity.

They require both specific supervisory competencies and an overall sense of competence. Throughout this book, you will learn about supervision in a manner that allows you to develop a clear mental map of your role as a supervisor. Ideally, you will have the opportunity to complement this book knowledge with the opportunity to practice supervised supervision, where you can reflect on your experiences of providing supervision with the aid of an experienced supervisor and begin to develop a cohesive vision of your role and confidence in your identity as a supervisor (Mann and Merced 2018; Stewart and Johnson 2023; Watkins et al. 2024a).

Once you launch your career as a supervisor you can maintain and update your supervisory knowledge and skills through both informal (e.g., consulting other supervisors) and formal (e.g., workshops) opportunities. With further development and experience as a supervisor you might eventually consider becoming a supervisor of supervisors. This role is valuable for the development of novice supervisors during their training and for beginner supervisors who are seeking licensure. While discussion of the competencies required for supervision-of-supervision is beyond the scope of this book, it is noteworthy that in supervision-of-supervision the supervisory working alliance remains central (Vandette et al., 2021), even as the focus of supervision incorporates a wider scope to encompass systems issues (Moral and Turner, 2019) and the evolving needs of supervisors in training for varying degrees of support versus challenge and autonomy versus direction (Stewart and Johnson, 2023).

Supervision Competence

According to the APA's supervision guidelines (2014), competence in supervision requires competency in several domains. Apart from the first domain, the APA domains listed below are described in greater detail in later chapters:

- the practice area being supervised (i.e., only supervise clinical activities you are competent to practice, as determined by your own professional training),
- working with individuals from diverse backgrounds (Chapter 3),

- establishing and maintaining a collaborative supervisory relationship (Chapter 3),
- modeling professionalism (Chapters 3 and 5),
- evaluating and providing constructive feedback (Chapters 4–6),
- identifying and addressing competency problems (Chapters 3, 5, and 6), and
- modeling ethical values, practices, and compliance with regulatory guidelines and laws (Chapters 3, 5, and 6).

Beyond Competence: Capability and Meta-Competencies

Although the competence construct offers a means of operationalizing professional development that is useful for teaching, evaluation, and gate-keeping (e.g., Fouad et al. 2009; Hatcher et al. 2013; Taylor and Neimeyer 2022), it has serious limitations (Humphreys et al. 2018). When competence is narrowly defined and focused on the execution of prescribed functions, it risks reducing the nuances of professional judgment to the relatively mindless execution of prepackaged skills within a predefined context. As well, merely possessing a set of micro-skills does not ensure that the practitioner will know how to choose wisely among them to permit the correct selection, application, and sequencing of competencies in response to an evolving clinical context (Huddle and Heudebert 2007).

To overcome these limitations, competent practitioners possess two higher-order executive abilities. The first is *responsiveness,* a meta-competency which exercises executive functioning to plan and monitor the selection and operation of individual micro-competencies judiciously in response to the evolving requirements of a dynamic circumstance. Below, we discuss how responsiveness is central to the work of both practitioners and supervisors. Second, *capability* refers to the ability human beings have to respond flexibly and adaptively to new problems that arise in unfamiliar contexts (Cairns and Malloch 2024; Lester 2014; Lozano et al. 2012). Thus, the capable professional is one who can not only *react* to changing circumstances but also demonstrates *autonomy* and proactive *agency* in identifying novel problems in their social and political context that require redress through the application of their competencies. Indeed, an essential capability in a diverse, multicultural society is the ability to address culture and diversity not only at the level of individuals (e.g., with clients and supervisees), but also to consider how to responsibly engage with larger systemic influences that impact one's community and work (Kaslow et al. 2022). Ensuring that professionals are capable as well as competent is essential as the pace of cultural and technological change continues to accelerate.

Regarding technological change, perhaps no area requires the exercise of capability more than maintaining one's digital literacy over time. Once, all that meant was knowing how to use a word-processor! Now, being a digitally literate supervisor requires you to know how to conduct therapy and supervision virtually, communicate, transfer, and store confidential information safely and securely across internet-connected devices; and how to instruct supervisees in these practices (CPA 2023b; Stewart et al. 2025). Maintaining digital literacy will also require supervisors to monitor developments in artificial intelligence (AI), including future research and professional guidelines on whether and how these may be used to support clinical practice as well as clinical supervision in safe, ethical, and effective ways (Ranihusna 2025; Maurya and DeDiego 2025). Thoroughly understanding the biases and limitations in AI tools is critical.

Responsiveness: Knowing What to Do When

Practitioners not only need to possess required competencies, they also need to be able to recognize, in response to the unfolding, dynamic, and somewhat unpredictable client responses typical of actual clinical practice, *which* competency from their repertoire to enact at each moment to achieve the best results. This ability implies the operation of an executive meta-competency, which acts like an internalized supervisor, that monitors, guides, and supports the practitioner's engagement with their client. This master skill of knowing what to do when, known as *responsiveness*, is the most important, yet least visible, aspect of competent practice with clients and supervisees (Hatcher 2021).

Responsiveness is a property of the natural world, defined as "behavior being influenced by emerging context" (Stiles 2021, p. 16).

Responsiveness means that one's actions depend on the circumstances. Applied to the therapy relationship, responsiveness highlights how therapists and clients mutually react to and influence one another. Although therapists' reactions could theoretically either facilitate or impede the goals of therapy, therapists' professional and ethical commitment to helping their clients means *therapist responsiveness* is in the service of always trying to "do the right thing given the context to enhance the outcome." The context includes client culture, identity, or treatment preferences, as well as their emergent responses to events occurring within or outside the therapy session.

Similarly, the skillful supervisor draws on responsiveness to successfully navigate the unfolding dynamic of each supervision session in response to the distinct context (e.g., learning needs, learning style, personality, supervisory relationship) of each supervisee (Friedlander et al. 2024). For instance, a supervisor might consider that although doing a role play might work well, there is not enough time in this session to use this strategy effectively, and so will use direct instruction instead and plan to use role-play in a future session if needed. In addition, supervisors must also develop both specific competencies and responsiveness within their supervisees. One way to do so is by asking the supervisee why they chose to respond (or not respond) to the client at various moments as they did, to identify what other choices they could have made in that moment, and to weigh their relative pros and cons.

How to Promote Learning and Competency Development

To know how to promote the kind of experiential learning central to supervision, it is necessary to have a good understanding of how people learn from experience. According to Bandura's (1989, 1997) influential social cognitive model, learning is advanced, and confidence is built, through specific types of learning experiences, particularly when they are properly structured. A key indicator of learning and developing competency and capability is the development of self-efficacy, which is the confidence that one can carry out a task successfully even in difficult or novel conditions. Research evidence suggests quality supervision contributes to supervisees' professional self-efficacy (Lo and Thompson 2025; Lohani and Sharma 2023).

Self-efficacy arises from four distinct types of experience: mastery, modeling, social persuasion, and physiological and affective arousal. Below, I describe each of these and discuss how they may be harnessed in supervision to enhance supervisee competency development.

Mastery emerges from repeatedly exercising a skill in different contexts and overcoming obstacles (think of learning to ride a bicycle through trial and error). Receiving corrective feedback on one's performance, either from experience itself or from a knowledgeable supervisor, is necessary for improvement. Success experiences breed confidence and the motivation to persist, whereas consistent failure discourages trying and can result in giving up. To increase their chances of success, supervisees need to be adequately prepared (e.g., with prerequisite foundational knowledge and skill preparation via modeling and role-playing) and provided with challenges that are provided in a graded fashion (e.g., by assigning easier clients and close supervision for supervisees who are either beginners or advanced trainees who are learning novel methods). Mastering tasks that are aligned with their stage of professional development generates confidence that persevering through periods of confusion and uncertainty will eventually yield clarity and a path forward. Conversely, when supervisees encounter difficult problems for which they are not prepared or not adequately supported, they are more likely to feel overwhelmed, become stuck, and withdraw. In a similar fashion, for novice supervisors, the challenge of learning a complex competency like supervision will be eased and their self-efficacy enhanced when they have learned a model of supervision and receive support to discuss their experiences applying it through supervised supervision (Stewart and Johnson 2023).

As noted earlier, *modeling* is a form of observational learning. Observation can convey nuanced, context-responsive skills that are difficult to put into words and must be seen to be fully appreciated. "By their behavior and expressed ways of thinking, competent models transmit knowledge and teach observers effective skills and strategies for managing environmental demands" (Bandura 1997, p. 88). Another reason that modeling is powerful is that it enacts skilled behavior in a context in which the observer is free from clinical responsibility and can therefore notice and reflect on the details of the skill display. As a supervisor, you can model skills in supervision (and subsequently rehearse them through role-play) or arrange for your supervisees to observe your work with clients. I recall a powerful experience of observing a supervisor conduct an intake interview. After asking the client what concerns brought them in, my supervisor waited for the client to respond ... and waited ... and waited. Perhaps three minutes of complete silence passed, which felt like three hours, before the client spoke. The tension was unbearable to me, even though I was on the outside looking in, but my supervisor was calm and cool. He maintained eye contact with the client, and his posture conveyed a patient, relaxed readiness. That experience not only taught me *how* to manage silences with clients, but instilled confidence *that* it was possible even in extreme cases, and thus taught me far more than a verbal description ever could. That said, sometimes an expert's skill level can be so far beyond what a novice feels they can achieve that observing them has little impact on their confidence. In contrast, observing a peer who is at a similar stage of professional development model acceptable, but imperfect, professional behavior can inspire supervisees that they can also achieve this more modest level of competence. Thus, in group supervision, supervisees can often gain self-efficacy vicariously from the experiences of peers and the performance feedback they receive. I say more about using modeling in supervision in Chapter 4.

The third source of self-efficacy, *social persuasion*, involves supportive messages from a credible source that the learner possesses the necessary ability to acquire or execute a skill. This messaging encourages them to persist in their mastery efforts. Most supervisors strive to be supportive and encouraging. Sometimes these messages, however well-intentioned, fail to develop confidence because they come across as unfounded, unrealistic, or consoling ("good try!"). For instance, my first experience of on-the-job feedback came when I was 16 and had completed a one-week stint as a junior camp counselor. The 17-year-old senior counselor I had worked with that week was tasked with giving me a page of written performance feedback. On it, he simply wrote, "Fantastic job, Ed! 10/10!!!!!!!". Although I was relieved to receive positive feedback, I learned nothing from it, nor did I feel more confident. In fact, it had a slightly undermining impact because I suspected the reason he was so effusively positive was that he felt I was insecure and needed it. In contrast, when learners receive realistic, positive feedback that specifies *what* was good about their performance and *why* it was good, the impact is to consolidate their learning and build confidence that they are on the right path and can take on new and greater challenges.

Social persuasion can also function at a systemic, professional level when professional standards are codified and become accepted practice. This is just what is occurring in professional training as a result of the competencies revolution. Thus, supervision has been recognized as a distinct competency that requires explicit training (Falender and Shafranske 2021; Pilling and Roth 2014). Moreover, accreditation standards for some professions (e.g., professional psychology) explicitly require supervision to be taught (APA 2015; CPA 2023a). Through the publication of guidelines and standards for supervision from APA (2014) and the Association of State and Provincial Psychology Boards (ASPPB 2015), along with supervision textbooks and manuals, the formerly nebulous role and responsibilities of supervision have been concretely specified. Together, these provide a form of social persuasion that enhances our collective supervisory self-efficacy as a profession. Concrete forms of support for development as a supervisor, such as these, are associated with greater pursuit of continuing education in supervision (E. A. Johnson and Stewart 2000) and with higher levels of perceived self-efficacy in supervisory roles (Bjornestad et al. 2014; E. A. Johnson and Stewart 2008).

The fourth influence on self-efficacy, *physiological and affective arousal*, occurs in response to both positive and negative experiences. Positive experiences of problem-solving, communicating, and collaborating in supervision can yield feelings of accomplishment, excitement, and connection in both supervisor and supervisee. These feelings support the supervisee's confidence that they are on the right track and are making progress and may elicit similar feelings in the supervisor about their own supervisory skills. However, the opposite impact can occur when supervisors provide unreasonably harsh criticism, make demeaning comments, act exploitatively, or engage in micro-aggressions. These destructive actions can elicit feelings of fear or harm in supervisees, which can diminish their trust that the supervisory relationship is a safe place for them to learn and grow. Similarly, when supervisors feel their messages are dismissed or ignored by the supervisee, this can lead to feelings of confusion, anger, and frustration that diminish their sense of efficacy as a supervisor. Collectively, these emotional experiences can affect both supervisors' and supervisees' perceptions of their efficacy and worth and attitudes toward supervision and one another. In Chapter 5 I elaborate on the kinds of problems that can arise in supervision and discuss how to address them.

In summary, your efforts to promote supervisee learning can benefit from applying the four sources of self-efficacy identified above. In Chapter 4, I discuss how Kolb's (1984) model of experiential learning draws on these learning principles to promote learning in supervision. For now, I invite you to deepen your understanding of the social cognitive model by completing the guided reflection exercise in the box below.

Exercise: Reflection on Learning Experiences

The purpose of this exercise is to help you better understand the social cognitive learning mechanisms described above by having you reflect on specific episodes in your own experiences of supervision where one or more of these sources have been present. Below, I have listed each of the four sources of self-efficacy that promote learning and the growth of confidence. For each of them, identify a personal learning experience in which that source was active and the impact it had on your learning and sense of efficacy. Once you finish, consider how these experiences might inform how you approach teaching and learning in your work as a supervisor.

Source of self-efficacy	Example of learning experience	Impact of experience
Mastery		
Modeling		
Social persuasion		
Physiological arousal		

Preparing Supervisees to Make Effective Use of Supervision

In a collaborative supervisory relationship, supervisees can only successfully play their part when they know what is required of them. This is especially true for novice supervisees, who often begin supervision with little preparation for, or understanding of, their role, rights, and responsibilities (Ellis et al. 2014) and what their supervisors expect of them (Mandel 2015). Supervisees' lack of preparation and role uncertainty can result in poorer supervision outcomes, including increased supervisee anxiety (Ellis et al. 2015), reduced learning and satisfaction from supervision (Nelson et al. 2008), and a weaker supervisory working alliance.

To get the most out of supervision, supervisees need to know what is expected of them and how they can contribute to its success (Crocker and Sudak 2017; Falender and Shafranske 2012; Rocha and Kemer 2022). They need to understand that supervision is a collaborative enterprise in which they are expected to be active, engaged participants. They must demonstrate a commitment to supervision by prioritizing time for supervision and their work with clients, recording progress notes, writing reports, and completing assigned learning activities. More specifically, they need to understand how their role and responsibilities relate to the three main functions of supervision discussed in Chapter 1.

Regarding the normative function of ensuring client welfare, supervisees need to understand that the supervisor bears ultimate responsibility for the client. To ensure supervisors can fulfill their responsibility, supervisees have an ethical and professional obligation to disclose information relevant to the client's well-being to the supervisor. Timely reporting is essential when working with clients who are at high risk of a critical incident (e.g., for self-harm or suicide, harming another person, or of being harmed). Note that some novice supervisees may have good intentions of reporting but lack the ability to spot subtle or indirect references to suicidality or intimate partner violence. Accordingly, novices benefit from discussing such indicators and from their being identified and categorized during video review of their work (see Chapter 4 for additional discussion of how supervisors help supervisees learn to categorize client behaviors). Supervisees also need to disclose their countertransference attitudes and feelings toward clients, as well as any strains or ruptures in the therapeutic alliance, as these may impact the quality of care they provide (Hayes et al. 2018). Finally, when a supervisor provides guidance on client care, supervisees are expected to be open to direction, make a conscientious effort to put it into practice, and discuss its implementation. If, however, the supervisee perceives the guidance as problematic (e.g., they feel ill-prepared to deliver it, don't understand the rationale, or think it is contraindicated), they are expected to express their concerns and seek to resolve them in a respectful manner. Later, I will address how and when supervisors can entrust more advanced supervisees with greater clinical autonomy.

Supervisees also need to understand how they can contribute to supervision's formative function to maximize their learning. Supervisees need to understand how they will improve. The main vehicles of improvement are:

- practicing skills (i.e., with clients, in supervision, and on one's own),
- accepting and integrating feedback and direction in supervision, and
- reflecting on experience.

Practice helps because it contributes to mastery. According to Dawes (1994), learning and mastery occur when two conditions are met: (1) there is clarity about what constitutes a correct versus incorrect response; and (2) immediate, unambiguous feedback is available when errors are made. Given the complexities of clinical work, such as psychotherapy, these conditions are typically not met. What constitutes a correct response varies depending on the therapeutic orientation. Even in cases of an unambiguous error, the client may choose to spare the therapist's feelings and not provide feedback that allows the therapist to perceive the error. Fortunately, supervision can overcome many of these limitations. First, supervision can help identify the extent to which trainee actions are correct or effective. Secondly, supervision can help trainees understand *why* or *if* a given action is helpful. In some circumstances, such as during live supervision, or co-therapy that includes supervisor and supervisee, supervisors can provide immediate corrective feedback or guidance when a supervisee makes a mistake. Through reflection during supervision, supervisees can consider and integrate their practice experiences and supervisory feedback. Finally, in addition to these three main drivers of learning, supervision also contributes to learning in other ways, such as through supervisor modeling of clinical skills, shaping of supervisee skills through role-playing, and conceptual development through direct teaching or assigned readings.

At the outset of a training experience, supervisees require support to identify their learning goals, so that relevant learning opportunities can be included in their training experience. This requires that supervisees clearly understand what learning experiences are available to them so they can align their goals with relevant opportunities. I recall my first supervisor asking me during our first meeting at an external site what my goals were for the training experience. As I had no idea of what learning opportunities were available to me at the site and would be most helpful for my development, I was unable to give an informed answer to the question.

Once training is underway, supervisees need to know how to prepare for supervision meetings. This involves such things as prioritizing their questions and concerns, identifying the parts of therapy recordings they wish guidance or feedback on, and completing assigned tasks. During supervision meetings, supervisees are expected to disclose difficulties they are encountering and be open to receiving constructive feedback. Subsequently, they must thoughtfully integrate feedback into their work with clients. Underlying these supervisee behaviors is a commitment to professionalism, evident in attitudes of openness, conscientiousness, and eagerness to learn, which facilitate learning across a wide variety of supervisors and supervisory styles (Kaslow et al. 2018). Supervisees must be willing to take sensible risks to advance their learning such as by trying new techniques or working with more challenging clients. It will help them to know that it is developmentally normative that they won't always succeed when taking these risks but can often learn a great deal from difficulties when they occur.

I wish my supervisors had better explained that struggles with clients and with learning new skills are common and expected of supervisees. When I was a trainee, I often succumbed to the need to look successful in supervision by selectively disclosing mostly the positive experiences with my clients to supervisors and the difficulties only when necessary. At the time, this felt like a necessary survival strategy. Looking back, I wish I could tell my earlier self not to fret about these developmentally normal growing pains and explain that, not only do they not mean I am a failure, but that supervision can help with managing and learning from them. I regret those missed learning opportunities. I share this story with my supervisees at the outset of our work together to encourage them to approach our supervision differently than I did. As it turns out, nondisclosure is a common occurrence in supervision. Supervisees often withhold information from their supervisors about themselves, their clients, or the supervision process in supervision (R. M. Cook et al. 2018; Knox 2015; Mehr et al. 2010). Research on supervisee nondisclosure documents how it is associated with higher levels of supervisee anxiety/shame and ambiguity about their role (Min and Kim 2024).

Another thing I wish I had known as a supervisee was how valuable, if occasionally painful, feedback would be to my growth and development as a therapist, especially when it was based on direct observation of my work. I recall receiving a somewhat blunt, but enormously valuable, bit of feedback from a supervisor concerning how little attention I gave to client affect. Ouch! However, that one observation completely reoriented my work with clients.

As the supervisory relationship is a key facilitator of the formative function (supervisee learning) of supervision, supervisees are expected to provide supervisors with meaningful feedback about their experience of supervision. This includes the supervisor's approach to supervision, especially concerning any issues that may interfere with the supervisee fully participating in or benefiting from supervision. Supervisees must also be prepared to learn how to process multicultural and diversity considerations as they arise with their clients and with their supervisor. Supervisors can encourage such discussions by broaching and modeling them, a topic we will explore further in Chapter 3.

Finally, to make effective use of the restorative function (supporting supervisee well-being), supervisees need to know that it is available to them and how it differs from therapy. Supervisees are expected to access the restorative function of supervision by disclosing unsettling experiences in their work with clients, which may have had an impact on their well-being and ability to function effectively in their role. These can include experiences of sexual harassment (Luke et al. 2020), vicarious trauma, microaggressions, or episodes of physical violence (Norcross and VandenBos 2018). Supervisors need to understand and validate these feelings and help supervisees process these experiences to allow them to regain their composure and well-being. Relatedly, supervisees are expected to formulate and work toward self-care goals to maintain their well-being. Supervisees should discuss their self-care practices (and struggles) in supervision so that they can learn how best to sustain them in the face of competing demands and the stresses of clinical practice. Supervisors and training programs also need to consider whether the demands and expectations they are placing on supervisees are realistic and sustainable (Hunt et al. 2025).

Chapter Summary

The competencies revolution has radically changed how supervisors and supervisees learn about their roles and responsibilities. What was once learned through osmosis is now formally articulated in models that are transmitted in courses, developed through research, and summarized in textbooks. These models represent a growing consensus concerning the attitudes, skills, and knowledge that contribute to effective supervision. Supervisory dyads can prepare for a positive and productive supervisory relationship by developing a shared understanding of their respective roles and how best practices will be incorporated into supervision.

Questions for Review and Reflection

1. What are the advantages of training supervisors to attain supervisory competence relative to an apprenticeship form of training?
2. Distinguish among competence, competencies, and capability.
3. What are meta-competencies, such as responsivity, and how are they distinct from competencies?
4. For each of the three functions of supervision (normative, formative, restorative), describe something you think it important for a novice supervisee to know about to be prepared for supervision.
5. Describe, in your own words, what a supervisee can do to maximize their learning within supervision.

CHAPTER 3

Starting Well: Building a Strong Supervisory Relationship

The start of the supervision relationship is a crucial moment. It is sometimes said that you only get one chance to make a good first impression. That is true, but it vastly understates what is at stake at the outset of supervision. The way you begin supervision sets the stage for everything that follows. By developing a positive working relationship with your supervisee and carefully planning how supervision will unfold you can create the conditions for a successful supervisory experience. With that in mind, this chapter offers guidance on how to start supervision well. Specifically, we will explore how supervisors and supervisees can accomplish three essential tasks during their first meeting(s). These are to: (a) initiate a positive supervisory relationship that attends to culture, diversity, and the potential need for accommodations, (b) agree on a shared plan for supervision and the training experience, and (c) set developmentally appropriate goals for the supervisee's training experience within a supervision contract (Watkins et al. 2024b).

A Positive Supervisory Relationship Is Essential

Supervision is fundamentally a relationship-based form of education and training. Like any meaningful relationship, its effectiveness hinges on trust, mutual respect, and a shared understanding of purpose. When these elements are present, supervision can strongly enhance learning and professional growth; when they are absent, little of value is likely to occur. Because supervisors hold greater power and authority than supervisees, they carry the primary responsibility for establishing the trust, respect, and rapport needed for a productive supervisory relationship (Chircop Coleiro et al., 2023).

A strong supervisory relationship shares many qualities with a strong therapeutic relationship. Bordin (1983) describes both as forms of a *working alliance*, grounded in an agreement to collaborate toward specific goals through shared tasks and methods. Over time, affective bonds—such as liking, caring, and trust—emerge and further strengthen the alliance.

This supervisory alliance is the vehicle through which most learning in supervision occurs. Highly effective teaching methods—such as modeling, role-plays, video review, feedback, and reflective discussion—are experiential by nature, and their impact depends heavily on the quality of the supervisor–supervisee relationship. A positive alliance amplifies learning, whereas a strained one diminishes it (Goodyear, 2014).

Given the inherent power differential, supervisors should not assume that a positive relationship will develop on its own. Intentionally cultivating the supervisory alliance from the outset helps prevent misunderstandings, fosters psychological safety, and sets the stage for meaningful learning and growth.

Warmth, Trust, and Safety: The Foundation

As discussed in Chapter 2, the ability to build and maintain a positive supervisory relationship is *the* core supervisory competency. This begins with the supervisor's interpersonal stance – approaching the supervisee with warmth, enthusiasm, and genuine interest. These qualities mirror conditions known to strengthen the therapeutic alliance, such as positive regard and affirmation (Farber et al., 2019; Lavik et al. 2018).

To foster a collaborative and open relationship, supervisors should directly communicate their intention to create an environment where supervisees feel safe discussing challenges. Psychological safety is essential for learning and growth, but it does not mean the absence of difficulty or risk. Instead, safety stems from trust—the confidence that attempts to grow, such as by experimenting with new skills or taking on more complex clients will be supported rather than punished. Trust deepens when supervisors respond to supervisees' disclosures of uncertainties or struggles with encouragement, constructive feedback, and openness about the supervisory relationship (Cucco 2020).

During initial meetings, setting this tone explicitly can be helpful. I often say,

> We will be working closely together. I am excited to get to know you and to support your development as a therapist. I see our work together as a collaboration based on mutual respect and a shared understanding of how we will work together. For supervision to benefit you fully, it's important that you feel enough trust and safety to be open about your clinical work -- including the challenges that every supervisee encounters. Discussing these struggles is part of your responsibility under supervision and an important avenue for growth. Trust also makes it easier to take appropriate risks in your learning, knowing that I will support, not punish, your efforts to learn and grow, even when you struggle. I will check-in periodically about how our relationship is going. If you ever have concerns about our work together or about anything that might interfere with your learning or client care, I encourage you to bring them up.

Talking so directly about the supervisory relationship may feel awkward at first, which may explain why it is often absent from routine supervision practice (Bailin et al. 2018) and even from recorded demonstrations of supervision sessions of master supervisors (Xu et al. 2021). With practice, however, these conversations become more natural, and supervisees typically appreciate them. They signal that discussing the relationship is both welcome and normal.

Once supervision is underway, periodic check-ins (e.g., "how are we doing?" "any concerns about how we are working together?") help maintain openness. When something seems off, a gentle inquiry (e.g., "I notice that sometimes you go quiet after I suggest an alternative way of responding to your client. Is there a better way I could support your learning?") can invite meaningful discussion while modeling skills that are also valuable in therapy.

Elsewhere, I address other relationship skills, including broaching culture and identity (further below), and addressing strains or ruptures in the supervisory relationship (Chapter 5).

Evaluation Procedures

A major challenge to establishing safety stems from supervisee concerns about evaluation. Supervisees often worry about both formal summative evaluations as well as supervisors' impressions of them. These concerns underscore how threatening evaluation can feel to supervisees.

Evaluation anxiety cannot be eliminated, but clear, transparent, and fair evaluation procedures can reduce it. The final evaluation process is covered in Chapter 6; here the emphasis is on what needs clarification at the outset. Supervisees should receive the final evaluation measure early so they can understand which competencies will be assessed. Two issues should be clarified.

First, competence must be evaluated developmentally, appropriate to training level. For example, the expectations of a novice beginning their first practicum should be much less than for someone preparing for autonomous practice. By identifying the supervisee's developmental level and adjusting the evaluation criteria accordingly, the supervisor can help make the goals of the training experience feel achievable, and the process of evaluation fair.

For instance, I typically tell novice supervisees that the primary criteria for success will be their ability to establish a positive therapeutic alliance with relatively uncomplicated clients, and to make good use of supervision by being open to feedback and conscientiously applying it. For a more advanced supervisee, my primary criteria expand to encompass more advanced goals, such as establishing a positive therapeutic alliance with more challenging clients, implementing therapeutic methods with greater autonomy and efficacy, and being more independent and proactive in the use of supervision. Of course, by highlighting these criteria, this does not negate the importance of the other professional competencies that supervisees need to acquire and which are also a focus of evaluation.

Second, nothing negative should appear in the summative evaluation unless previously identified and communicated to them through formative feedback. This is the *no surprises* rule of evaluation. It ensures the trainee has had the opportunity to address any identified concerns well before the final evaluation. A midpoint evaluation, in which any areas not meeting expectations are identified, supports correction of concerns through additional focus. The no surprises rule also implies that ongoing constructive feedback will be provided throughout the training period (see Chapter 4).

Supervision Boundaries and the Limits of Confidentiality

It is best to address the boundaries of the supervisory relationship at its outset (Wood 2007). Supervisors differ in how firmly and explicitly they set boundaries within supervision. Whatever your preference is, though, you should be aware that there is a limit beyond which a professional supervisory relationship should not pass. Harmful boundary violations, including sexual intimacy or harassment, abusive, or exploitative relationships, occur too often in supervision (Ellis et al. 2014, 2017b). A major reason such exploitation is possible is due to the immense power of the supervisor to affect the career of the supervisee, which diminishes the supervisee's ability to say no to the supervisor. Establishing an open and mutually respectful dialogue about the supervisory relationship from the outset helps to ensure the relationship remains positive and professional.

Another way to prevent boundary violations is to identify and discuss how to manage any non-supervisory relationships that exist between you and your supervisee. These may include professional relationships such as research employer/employee, instructor/teaching assistant, thesis advisor/ student, as well as non-professional relationships, such as team-mates in a recreational sport, members of a social or religious organization, and so on. While some of these relationships may be unavoidable or mutually beneficial, they nonetheless can complicate your relationship and have the potential to negatively interact with the supervisory relationship. Accordingly, it is ethically prudent for supervisors when considering such multiple relationships to reflect on whether such relationships are war-ranted, and to discuss them proactively with the supervisee to prevent or minimize potential harm (Falender 2016). For example, this might involve agreeing that supervision time will be protected and not devoted to other roles and responsibilities.

The limits of confidentiality of the supervisory relationship differ from the limits within a therapeutic relationship and therefore require discussion to avoid misunderstanding (Falender, Shafranske, and Ofek 2014; L. Forrest et al. 2022). Whereas clients are entitled to a high stan-dard of confidentiality, the same does not apply to trainees. Trainees are not clients. Trainees are seeking to enter a profession; by doing so, they agree to be evaluated by training programs and licensing boards (Vacha-Haase et al. 2019). Consequently, confidentiality within supervision is limited by the requirement for supervisors to evaluate supervisees and report these evaluations to relevant educational or professional regula-tory authorities. L. M. Forrest and Elman (2023) recommend transpar-ency on this point by making an explicit statement to trainees such as, "a decision to become a professional involves recognizing that you have no confidentiality related to your professional competence, performance, or behaviors" (p. 139).

Because the person of the trainee is central to their functioning and effectiveness as a therapist and because issues of personal character can affect their professionalism (e.g., integrity, responsibility, accountabil-ity), personal matters (e.g., attitudes, deportment) may become a focus in supervision (L. Forrest et al. 2022). Consequently, when considering supervisee confidentiality, it is helpful to distinguish between the *personal/ private* issues that don't affect or influence the supervisee's professional functioning and the *personal/professional* ones that do. On those (hopefully rare) occasions when personal issues undermine professional functioning, supervisors must respect their gatekeeping obligations by reporting com-petence problems or professional violations, as necessary, to the student's program, the health care institution, and/or the profession's regulatory body. These reports may require the disclosure of some of the supervis-ee's personal/professional information. Ideally, this is done with the con-sent and cooperation of the supervisee; however, the ultimate decision to report professionalism concerns rests with the supervisor (L. M. Forrest and Elman 2023). However, the disclosure of personal information is only to the extent necessary to achieve a legitimate supervisory or professional purpose. These limitations to confidentiality in supervision should be clearly outlined in the supervision contract, the professional disclosure statement (PDS; both described further below), and discussed at the outset of supervision. It is helpful to let the supervisee know what personal/professional information you intend to share about them prior to doing so for the sake of transparency and to give them a chance to voice any concerns. Further guidance on how to manage serious difficulties with supervisees is provided in Chapters 5 and 6.

Conversely, supervisors need to consider whether and when to make personal disclosures to their supervisees. Supervisor disclosures about professional experiences can be helpful in normalizing difficult training experiences (Knox et al. 2008). In doing so, supervisors need to be mindful not to inadvertently sideline or dismiss the supervisee's concerns (Boyle and Kenny 2020) and consider whether the disclosure is congruent with the supervisee's needs and whether the level of intimacy of the disclosure is acceptable (i.e., not too high or too low) (Knox 2015). Supervisor self-disclosure is generally well-received by supervisees and tends to strengthen the supervisory working alliance, particularly the bond (Knox 2015). Although some supervisors believe that supervisor self-disclosure promotes supervisee self-disclosure, the limited evidence available does not support this view (Mehr and Daltry 2022). Supervisor disclosure may also serve a mentoring function by describing the supervisor's experience with various professional training or development opportunities. In the personal domain, there may also be good grounds for disclosure. For example, supervisees have a right to know when a supervisor's availability or abilities are compromised by life events, though supervisors may use discretion in sharing the reasons for their limitations. Also, a supervisor may choose to disclose a personal issue or circumstance to facilitate a supervisee's practicing therapy skills in a role-play in supervision. In doing so, supervisors should consider that although supervisors may request that supervisees treat such disclosures confidentially, the supervisee is not necessarily obligated to maintain the supervisor's confidentiality. Indeed, a supervisee may be entirely justified in breaching a supervisor's expectation of confidentiality in instances of harmful or exploitative supervision. Also, it is not appropriate for supervisors to use supervision to obtain ongoing free therapy for their personal issues from their supervisee during supervision, as this constitutes a dual role conflict and an exploitative ethical violation.

Counseling Within Supervision

While we are discussing the boundaries of the supervisory relationship and the overlap of personal and professional functioning, this is a good place to discuss the nature of counseling within supervision and how it is similar to, yet distinct from, a therapy relationship. As outlined in the definition of supervision, supervisors at times assume a counselor role in supervision to assist supervisees in processing their personal reactions to their clinical work as part of supervision's restorative function (Bradley and Becker 2021). This helps the supervisee enhance their clinical functioning, for instance, by learning to distinguish their countertransference responses to a client from responses that anyone might have to the client's behavior. These discussions depend on supervisees feeling enough safety to be willing to take the risk of opening up about their feelings toward their clients or perhaps toward you as a supervisor. By inviting and encouraging exploration of these disclosures, supervisors can promote a deeper sense of safety within the supervisory relationship that is freeing and emboldening for supervisees in a way that has been likened to a corrective emotional experience in therapy (Feldman et al. 2024).

Discussions of feelings toward clients can also lighten the emotional burden that sometimes accompanies clinical work. If unprocessed, negative impacts of clinical work can contribute to burnout, which is a "work related mental health impairment" (Awa et al. 2010, p. 184). Burnout is characterized by three inter-related dimensions: feelings of emotional exhaustion (including mental fatigue and somatic symptoms), negative feelings toward the people one works with (e.g., cynicism, detachment, or depersonalization), and a reduced sense of accomplishment or efficacy (Maslach et al. 2001). High levels of burnout are frequently reported by mental health workers (Volpe et al. 2014; Westwood et al. 2017). Trainees, despite (or because?) they are new to clinical work, are also vulnerable to burnout, especially those plagued by perfectionistic standards (Kaeding et al. 2017). The high prevalence of burnout among clinicians affects their functioning, reducing the efficacy of therapy for clients (Delgadillo et al. 2018). Given burnout's cumulative impact on the functioning and well-being of trainees, supervisors have an ethical responsibility to help those they supervise manage these emotional demands and avoid burnout (Simionato et al. 2019). Moreover, there is evidence that providing quality supervision may help reduce burnout symptoms (Forshammar Geisler et al. 2025; J. Johnson et al. 2020).

To introduce the counseling role within supervision, I usually say something like,

> Working with people suffering from psychological disorders can be emotionally demanding. When these emotional strains accumulate without being processed and worked through there is a risk that you will experience symptoms of burnout. These symptoms could include emotional exhaustion, detachment from your work, feeling ineffective, mentally fatigued, as well as physical symptoms of stress like headache and muscle tension. One of my responsibilities as your supervisor is to help you avoid burnout and to learn effective ways of addressing these emotional demands. To do this, I will sometimes ask you about how your work with your clients is affecting you and invite you to explore that impact in supervision. How does that sound to you? Do you think you'd feel comfortable doing that? Do you have concerns or questions about this aspect of supervision?

A statement like this that includes an invitation for supervisee questions and input will hopefully open the door to a productive conversation about the counseling role in supervision. Another element of that first conversation should touch on is the distinction between counseling in supervision and psychotherapy. To convey this, I will say something like,

> Sometimes these discussions may feel a little like therapy, so we need to be clear about how they are different from therapy. First, and most obviously, you are not my client and I am not your therapist. Supervision is not the place for a broad and deep

exploration of your personal issues and conflicts. Therapy is the place for that, and it is something I recommend all therapists engage in from time to time for their own mental health and well-being. Here in supervision, when we are discussing the emotional burden of your work, we will maintain a focus on the emotional responses and attitudes you experience toward your client(s). Sometimes these will involve countertransference feelings in which you might experience strong emotions toward a client (e.g., attraction or repulsion) or alternatively, boredom and disinterest. At other times the feelings you may be grappling with may arise from worries about your client's well-being and safety. You may also experience vicarious trauma when working with trauma victims, or feeling discouraged and ineffective when working with an unresponsive client. All these issues are suitable subjects for our discussions insofar as they can distort or erode your work with clients. I encourage you to take advantage of the opportunity to explore these issues in supervision for the sake of your well-being and your work with your clients.

A final aspect of supervision that can be considered part of the counseling role relates to monitoring and encouraging the supervisee's self-care. Self-care is an ethical and professional obligation that should be taught, encouraged, and reviewed in supervision. Discussions about self-care can often be initiated with a simple "how are you?" (Seabrook 2022) and explored with "what do you want (or need)?". Because self-care is also relevant for supervisors, it is reasonable to include some self-disclosure about how you manage self-care when introducing the subject. I will usually say something like,

An important way you can contribute to your own well-being in an ongoing way is to establish good self-care habits now while you are in training. In fact, that's one of the professional competencies that you are expected to develop in training. It's fair to say that many mental health workers struggle with self-care in part because they place more value on others' well-being than their own. This is an attitude that we all need to challenge. Here in supervision,

I invite you to discuss your self-care activities and to reflect on whether they are genuinely helpful and effective in restoring your well-being and re-energizing you. I will share with you some of my own experience and challenges with self-care along the way and perhaps together we can each make some progress in improving our self-care.

Creating a Welcoming Space for Discussions of Culture and Diversity

Culturally competent clinical supervision requires explicit attention to culture from the outset of supervision (Greene and Flasch 2019; Jacquart et al. 2024; Wilcox et al. 2023; M. T. Williams et al. 2023). Culture may be thought of as the subconscious habits of perception, thought (e.g., worldviews and ideologies), adaptive behavior, and community identification that we tacitly absorb during development within a given time (i.e., historical moment), place (e.g., country; locale: rural, urban, suburban), and community (Bruner 1996; Falicov 2014). In these few pages, I can only briefly address this complex topic, but trust that the references provided will point you toward more comprehensive discussions.

As cultural influences are subtle, numerous, interacting, and continuous, it is helpful to separate and categorize them for the purposes of promoting reflection, learning, and self-awareness. Just as each culture divides up the continuous color spectrum into discrete colors in slightly different ways, so too the way culture and identity are categorized varies over time and across places (Bruner 1996). Currently, the following dimensions of identity are commonly distinguished: gender identity, race/ethnicity (including Indigeneity), sexual orientation, religious or spiritual affiliation, age, disability, neurodiversity, and socioeconomic level (Falender, Shafranske, and Falicov 2014). Each of these identity categories, and the subcategories within them, has been the subject of growing analysis and commentary. For those who focus their clinical work on a particular identity community, it is vital to attain cultural competence by learning about the focal culture (or subculture) not only from the academic and professional literatures, but also experientially through engaging with the culture in community practices and events. As a culturally competent supervisor, you can guide and scaffold your supervisee's learning by recommending readings and facilitating contact with members of the culture and cultural events both within and outside of clinical service settings.

Supervisors, especially those whose identities reflect privilege, need to appreciate the systemic context of bias and oppression that may subconsciously influence their approach to supervisees. One study found that trainees who identified as White or heterosexual reported fewer experiences of bias or microaggression from supervisors than trainees who identified as Black, Indigenous, people of color, or lesbian, gay, bisexual, transgender, and queer (Chong et al. 2025). Similarly, a study of 175 supervisees of color found that those working with White supervisors (relative to those working with supervisors of color) reported more racial microaggressions in supervision, perceived their supervisor as less multiculturally competent, and experienced a weaker supervisory working alliance (Sukumaran et al. 2025). These results highlight a need for all supervisors, particularly those whose identities reflect privilege, to engage in training and self-reflection to promote their multicultural competence.

Because identity reflects the complex intersection and interaction of all the distinct dimensions identified earlier, the range of distinct identity combinations is large. For instance, to name but a few aspects of my own identity, I am White, cisgender, male, straight, neurotypical, older, able-bodied, and an English-speaking Canadian. Which one of these identities, or which combination of them, are most central or influential to my experience varies depending on the context in which I am interacting. That is, each context elicits a different set of operative biases, expectations, and norms. Being culturally competent means becoming sensitive to the shifting influences of identities on my experience, to note and try to correct for my biases, especially as they may influence my perceptions of and interactions with those who differ from me. Indeed, I recognize that people who share some of my identities have historically contributed to creating unjust social and cultural contexts that have enabled me to experience privileges denied to others. Consequently, it means that my own journey to cultural competence requires a sometimes-painful acknowledgment that many of my privileges in life (that are often invisible to me) rest on a legacy of harms that the cultures I identify with have historically perpetrated on members of other cultures. For those who identify as White, or wish to gain insight into the experience of Whiteness, I have found completing the *White Privilege Checklist* (McIntosh 1989/2015) a helpful way of identifying and reflecting on aspects of White privilege. In addition, there are various self-report scales that measure Whiteness attitudes that can be used to raise awareness (Hays et al. 2023). Doing the ongoing work of learning about other cultures and reflecting on one's own is essential for supervisors and supervisees alike (Greene and Flasch 2019; McMahon 2020). Of course, race and ethnicity represent only one dimension of identity. Supervisors also need to deepen their understanding and awareness of other dimensions, particularly of those whose members may have experienced social exclusion, such as those who identify as lesbian, gay, bisexual, transgender, or gender-diverse (Boe et al. 2024).

As individual supervisors and trainees, our critical self-reflection and cultural learning are necessary and important. However, for broader impact, critical self-examination needs to occur at a systemic level within our mental health professions and the education and training programs that support them (Rajesh et al. 2024). Some initial steps in this direction have been taken. For instance, researchers have described the operation of systemic biases against people of color and how these have contributed to the exclusion of racialized individuals from organized psychology in Canada (Faber et al. 2023). Researchers have urged that efforts to promote inclusiveness should include the perspectives and lived experience of racialized trainees (Martinez et al. 2024) and be concretely implemented in training programs to meaningfully increase diversity in our profession (e.g., Cullinan et al. 2024; Reid et al. 2024; Rodriguez Espinosa et al. 2024).

Such recommendations have greater impact when they receive the support of an organization and the institutional authority it offers. For instance, CPA organized a task force to create "a statement of accountability and responsibility to Indigenous Peoples on behalf of the profession of psychology in Canada and developed guiding principles for psychological practice with Indigenous Peoples in Canada" (CPA 2018, p. 6). This task force report is required reading in many Canadian psychology training programs and offers concrete guidance for practitioners, educators, supervisors, and leaders. As a small step in the direction of decolonization and reconciliation, supervisors and supervisees may find it helpful to learn about and reflect on how the Indigenous Seven Sacred Teachings of love, respect, courage, honesty, wisdom, humility, and truth apply to supervision and facilitate Two-Eyed Seeing (Marsh et al. 2015; Kennedy et al. 2023; McMillan 2023; Rogers et al. 2019).

Multicultural Competence, Cultural Humility, and Broaching Culture and Identity

Multicultural competence consists of culturally relevant knowledge, skill, and attitudes/self-awareness that facilitate safe and effective attention to diversity in clinical practice and supervision (Falender, Shafranske and Falicov 2014). It is widely agreed that multicultural competence is an ethical expectation for therapists (e.g., W. B. Johnson et al. 2012) and that educators, including supervisors, must promote multicultural competence in trainees (Mitchell and Butler 2021). Although trainees and practitioners alike report that they possess high levels of multicultural competence, in practice, few demonstrate expected skills and attention to clients' culture (Wilcox et al. 2020). This suggests a gap between self-assessed versus demonstrated competency when it comes to putting multicultural competencies into practice.

Cultural competence encompasses the professional's cultural awareness and beliefs, cultural knowledge, and cultural skills (American Psychological Association 2017; D. W. Sue et al. 2022). Similarly, Constantine (2003) defined multicultural supervision competencies as supervisors' awareness, knowledge, and skill in addressing multicultural issues in the supervision triad (supervisor, supervisee, client). Relevant attitudes and self-awareness include openness to reflecting on cultural knowledge as it relates to one's own cultural background and to exploring how that differs from one's client, supervisor, or supervisee. Relevant knowledge includes information about cultures, identities, and their intersections, especially regarding how these relate to clinical practice. Relevant multicultural skills include the ability to discuss culture and diversity issues with comfort and skill in clinical (Day-Vines et al. 2007; Newton et al. 2025) or supervisory (Jones et al. 2019; K. M. King and Borders 2019) contexts. Culturally responsive supervision assumes that culture permeates clinical practice and supervision. It involves modeling, reflective discussion, and attention to issues of culture (Sisko and Rosenfield 2025).

Supervisees appear to benefit from supervisors' multicultural competence. Supervisees report greater satisfaction with supervision from supervisors who are more culturally responsive (Vekaria et al. 2023) and multiculturally competent (Soheilian et al. 2014). One way that supervisors' multicultural competence contributes to greater supervisee satisfaction with supervision is by enhancing the supervisory working alliance (Crockett and Hays 2015). More concretely, supervisees who reported greater depth of discussion of multicultural identity issues in supervision reported higher levels of supervisory working alliance and multicultural intervention self-efficacy (Phillips et al. 2017).

Society's response to diverse groups (e.g., bias, discrimination) affects equality between groups and their relative inclusion versus exclusion from society. Individuals who belong to marginalized, undervalued groups are likely to have poorer access to societal resources like quality education, employment, health care, justice, and political advocacy (Benner et al. 2018; D. R. Williams et al. 2019). Clients, supervisees, and supervisors who belong to these groups may have experienced discrimination, intolerance, exclusion, or even acts of hatred (Faber et al. 2023). Identifying, acknowledging, and skillfully addressing issues of difference, inequality, and exclusion in the context of therapy or supervision represent features of social justice competency, which complements multicultural competencies (Peters et al. 2022).

What does supervisory multicultural competence look like in practice? In a qualitative study, supervisors identified as highly multiculturally competent were described by their supervisees as being aware and knowledgeable about multicultural issues and open and interested in discussing them in supervision. These discussions were characterized by attitudes of respect for potentially different beliefs of the supervisee and client (Ancis and Marshall 2010).

Complementing multicultural competencies is an attitude of cultural humility, defined as "an interpersonal stance that is other-oriented rather than self-focused, characterized by respect and lack of superiority toward an individual's cultural background and experience" (Hook et al. 2013, p. 353). In practice, it is often helpful for both supervisees and supervisors to work toward cultural competence by first cultivating an attitude of cultural humility and cultural responsiveness, rather than focusing on learning decontextualized facts about different cultures. Cultural humility involves explicitly positioning oneself as a cultural learner with respect to a client or supervisee whose identity and experience differ from one's own (Zhu et al. 2023). Cultural humility allows supervisors to create a safe space to discuss differences in supervision and to model receptivity to learning from each other (Watkins and Hook 2016). Evidence shows that supervisor cultural humility strengthens the supervisory working alliance and supervisee satisfaction with supervision (Watkins et al. 2025; Wilcox et al. 2024). Moreover, among supervisees who identify as a person of color and had been supervised by a White supervisor, their perceptions of supervisor cultural humility contributed to greater counseling self-efficacy, and this effect was mediated by the quality of the supervisory working alliance (Vandament et al. 2022). Supervisors who can exhibit and teach cultural humility can help supervisees overcome some of the gaps in cultural humility skills that have been identified in training programs (Galán et al. 2024).

Ideally, supervisors not only welcome cultural discussions but actively look for opportunities to discuss culture with supervisees in an inviting way as part of their commitment to a broader multicultural orientation (Owen 2013; Watkins et al. 2019). In contrast, lack of attention to multicultural issues in supervision represents missed cultural opportunities and ineffective supervisory behaviors, both for White trainees (Ladany et al. 2013) and racialized trainees (Wong et al. 2012). The absence of cultural responsivity in supervision has been identified as particularly problematic for White supervisors working with supervisees of color and has been linked to reduced supervisee satisfaction with supervision (Phillips et al. 2017; Wilcox et al. 2024). These findings suggest that while all supervisors may benefit from continuing education and attention to developing multicultural supervisory competencies, this benefit may be larger for White supervisors.

Supervisors need to not only maintain and develop their own cultural humility, but also help supervisees develop it. Winkeljohn Black et al. (2025) suggest that supervisors focus on four key elements to help build cultural humility in supervisees. First, they suggest collaboratively exploring supervisees' cultural strengths as well as gaps in their awareness of culture through activities such as cultural genograms and providing feedback on cultural dimensions of work with clients. The next element they highlight for development is the ability to receive feedback nondefensively, which they define as being able to:

> (a) recognize and regulate one's defenses; (b) maintain enough ego strength or the capacity to, among other things, adapt, manage stress, and tolerate frustration in challenging situations; (c) develop critical self-compassion ..., and (d) [respond] with curiosity and openness rather than with anger, denial, or being upset. (p. 57)

To promote this capacity, which is essential for learning from constructive feedback on cultural and other competencies, the authors suggest encouraging the use of mindfulness to observe one's own responses to feedback and the use of in-the-moment processing to explore defensive responses in supervision. The third ingredient the authors propose as essential to developing cultural humility is the capacity for accurate empathy. They note that countertransference and poor emotion regulation can both impede empathy and suggest that supervisors assess for the presence of these in supervisees. Empathy can be developed through a mixture of didactic methods (Ngo et al. 2022) and practicing empathic responses in supervision with role play. The fourth and final ingredient for cultural humility is to cultivate the supervisee's capacity for curiosity about clients' cultural experiences. As expressing curiosity about a cultural dimension of a client's experience requires risk-taking, supervisees will likely require guidance on how to express such humble curiosity in a way that reflects genuineness, rather than a stance of mere intellectual curiosity.

Broaching is a useful skill for safely introducing cultural identity as a potential topic for exploration in clients as well as similarities or differences in identity between counselor and client (Day-Vines et al. 2007; K. M. King and Borders 2019) or supervisor and supervisee (Jones et al. 2019). Broaching in the context of supervision has been described as:

> a strategy or skill that is intended to begin and/or continue ongoing facilitation of dialogs concerning how the supervisors and supervisees' cultural make-up may impact the working relationship and

alliance throughout the supervisor-supervisee relationship, supervisee and client relationships, and supervisees' overall development (Jones et al. 2019). Supervisors can utilize broaching to initiate conversations concerning cultural similarities and differences with genuine and respectful inquisitiveness (i.e., positive factors of cultural humility) (Jones and Branco 2020, p. 201)

Supervisors are encouraged to broach culture and identity issues in supervision from the outset in the first meeting to begin to foster such discussions. Here is an example of an initial broaching statement:

> As we begin our supervisory relationship, I want to take some time to point out that I intend for this to be a safe space. Every relationship we enter into will be intercultural, and the supervisory relationship is no different. Culturally we may have similarities and differences, and I welcome having discussions concerning those cultural similarities and differences. If at any time you feel as though I have offended you or failed to acknowledge the impact of your cultural perspective, please do not hesitate to let me know (Jones et al. 2019, p. 9)

A few things are noteworthy about this statement. First, it identifies safety as a relational goal. It contextualizes the supervisory relationship as intercultural and thus that both similarities and differences between supervisor and supervisee are likely. It also signals the supervisor's openness to discussing those sociocultural dimensions of the supervision relationship and invites the supervisee's input. Here is another example that includes an invitation to teach the supervisor about times they may be the source of bias, another expression of humility:

> I believe that to learn and care for patients to the best of our abilities, we all need to feel comfortable and supported in our work environments. I wish that expressions of bias never occurred; unfortunately, they do. Patients and families may say things that reveal their biases, and sometimes I myself may be the source.

I want to know when you are not feeling comfortable or supported. I hope you will teach me as I teach you. (D. J. Wheeler
et al. 2019, p. 1113)

While examples like this can provide a useful starting point, ultimately it is essential to communicate these kinds of messages using words
that feel true to who you are, and which are a good match for your supervisee and as a model for them to do likewise with their clients (Day-Vines
et al. 2018). Once you and your supervisees find broaching statements
that communicate these ideas well, it helps to practice them, perhaps in
a role-play, so you can overcome fear and avoidance of this topic and feel
comfortable using these statements (Jacquart et al. 2024; Jin et al. 2024).

Supervising Students With Disabilities and Identifying Useful Accommodations

Disability is a distinct dimension of culture and identity that has many
tangible implications for supervision that need to be considered at the
outset. These include creating a welcoming environment for supervisees
with a disability to share their need for accommodations, facilitating
their access to accommodations, as well as less tangible considerations
such as helping them recognize and address discriminatory attitudes
and stigma (Lund et al. 2020; Pearlstein et al. 2022). Unfortunately,
most supervisors have had no training in how to work with trainees with
disabilities, are uncertain about how to do so, and feel they lack dis-
ability-specific supervisory competence (Wilbur et al. 2019). Given that
supervisors are responsible for exercising leadership, guidance, and advocacy for supervisees with a disability, there is a risk that they may experience inadequate or harmful supervision (Pearlstein and Soyster 2019;
Wilbur et al. 2019).

In this section, I will only highlight a few of the key issues for supervisors working with supervisees with a disability, and the references cited
above and below can help you fill in some of the gaps. A good starting
place is to read about disabilities and disability culture to develop greater
awareness of the attitudinal stigma and practical barriers that those with a

disability encounter in much of life and to learn how you, as a supervisor, can support and advocate for reasonable accommodations for trainees (Wilbur et al. 2019). This step will require you to honestly reflect on your own attitudes toward trainees with disabilities. Do you perhaps believe that those with disabilities are inherently less capable? If so, it may help to read about individuals with disabilities who have achieved success in their occupations (e.g., Steven Hawking, Oprah Winfrey, Frida Kahlo, and Andrea Bocelli) or, closer to home, the accomplishments of mental health professionals with lived experience of mental illness (Boyd et al. 2016). Or perhaps you feel providing accommodations is unduly burdensome, unnecessary, or not your job, in which case you should learn about trainees' legal rights to reasonable accommodations (Lund et al. 2020; Olkin 2009). If you are feeling unsure of how to proceed, it can be helpful to consult with relevant offices at your employing institution (e.g., student accessibility services, human resources).

Some disabilities are visible (e.g., people who use mobility devices); however, many are not (e.g., people living with a learning disability, chronic or episodic illness, or mental health challenges). Thus, supervisors should not assume that the absence of a visible disability equates to no disability, but should indicate to all trainees at the outset that reasonable accommodations are available should they need them. Because of the power differential, the supervisor should open the door to that discussion, as some supervisees may be reluctant to request required accommodations. Also, it helps to frame the discussion around the need for accommodations rather than about having a disability. Because a disability is related to a health condition, it is private information that trainees are not required to share. While some trainees may be at ease with voluntarily discussing their health condition or disability status, others will not, and that is their right.

Supervisees with a disability have a legal right to reasonable accommodation (Lund et al. 2020). That includes the right to be involved in discussions about their needs. It's essential that supervisees participate in these discussions as they will typically know what they require. Trainees who are university students may have documentation from their university's accessibility office, typically identifying required accommodations. However, these may be standard academic accommodations (e.g., additional time for completing a test or assignment) and may not address the idiosyncratic needs for non-standard accommodations a supervisee requires for success at the trainee's practicum or residency experience. Establishing reasonable non-standard accommodations should be collaboratively discussed and brainstormed among the trainee, the supervisor, and the training director, and a written plan included as part of the student's written training contract. The student's university training program director should also be informed of the plan as appropriate. Ideally, accommodations will be individualized to allow the trainee to learn and demonstrate essential competencies. To illustrate, some of the accommodations required may include supervisor behavior (e.g., speaking louder and more distinctly to a supervisee who has reduced hearing capacity and can read lips), environmental supports (e.g., adaptive technology, accessible physical spaces, availability of interpreters who can sign, information provided in an alternative format), and adjustment of task demands and time frames (Pearlstein et al. 2022).

The search for reasonable accommodations that do not compromise the educational activity or the welfare of the client raises the question: What is an essential competency, and what does it mean to demonstrate it? Essential competencies are abilities in each competency domain (e.g., assessment) that are distinct from the specific tasks that may be used to fulfill them (e.g., administering an intelligence test). For instance, a student who has a visual impairment may be accommodated by having a psychometrist (or the supervisor) perform the portions of test administration of an assessment that require vision (e.g., block design). The student may then administer verbal components of the assessment, synthesize assessment results, complete report writing, and communicate the results of the assessment. These strategies enable the supervisee to demonstrate their assessment competency. In other cases, where accommodations concern time for task completion, supervisees may be able to demonstrate essential competencies with flexibility around time demands. This might mean additional time to complete tasks or permitting a modified schedule so the trainee can conduct their work at the time of day in which they are better able to function. In some cases, these accommodations may entail that the supervisee be given longer to complete their training experience.

Reasonable accommodations are required unless they create an *undue burden*, meaning they would compromise client welfare, fundamentally alter essential training competencies, or demand resources or supervisory time beyond what the site can realistically provide. Accommodations can change *how* a trainee demonstrates competencies but cannot eliminate the obligation to meet professional and ethical standards. Most supports—such as structured feedback, scheduling flexibility, or assistive technologies—are feasible and expected. Undue burden applies only when no reasonable alternative can preserve both the trainee's access needs and the program's responsibility to ensure competent and safe clinical care. In cases where a trainee cannot demonstrate essential competencies with the aid of reasonable accommodations, supervisors will need to consider remediation or gatekeeping (see Chapter 6).

The Goals and Tasks of Supervision

Beyond establishing a positive relationship, a strong supervisory working alliance requires agreement on the goals and tasks of supervision. Goals describe *what* supervision is meant to accomplish and tasks operationalize *how* these goals will be met. While many of the goals (and their associated tasks) that are important for supervisee development are common across supervisees, each supervisee also will seek to fulfill certain unique goals. Therefore, supervisors need to collaborate with supervisees to agree on the set of common and unique goals that will be undertaken during the training experience. I have found that an efficient way to do this is to comprehensively address the many common goals and tasks that every supervisee I work with needs to understand in one document, known as a Professional Disclosure Statement (PDS). Complementing the PDS, the supervision contract addresses supervisee-specific goals and is uniquely designed for each supervisee. Discussing both in an initial meeting helps establish shared expectations. A description of the purpose and content of both the PDS and the supervision contract follows.

Clarifying Expectations With the Professional Disclosure Statement

The PDS offers a general description of a supervisor's approach to supervision and expectations of supervisees—the framework of supervision. Using a PDS helps ensure supervisors communicate all the essential information that supervisees require to understand what is expected of them and what they may expect from supervision at the outset and it provides a clear plan to follow. This comprehensive information about plans and mutual expectations goes a long way toward demystifying the training experience. This transparency provides predictability, reduces uncertainty, and reduces the power imbalance It also is akin to informed consent.

Through sharing and discussing their PDS, supervisors help to create conditions for trust and safety which are essential to successful supervision (Egan et al. 2017; Watkins 2020a). Without them, little learning or growth can occur. When supervisees experience a safe relationship with a trustworthy supervisor, they are more likely to disclose challenges (Gibson et al. 2019; Park et al. 2019), accept input, develop confidence (Park et al. 2019), and take sensible risks in their work.

For additional clarity, the supervisor also needs to describe the institutional and systemic factors that influence the training and supervisory experience. These contextual aspects include the requirements of the

- supervisee's graduate training program,
- professional regulatory body of the trainee and supervisor,
- clinical setting's policies and procedures,
- ethical code of the profession, and
- relevant legislation in the jurisdiction (e.g., laws regarding privacy and health information).

These requirements are typically laid out in publications made available by each organization. Supervisees should be alerted to these requirements and to the source publications. Supervisors should ensure that the relevant aspects of these regulations for the training experience are reviewed and discussed at the outset of training and as needed along the way.

Orienting the Supervisee via the Professional Disclosure Statement

The PDS informs supervisees about the supervisor's qualifications, approach, expectations, and responsibilities. Along with the supervision contract it documents informed consent (Barnett 2023). Table 3.1 lists typical PDS elements (see also Watkins et al. 2024).

Table 3.1 Template for supervisor's professional disclosure statement

---

Supervisor Name/Title/Address and emergency contact information

Overview and purpose of PDS

Supervisor's qualifications:
- Degrees, credentials, and licenses.
- Clinical training and previous supervision.
- Clinical interests and declared competencies.
- Supervision training and experience.

Supervision teaching and research experience (if any)

Goals of supervision and model(s) and methods of supervision used

Structure and content of supervision meetings:
- Frequency, duration, and format (e.g., individual/group, in person/online).
- Types of foci (e.g., intervention, cultural competence, countertransference).
- Supervisory roles, including limits of counselor role.
- Expectations for supervisee activity within and between meetings.
- Supervisor's responsibilities (including how dual-roles will be managed).

Feedback and evaluation procedures

Confidentiality policies/procedures:
- Client informed consent and confidentiality.
- Procedures for the secure storage and transfer of client documents and communications.
- Limitations of confidentiality in the supervisory relationship.

Disclosure of services delivered under supervision

Emergency procedures

Ethics, professionalism, concerns, and evaluation appeals:
- Ethical codes adhered to by supervisee and supervisor.
- Procedure for addressing concerns and complaints.

Supervisee's signature acknowledging receipt and understanding of the document

---

To illustrate, I offer descriptions and examples from my own PDS. I state that the purpose of my PDS is to "provide you, my supervisee, with an understanding of the process of clinical supervision, including our mutual responsibilities to one another and our clients, as well as to acquaint you with my background in supervision and how I approach it." In the Supervisory qualifications section, supervisors describe their professional education and training, including the therapeutic approaches they use and their areas of competency. This section concludes with a description of the supervisor's education and training in supervision that may include coursework, workshops, self-study, and supervised supervision experience, as well as the number of years of supervision experience and the range of supervisees supervised (e.g., from first practicum through postdoctoral supervisees).

In the *Goals of supervision and models used* section of my PDS, I describe my goals as being to:

> ...create a safe, supportive, respectful, and stimulating supervisory relationship as the foundation for ensuring client welfare and quality service delivery, promoting your competency development, supporting your coping with the demands of clinical work, and doing so in a manner consistent with professional standards, ethics, relevant legislation, and site-specific regulations and policies.

Regarding my approach to supervision, I include two paragraphs, the first providing a conceptual overview where I state, among other things, that it is "informed by a developmental perspective, which seeks to tailor supervision to your level of professional development and training needs and goals." In the second paragraph, I specify, in detail, how my supervisee and I will work together. I include here a lengthy verbatim extract to give you a sense of the types of things one might choose to specify:

> We will meet each week for a two-hour supervision meeting. Early on in our work we will spend a good deal of time discussing case-conceptualization and treatment planning for your clients. I may assign you readings as part of this, which should be completed prior to our next meeting. Part of our meeting will be reserved for us to review your work with clients. My approach to this part of our meeting is informed by an events-based model of supervision (Ladany et al. 2005), which emphasizes identifying, understanding, and dealing with small but significant events that crop-up in the course of therapy as well as events within supervision that require discussion. Both you and I will collaborate in identifying events for discussion in supervision at the outset and put them in our agenda. Events should be selected that meet your learning goals, concern supervision, or address client welfare or service delivery quality/ effectiveness. Categories of events to consider include
>
> • problems in the therapeutic alliance or client commitment to therapy,
> • successes and difficulties carrying out intervention,

- client response to treatment/therapist,
- therapist response to client (e.g., countertransference),
- crises,
- previously assigned tasks in supervision,
- issues relating to the supervisor, supervision, or supervisory alliance;
- ethical dilemmas,
- issues related to culture or identity, and
- professional identity and professionalism.

As part of this portion of our meeting I will want to see brief (3–5 minute) selections of video relevant to the focal issue. Over time I will need to see selections of your work with each of your clients. I encourage you to include examples of when things have gone well because understanding such successes promotes a well-founded confidence that is essential to being effective. Note that at times it will be valuable for us to process your personal (emotional, behavioral, attitudinal) reactions to things your clients say or do. To facilitate this, I will adopt a counselor role within supervision. The focus of this work is necessarily limited to your response to the client and to ensuring this does not interfere with your work with the client. Should it become apparent that deeper personal problems or issues underlie such reactions I may suggest that you explore these in the context of your own personal therapy as this goes beyond the limits of what is appropriate for the supervision context and our respective roles. It is expected that psychologists and psychologists-in-training will engage in self-care to support their own mental health, including seeking therapy or counseling as-needed.

For some of the supervisee tasks and expectations outlined above supervisees' ability to meet them will depend in part on their capacity for self-awareness and insight. When these supervisee qualities are weaker the supervisory alliance may suffer unless self-reflection is specifically encouraged and promoted within supervision (Brien et al. 2025).

I go on to list other ways I expect supervisees to be prepared for our meetings, such as having completed previously assigned tasks, identifying learning needs and clinical priorities, and maintaining a journal or log to record plans and assignments for future reference. I also list my responsibilities, which include being punctual, respecting the scheduled time (e.g., not dealing with other matters unless absolutely necessary), being prepared, engaging in collaborative agenda-setting, basing clinical guidance and feedback on observations of the supervisee's work, and being open and responsive to feedback about supervision.

Concerning feedback, I indicate that supervisees will receive ongoing formative feedback and that any areas of performance that fall below expectations will be promptly identified to permit corrective actions and learning to occur. Areas exceeding expectations will also be identified and positively acknowledged. An informal evaluation at the midway point will be given. The final, summative evaluation will be based on previous feedback (and the supervisee's response to it) using the evaluation measure identified at the outset of training.

In the *Confidentiality* section, I review my expectation that my supervisees will be familiar with, and adhere to, relevant health care legislation and clinic policies regarding client confidentiality and its limits. I also outline the limited nature of confidentiality for supervisees within supervision. Here is what I say:

> In general, confidentiality in supervision is limited by the requirement for supervisors to (a) evaluate supervisees; and (b) report on these evaluations to relevant educational or professional regulatory authorities. Nonetheless, I will not disclose personal details of your private life that have no bearing on your professional or educational functioning. If I believe personal material does have a bearing on your performance or professionalism and needs to be included, I would discuss my intention to include such personal information in an evaluation with you so you are aware and have an opportunity to respond before it goes beyond supervision.

The *Services delivered under supervision* section simply outlines how the supervisee must disclose to clients that services are provided under my supervision and that the clinician is a student trainee (when that is the case). I include the following statement for clarity:

> As the registered psychologist providing supervision under the authority of my registration certificate, I am responsible for all of your work. As such, all clinical decisions and courses of treatment must have my approval. If you have any concerns about your clients or doubts about the appropriateness of a course of action you are considering, please consult me at your earliest opportunity.

Regarding emergency procedures, I indicate that we will verbally review what constitutes a crisis and develop a plan for whom to contact in such cases. Concerning ethics and professionalism trainees are expected to have read the *Canadian Code of Ethics for Psychologists* (CPA 2017a), the *Ethical Guidelines for Supervision in Psychology* (CPA 2017b), and the profession's practice guidelines, so that they are prepared to identify, raise, and discuss ethical and professional issues. I expect supervisees to conform their professional decision-making and behavior to these ethical principles For clarity, I state, "You should be aware that unprofessional and unethical behaviour may result in both a negative evaluation in this practicum as well as sanctions from the university (including possible mandatory withdrawal from the program)." Although this is no doubt a little unsettling for supervisees to read, I think that the value of knowing all the parameters of supervision creates a degree of predictability and control for supervisees that outweighs any short-term anxiety produced.

What is most important about the PDS is not simply providing it but using it. By using it as a basis for a discussion supervisors can assess and deepen the supervisee's understanding. With that in mind, I suggest that you take this opportunity to write up your own PDS using the headings provided above, or to update it if you already have one.

Creating Unique Goals and Plans in the Supervision Contract

The supervision contract complements the general framework for supervision described in the PDS by describing how the training experience, including supervision, will be tailored to the unique learning goals for the supervisee. It should be developed in collaboration with the supervisee to ensure it captures their learning goals and expectations. To avoid redundancy with the PDS, supervisors can reference and attach the PDS when material overlaps. In the absence of a PDS, supervision contracts should include many of the PDS details described above.

Like the PDS, supervision contracts serve to:

- advise supervisees of clinical expectations and responsibilities,
- clarify expectations for supervision (such as methods, goals, structure, and purpose), and
- provide a context for communication and a basis for the development of trust.

If you are providing supervision within an institution, chances are they have a standard contract. However, if you ever need to construct or revise a contract, you can find the specifics of what should go into a contract in the supervision guidelines of APA (2014) or Association of State and Provincial Psychology Boards (ASPPB 2015). A sample contract that meets the ASPPB recommendations can be found in Appendix IV of the ASPPB guidelines (2015). Other sample contracts are also publicly available (e.g., Bernard and Goodyear 2019; Falender and Shafranske 2021).

A good contract is clear, concise, and specific about the nature and goals of the training experience and who is involved. A contract should identify the primary supervisor, the supervisee, the setting, the client population, the supervisee's time commitment and caseload, the goals and requirements of the training experience, and the details concerning supervision (e.g., how much time per week, along with information about feedback, evaluation, and expectations of the supervisee). The specific goals and requirements of the supervision contract should align with the requirements of the student's training program, and the policies and procedures of the training site.

When a training experience includes multiple supervisory assignments (e.g., during residency) an individual should be identified who will take responsibility for coordinating the training experience and facilitating problem-solving as necessary. This individual, or their designate, should take responsibility for integrating the evaluations across multiple supervisors and summarizing them in a written report for the student and their training program. In simpler cases, there may only be a primary and secondary supervisor. In these, the primary supervisor assumes overall responsibility for the training experience including integrating the secondary supervisor's evaluation into the overall evaluation of the supervisee. Details of secondary supervision arrangements should be noted in the primary supervision contract.

Where the contract needs to go beyond the PDS is in the specification of unique learning and training goals for each supervisee. This process begins with consideration of the supervisee's baseline competencies (described below). The dyad must identify which of these competencies will be a focus for development in this training experience and how this development will occur. This plan must consider the supervisee's needs and interests, the limits of the supervisor's competencies, the clinical opportunities afforded by the clinical site, and the resources (e.g., duration of training experience) available to the dyad. The type of learning opportunity and the degree of challenge involved will need to reflect the stage of the supervisee's development. Once a supervisor has had the opportunity to develop an understanding of the supervisee's level of competency (e.g., through observation of clinical work and discussion of past training experiences), supervisors can make informed decisions about how much autonomy the supervisee can be entrusted with. Whereas novices require close monitoring and careful scaffolding of work with easier clients, more advanced supervisees benefit from increasing autonomy and the opportunity to work with more challenging clients. Advanced supervisees can benefit from taking symbolic ownership of responsibility for their client's care, treating the client as if they were their own.

Assess Baseline Competencies and Set Training Goals

Assessing baseline competencies sets the stage for an impactful training experience and for effective supervision. It does so by clarifying supervisee strengths, identifying training targets, guiding client assignments, and establishing a reference for later evaluation.

When considering the supervisee's baseline competencies, supervisors need to consider whether the supervisee is developmentally on course—that is, whether the supervisee is where they should be relative to their stage of professional development. For context, supervisees tend to develop their foundational competencies more rapidly than their functional competencies (Hitzeman et al. 2020). This suggests that attention should be given during this initial assessment to the supervisee's functional competencies through direct observation of their work with clients. When considering what level of ability is typical or expected for a supervisee at a given stage of professional training, experienced supervisors will have internalized a developmental frame of reference they can consult. However, less experienced supervisors may benefit from consulting with more experienced supervisors.

Fouad et al. (2009) describe three transition points that serve as useful frames of reference when deciding whether a trainee is on track in the development of their foundational and functional competencies. These include readiness for: practicum, residency, and entry to practice. Fouad et al. propose detailed behavioral anchors consistent with readiness for each of the three levels (see also Hatcher et al., 2013). In general, the essential component at the readiness for practicum level is understanding of relevant foundational knowledge (e.g., ethical and professional standards), whereas the readiness for residency level involves awareness and application of that knowledge to practice (i.e., functional competency), and at the readiness for entry to practice level, it requires independent application of knowledge to practice. Applying these readiness tests to your supervisee allows you to evaluate whether your supervisee's baseline competencies are developmentally on course. This, in turn, sets the stage for targeted goal setting to occur.

To evaluate the supervisee's baseline competencies, supervisors need to familiarize themselves with the supervisee's prior learning. To do so, supervisors may ask supervisees to summarize their past training experiences, and note any areas previously identified by supervisors as areas of strength or in need of improvement. It may also be valuable to have supervisees self-evaluate their competencies using the training site's evaluation form. Supervisees should also report on their past training experiences with specific client demographics (e.g., children and youth, adults, seniors; individuals from different racial and ethnic populations; genders and sexual orientations; religious traditions; persons with disabilities; etc.), diagnostic presentations, and the range of therapies and modalities they have delivered (e.g., group, individual, couple). This information can help ensure they are getting the opportunity to work with a diverse range of clients.

Finally, supervisors will benefit from directly observing their supervisee's work with one or more clients. Even brief samples of direct observation provide supervisors with a wealth of behavioral and stylistic information that simply cannot be conveyed through supervisee self-report. These rich observations can be used to inform goal setting and to gauge subsequent learning and development. For advanced supervisees who may be accustomed to a high degree of clinical autonomy, this level of scrutiny may feel as if their new supervisor doubts their abilities or is not respecting their accomplishments from previous training. Consequently, it may be helpful to explain that this is a standard assessment designed to support their development, and that greater autonomy will follow.

Chapter Summary

Establishing a positive supervisory relationship is essential to a successful supervision experience. It includes a warm, positive bond that includes feelings of trust, safety, mutual respect, and initial discussion of all aspects of the relationship, including diversity and need for accommodations. It also includes a clear understanding of and agreement on the goals, methods, and tasks of supervision. This understanding is facilitated by reviewing the supervisor's PDS where their approaches to, and expectations for, supervision are stated. With this context, the dyad can effectively gauge the supervisee's baseline competencies to set relevant goals for the training experience and document these in the supervision contract.

Questions for Review and Reflection

1. Why is it essential to have a positive supervisory relationship? How will you promote a positive relationship with your supervisees?
2. In what ways is the supervisory relationship like, and unlike, the therapeutic alliance? How would you make this clear to a supervisee?

3. What is the purpose of the PDS? How does it complement the supervision contract? What part of your own PDS do you think will be most important or helpful for your supervisees?

4. Why is it helpful to inform all supervisees about the availability of reasonable accommodations at the outset of supervision? How might you follow up with a supervisee who indicates they require accommodation?

5. What is the purpose of assessing a supervisee's baseline level of competence? How would you go about that? How would you use the results of that assessment?

6. Part of the supervision contract involves explicitly specifying the supervisee's goals. Sometimes, however, once written into the contract, the goals are often forgotten when dealing with the immediate demands of clinical work. How might you keep supervisee goals in view during supervision?

CHAPTER 4

Making Supervision Meetings Effective

Recall the three primary goals of supervision: normative (client care), formative (supervisee learning and development), and restorative (supervisee well-being). The supervision meeting is the key place where these goals are planned, addressed, monitored, and evaluated. In this chapter, I discuss how to collaboratively structure supervision meetings to achieve these three goals. As an organizational aid, I relate these goals to the typical timeline of a course of psychotherapy, which dictates the sequence of the supervisee's work with the client, and thus a focus of supervision meetings.

Collaborating and Planning to Achieve the Goals of Supervision

Working collaboratively means the perspectives of both members of the dyad are respected, that both can initiate discussions, clarify issues, and bring in relevant materials. Both supervisor and supervisee should contribute to supervisee learning and development when planning and conducting supervision. The benefits of working collaboratively include a stronger supervisory alliance, deeper and more enduring learning, and a richer, more creative process (E. A. Johnson 2019).

The Timeline of Psychotherapy Supervision

To meet the three supervision goals requires attention to a predictable sequence of tasks over the course of the training experience. Supervisors and supervisees need to attend to this sequence to anticipate upcoming developments and plan appropriately. The sequence begins prior to the first supervision session and continues beyond the last supervision session, as shown in Table 4.1.

Table 4.1 Phase of training and associated supervision tasks

Phase of training	Supervision tasks
Preparatory	• orienting the supervisee • sharing mutual expectations • planning/contracting/goal setting
Early	• building the supervisory alliance • assessing the supervisee's baseline competencies • selecting clients and conducting intakes • conceptualizing clients and treatment planning
Middle	• implementing treatment/outcome monitoring • fostering professional development, formative feedback • dealing with challenges in therapy and supervision • completing midterm evaluations and identifying goals or competency problems for additional attention
Late	• consolidating client and supervisee gains • preparing for termination/transfer • completing final evaluations • concluding supervision
Post-Supervision	• gatekeeping • maintaining a post-supervision relationship

As discussed in Chapter 3, the organizational meeting in the preparatory phase orients the supervisee to supervision and to the training site. The dyad needs to develop a contract to specify and agree on the goals and methods of the training and supervision experience. The early phase of training, in which new clients are evaluated, provides an opportunity for the supervisor and supervisee to observe one another's work. This allows the supervisor to deepen and refine their assessment of supervisee baseline competencies. It can aid in selecting clients who offer a suitable level of challenge for the supervisee's competency level and meet the training goals. The early phase concludes with case conceptualization and treatment planning. Prominent ethical and professional issues during this phase include obtaining informed consent for treatment, discussing confidentiality and its limits, and consulting with referral sources or other team members. The middle phase of training, discussed in this chapter, involves implementing treatment plans and monitoring client outcomes throughout therapy. It requires the dyad to address challenges in therapy and supervision but also to attend to and learn from what is working well. Challenges that strain either the therapeutic or supervisory working alliances require immediate and careful attention to help heal any rupture in the alliance (see Chapter 5). The middle phase of training includes a midterm evaluation of the supervisee's progress in meeting goals and developing competencies and the adequacy of supervision and the training experience. The final phase of training involves helping the client and supervisee consolidate the gains they have made and preparing the client for termination or transfer at the conclusion of the training experience. The end of the training experience (as discussed in Chapter 6) involves a final summative evaluation for the supervisee as well as an opportunity for the supervisee to provide feedback to the supervisor about the training experience and supervision. After supervision ends, the supervisor may have a gatekeeping role that can include providing letters of reference for the supervisee to assist with obtaining other training opportunities (such as residency), employment, or licensure. Eventually, the supervisee may become a colleague, creating new opportunities for professional collaboration and a change in the professional relationship.

Normative Supervision: Ensuring Safe and Competent Client Care

Ensuring client safety means that the supervisor and supervisee work together to prevent clients from experiencing harm while in treatment, or to mitigate harms that do occur. Harm can be physical or psychological. Preventing harm is an essential responsibility that is mandated by our professional ethics.

Client Safety: Avoiding Harm

Before exploring how to avoid harm to clients, it is helpful to place this issue in perspective. Research clearly shows that most clients benefit from treatment, and this finding does not vary much across *bona fide* forms of treatment. Nonetheless, a minority of clients fail to improve, and some will worsen during therapy (Gazzola and Iwakabe 2022). As Barlow (2010) noted, "In general, deterioration of various kinds is much too common to be ignored" (p. 250). The evidence suggests that client characteristics and therapist qualities are the primary contributors to client deterioration. The implications for supervision are that supervisors need to select clients for their supervisees, bearing in mind the client's risk for deterioration, the supervisee's baseline competency level, and the degree of support available to the supervisee from the supervisor and the service environment (e.g., inpatient vs. outpatient treatment). Further, supervisors and supervisees need to monitor client outcomes throughout treatment to identify clients who are deteriorating early on.

Several client factors have been identified as contributing to the risk of client deterioration during treatment (Constantino et al. 2021). Severity of disturbance is the client factor most strongly related to risk of deterioration (Lambert and Hawkins 2001a). In general, clients with chronic or recurring mental health problems such as schizophrenia, schizo-affective, bipolar, and personality disorders tend to show the poorest response to psychotherapy. Other client variables linked to poor outcomes include extrinsic motivation, low expectancy for success, limited ability to relate to others, weak ego strength (e.g., lack of persistence and determination), low psychological mindedness, and limited ability to recognize problems or patterns (Garfield 1994). In general, clients with fewer of these challenges are more suitable for novice supervisees in an outpatient setting. More challenging clients may be safely assigned to more experienced supervisees when adequate supports are in place.

Some cases of client deterioration are associated with therapists' style or qualities. D. G. Martin and Johnson (2024, pp. 375–376) summarized therapist actions or qualities that have been associated with damage to clients and worsened outcomes. These include:

- Therapist's *take charge* attitude early in therapy (as evidenced by)
  - confrontation,
  - negative processes (e.g., hostility, mocking, blaming, criticism),
  - assumptions (e.g., that clients are satisfied and doing well),
  - therapist-centricity (arrogance about knowing what's best for client),
  - rigidity (in adherence to rules and procedures of therapeutic approach), and
  - cultural arrogance (imposing one's own cultural beliefs).

- Insight or interpretations offered prematurely.
- High concentrations of transference interpretations.
- Arguing with clients.
- *Aggressive stimulator* style: intrusive, confrontational, challenging, caring, self-revealing, charismatic, authoritarian, focusing on the individual.
- High focus on the client–therapist relationship, combined with low empathy, genuineness, and warmth.
- Cold therapists.
- Therapist irritability.
- Lack of empathy.
- Negative countertransference.

Two main themes appear in the list: therapist actions that involve real or perceived attacks on the client, and therapist coldness and lack of caring or compassion for the client.

Therapists who behave in these ways are more likely to do harm to clients. Supervisors who observe any of these potential indicators of harm need to address them immediately and determine whether client safety or well-being has been compromised and whether the supervisee requires additional training or oversight to avoid future reoccurrences.

One of the ways client harm or a deterioration in the therapeutic relationship is manifested is through ruptures in the therapeutic alliance, which, if not repaired, are associated with a weaker therapeutic alliance and worse outcomes (Eubanks et al. 2018). Ruptures arise not only from therapist harm, but also from disagreements and misunderstandings between therapist and client. These can range from relatively minor misunderstandings on the therapist's part (e.g., empathic misses) to severe, acrimonious conflicts. Therapy being a human enterprise, such strains and ruptures are likely inevitable. Thus, being able to notice them when they occur allows them to be repaired. To recognize a rupture, it helps to understand the two main types of client responses to a rupture: *withdrawal* and *confrontation*. In a withdrawal, the client pulls back from the therapist and emotionally distances themselves. Markers of withdrawal ruptures include when the client goes unusually quiet, abruptly changes topic, talks abstractly, or hastily agrees ("yes, yes"). Withdrawals are an effort to maintain the relationship by suppressing or avoiding overt conflict. Whereas with-drawal ruptures can be hard to detect, confrontation ruptures involve overt expressions of hostility and anger toward the therapist or therapy and may include efforts to exert control. Confrontation ruptures can be understood as self-assertion at the cost of relatedness (Muran et al. 2021). Markers include criticisms of the therapist or therapy, manipulations, microaggres-sions, and objectifying the other. Perhaps the simplest and most obvious form is when a client says *no* to a therapist suggestion.

Supervisors who observe indicators of alliance rupture need to explore these with the supervisee and determine how best to repair the alliance. Repairs to the alliance improve client outcomes and can sometimes be accomplished with a simple and genuine acknowledgment of error by the therapist when appropriate. Other effective repair strategies involve nondefensively

- revisiting the therapeutic rationale when an intervention is misunderstood,
- revising tasks or goals when the client disagrees with assigned tasks or goals,
- addressing misunderstandings, for instance, when a client feels criticized by the therapist; and
- nonjudgmentally exploring how the rupture may reflect relational themes or common patterns in the client's life (Safran, Muran and Eubanks-Carter 2011).

Supporting Competent Care

Beyond ensuring safety, supervisors are responsible for seeing that clients receive competent care. But what does this mean when the trainee may be a beginning therapist struggling to master the basics of the craft? It means that the supervisor makes an *entrustment decision* based on an assessment of the supervisee's baseline competencies. This enables the supervisor to choose clients or clinical activities for the supervisee that are suited to their competency level and to provide the right amount and type of sup-port required for competent care. For example, a novice therapist may need to observe the supervisor work with clients at first as a co-therapist before taking a more active role with clients. Later, once the supervisee has demonstrated some understanding and confidence in this highly supported environment, more autonomy may be given.

In contrast to the emphasis on avoiding harm, which is the focus of ensuring client safety, the emphasis in promoting supervisee competence is on developing the supervisee's competencies as they relate to well-established approaches to therapy. Supervisors train their supervisees within their area of competence using their preferred evidence-informed therapeutic approach. In doing so, it is helpful for supervisors to focus on common factors, especially the therapeutic alliance, within their preferred therapeutic orientation.

One reason for focusing on common factors rests on the finding that common factors contribute more to therapy outcome than specific factors (Wampold 2015). Although many now equate common factors with therapeutic relationship variables, Lambert and Ogles (2014) note that the common factors category encompasses many other types of variables, such as the therapeutic setting (a private space that permits safe disclosure of embarrassing material), or exposure methods, which are employed in various ways in many therapies. Lambert and Bergin (1994) note that the common elements of many therapies can be classified into support, learning, and action. That is, distressed clients who receive support from a trustworthy helper can be emboldened to acknowledge and reconceptualize their problems and, with the aid of a systematic approach, identify and try out new solutions.

Research on common factors has identified the quality of the therapeutic alliance as perceived by the client to be among the strongest predictors of psychotherapy outcome, independent of treatment orientation. In an influential review, Norcross and Lambert (2018) identified the following elements as demonstrably effective: the alliance, therapist empathy, positive regard, affirmation, and collecting client feedback.

Another rationale for supervision to focus on common factors concerns supervisee development. As supervisees progress through different training experiences and supervisors, they will necessarily be learning different therapeutic approaches and methods. Consequently, a focus on common factors enhances the continuity and integration of learning across training experiences and supervisors. It also increases the likelihood that clients will receive competent care.

Using Client Feedback in Supervision Through Outcome Monitoring

A growing body of evidence indicates that client outcomes improve when therapists employ outcome monitoring (OM; Barkham et al. 2023; Lambert et al. 2018). OM involves obtaining quantitative measurements from the client on one or more outcome domains prior to initiating treatment and measuring the client's progress repeatedly across sessions. OM helps primarily by identifying clients who are not improving or who are deteriorating. These clients are at heightened risk of dropout, premature termination, and having a poor outcome (Rognstad et al. 2023). Because therapists tend to be overly optimistic about their clients' progress (Hannan et al. 2005), they tend to miss deterioration when it occurs and with it the opportunity to address the issue with clients. In light of these benefits, and their trans-theoretical compatibility, several writers have recommended incorporating OM for routine use within all forms of therapy and supervision (E. A. Johnson 2019; Tasca et al. 2019; Wright et al. 2020). Unfortunately, many training clinics in Canada do not use OM, in part because supervisors lack familiarity with OM (Madsen et al. 2023). Although space constraints limit what follows to a brief overview, I hope that the references supplied will help interested supervisors learn more about OM.

Sophisticated automated systems are available (e.g., Lambert 2015); however, they are not necessary to use OM. Incorporating OM in both therapy and supervision provides several potential benefits. First, it conveys a strong message that OM is beneficial for client welfare and therapist learning. Second, using it in supervision provides an opportunity to teach how to implement OM effectively. This is vital given the practical nuances of using OM (Aafjes van Doorn & de Jong, 2022) and because the benefits derived from OM depend on how effectively it is implemented (Lutz et al. 2022). A practical benefit is that OM-informed early identification of deteriorating clients allows supervisors and supervisees to reconsider the treatment approach or enhance the therapeutic alliance. A study by Reese et al. (2009) examined the impact of OM on clients and supervisees. Relative to a no OM condition, incorporating OM into supervision was associated with better client outcomes, and did not harm supervisee counselling self-efficacy, satisfaction with supervision, or supervisees' perception of the supervisory alliance. Additionally, supervisees in the feedback condition exhibited a stronger correlation between their self-efficacy scores and client outcomes than those in the no feedback condition, suggesting that OM may enhance accurate self-appraisal in trainees.

As OM methods and technologies proliferate, supervisors are faced with decisions about how to choose among OM methods and incorporate them into supervision (McAleavey et al. 2024). Some supervisors have noted practical challenges with incorporating OM into supervision, highlighting the need for ongoing research on implementation and training issues (Valdiviezo-Oña et al. 2025). Helpful guidance on incorporating OM in supervision can be found in Swift et al. (2015). Implementation and use of OM are more likely when trainees and supervisors are well-supported with the infusion of training materials and opportunities throughout the training program (Cooper et al. 2021).

Formative Supervision: Developing Supervisee Competencies

The Role of Supervision Models in Promoting Professional Development

During formative supervision, promoting the supervisee's professional growth and development is the focus. How this is accomplished, and for what purpose, varies somewhat with the supervision model in use. First-generation supervision models include psychotherapy-based, developmental, and process models (Bernard and Goodyear 2019). Second-generation models have focused on either integrating first-generation models by combining them or seeking common factors among them or addressing more specialized issues in supervision, such as multicultural supervision. As descriptions of these models are widely available,

I will not review them here. Nonetheless, supervisors are encouraged to thoughtfully synthesize formative approaches and methods from models that support their goals and preferences (and those of their supervisees) in a coherent manner. This emphasis on formative supervision aligns well with virtually all supervisees' preferences to use supervision to improve their competence (Spännargård et al. 2025). To illustrate how formative supervision goals can be met, I will describe a model that integrates several experiential learning approaches, which are known to be effective formative supervision methods (Bradley and Becker 2021).

The Experiential Learning Cycle

In his model of evidence-based clinical supervision, Milne (2009) updates Kolb's (1984) model of experiential learning to propose that learning in supervision best occurs through a cycle that involves five distinct mechanisms of change known as modes: experiencing, reflecting, conceptualizing, planning, and experimenting. These modes are not unique to Milne's model, but rather appear in many models of supervision. Learning in supervision is thought to occur through repeated cycles through this sequence. Below, I describe each of the five modes and offer suggestions, drawn from Milne and other sources, for how various methods can be used to enhance supervisee learning and development. Across all modes, the focus is on supporting the supervisee's evolution toward becoming an autonomous clinician.

Experiencing

Experiencing refers to the affective, attitudinal, and motivational dimensions of experience. The primary goal in working with the experiencing mode in supervision is to heighten supervisee awareness of these dimensions of experience. One could alternatively describe it as helping supervisees become more mindful of their experience in therapy and supervision.

Enhancing supervisee awareness of psychological states can be undertaken through open-ended questions such as "what were you feeling when the client went silent?" These do not make assumptions about the supervisee's experience and thus, provide a safe, supportive starting place.

Activities such as recalling and describing specific feelings, gathering information, and processing affect can further raise supervisee consciousness. Supervisors can also ask more focused, awareness-raising questions that direct the supervisee to pay attention to specific aspects of their experience, such as their motivation or attitude. Recognizing that these questions can feel more pointed, supervisors need to be mindful of the need to conduct the inquiry in a safe and supportive manner.

A richer, more systematic way of heightening attention to experience, known as interpersonal process recall (IPR; H. Kagan and Kagan 1997; N. I. Kagan and Kagan 1990), involves reviewing a client recording in supervision and pausing the recording at key moments and inviting the supervisee to discuss what they were thinking, feeling, or experiencing in that moment with the client. Supervisors can facilitate supervisees' disclosure and exploration of difficult or uncertain experiences with clients by paraphrasing and validating their responses and being nonjudgmental (Foskett and Van Vliet 2021). IPR can also be adapted as a means of exploring supervisees' experiences that are relevant to addressing multicultural issues with clients (Ivers et al. 2017).

Supervisees can actively participate in this mode of learning by being open and non-defensive in responding to questions and by internalizing this process by learning to ask the same types of questions of themselves after client sessions. In addition to these retrospective activities, supervisees can also use a brief presession mindfulness centering exercise to enhance their ability to remain present to their experience in therapy. Doing so enhances both therapist's in-session presence and session effectiveness as perceived by the client (Dunn et al. 2013). Conceivably, mindfulness exercises may also enhance therapists' post-session recall and awareness of experiences.

Reflecting

Reflecting involves thinking about experiences and behavior to generate novel ideas, insights, or hypotheses. Reflecting can be directed at one's own or others' (e.g., client, supervisor) behavior or experience. Reflecting is valuable when an experience or behavior does not make sense, is confusing, or contradicts other information. Reflection on emotional responses to clients, also known as countertransference responses, can be an especially fruitful topic for exploration in supervision via reflection (Hayes et al. 2023).

The use of reflective discussion can be particularly useful when reviewing therapy recordings. Whereas IPR focuses primarily on raising awareness of supervisee's in-the-moment experience with a client, reflective questioning and discussion seek to expand on such awareness by developing a broader conceptualization of the therapist's subsequent decision-making and action in specific moments. Hill et al. (2016) found that having supervisees answer a list of written questions about the recordings prior to supervision provided a helpful way of deepening the subsequent discussion in supervision. Hill et al.'s list includes reflective questions related to the supervisee's thoughts and feelings during the chosen portion of the session, their actions and what they intended them to accomplish, the values or principles that prompted their actions, as well as what they didn't say or do (and wish they had), what they would do differently next time, and what reflections they wish to share in supervision. By priming supervisees to consider these questions ahead of time, the subsequent discussion in supervision can be enriched. For instance, it may uncover supervisee feelings of anxiety that may have previously been undisclosed and offer an opportunity to explore and contextualize such feelings.

Socratic questioning is another common method for stimulating reflection in supervisees. When done well, it offers a subtle, yet powerful means of engaging a learner in a process of reasoning that can generate productive new ideas. Done poorly, however, it can feel like a tedious or condescending game of "guess what I am thinking." Socratic questioning can be facilitated by beginning with drawing attention to a relevant set of observations (e.g., "It seems like you are having a lot of mixed feelings about your client leaving therapy") and inviting the supervisee to reflect on that with an open-ended question (e.g., "how do you make sense of that?"). Frequently, the supervisor will need to add other information to prime the supervisee's reflection, such as a relevant theoretical or conceptual perspective ("Is it possible your different feelings may relate to the different roles you have with your client as therapist, supervisee, and fellow-human?"). While this process may sound as if it is designed to lead the supervisee to a predetermined conclusion, in practice this rarely occurs, as there are always many more plausible explanations that fit a given set of facts than one might initially suppose, particularly if one is open to just that possibility.

Abductive inference is a distinct form of reflective reasoning that seeks to explain a surprising or confusing phenomenon by hypothesizing the existence of a cause, which, if it existed, would account for the phenomenon (Vertue and Haig 2008). This type of reasoning is often employed in constructing case formulations using if-then statements. Suppose a client seems surprisingly upset over receiving a grade of A– on a paper. One might hypothesize that *if* they held very high, rigid expectations for their performance on the paper (e.g., only an A+ is good enough) *then* this would explain why they are upset. If the client displayed a similar pattern in other situations, one might also hypothesize a more general cause, namely, that they are a perfectionist. Supervisors can promote this type of thinking by asking questions such as "what, if it were true, would make sense of the client's response?"

Perhaps my favorite means of generating new insights and meaning in both supervision and therapy involves attending to metaphor. In the face of an initially perplexing or confusing situation, a novel metaphor will often suggest itself and may shed new understanding. Although there is no shortage of well-worn metaphors, such as "he is an open book," these are not what typically emerge for me. Rather, a novel metaphor arises on the spur of the moment in response to the particulars of the experience. To illustrate this in supervision, I once shared with a supervisee a story about a perfectionistic client I had worked with on becoming less rigid about always correcting his children's manners. He acted on this compulsion even when it interfered with his children sharing their feelings with him. I suggested to the client that for him, seeing any metaphorical unmade bed triggered an urgent need in him to correct the issue with his child and that he could not unsee it until it was resolved. The client eagerly adopted the metaphor, and noted how the metaphor helped put his habit in perspective. Supervisors can help supervisees cultivate attention to metaphor by asking questions like "what does this situation remind you of?" or "what is this similar to?"

Conceptualizing

In clinical practice and supervision, conceptualizing refers to the cognitive activity required to integrate specific observations or experiences with more general theories, models, or understandings. Doing so often involves accommodation, the Piagetian process in which an existing schema or model is adjusted or revised to integrate new experience. As a result, the revised theory or model becomes richer and more meaningful to the learner. As an illustration, consider a supervisee who, upon observing a supervisor use humor appropriately with a client, discovers that therapy can at times be a richer, more human interaction than they had previously supposed.

Conceptualizing therefore brings together previously private, subjective experiences of the supervisee, such as those noticed in the mode of experiencing, or pondered when reflecting, with publicly available knowledge. Public knowledge may come from scientifically established theories, models, or empirical findings, as well as the supervisor's knowledge of therapeutic methods, approaches, strategies, ethics, and standards. One particularly helpful aspect of conceptualization occurs when supervisors help supervisees recognize key events in therapy (e.g., strains in the alliance, client disengagement or withdrawal, changes in client affect, therapist misses) that may not have previously seen or noticed (Gaete and Strong 2017). Much as an experienced radiologist can read an X-ray and see things that are undetected by a novice, so a supervisor must help a supervisee learn to read the key moments of a therapeutic interaction and properly encode them as instances of theory-related categories such as defensiveness, alliance-ruptures, felt-shifts, catastrophizing, and so on.

Supervisors can promote supervisees' conceptualizing activity by asking questions that require synthesizing experiences and observations with theories or models. "How might a CBT conceptualization of this client's grief differ from a psychodynamic one?" "What does the evidence suggest are effective therapeutic approaches for this problem and client?" "What in the client's cultural background might help to explain their reluctance to challenge their parents?" Conversely, supervisees can take the initiative to search the literature for new findings and approaches relevant to their clients and bring them to supervision.

Planning and Experimenting

In preparing for battle I have always found that plans are useless, but planning is indispensable.

Eisenhower

Eisenhower's remark reflects the fact that in real life, events almost never unfold as anticipated. This applies to planning therapy sessions with clients. Our plans often need to be modified or set aside when our clients come in with new, previously unexplored problems, crises, or changes in their condition. Doing so can be difficult, particularly for novices who may lack the creativity and skill needed to flexibly adjust plans to suit the circumstances.

With this in mind, supervisors guide or oversee treatment session planning with an eye to ensuring the supervisee not only has a clear idea of how to implement the plan, but also whether or how to do so under a range of conditions, and how to make such decisions in the moment. Such contingency-planning needs to be explicitly taught to novice supervisees, whereas in more advanced supervisees, the supervisor may adopt a consultant's stance—ready and able to assist, if needed.

The purpose of planning, with respect to the supervisee, is to help them prepare to implement or test out with a client a treatment strategy or technique that is new or not yet fully mastered. Doing so may require supervisors to draw upon a range of teaching strategies, including assigning reading, instructing, modeling, and role-playing. Modeling and role-playing new skills are particularly helpful for skill mastery prior to implementation. Unfortunately, modeling is often used without role-play in supervision (Bailin et al. 2018; Caron et al. 2021; Dorsey et al. 2018). Modeling's value is limited unless it is paired with role-play to consolidate the learning and allow the supervisor to evaluate mastery. By following modeling with role-play, the supervisee can practice implementing the new skill in a way that feels authentic and doable to them.

With respect to Kolb's learning cycle, planning bridges the gap between conceptualizing (an abstract process that deals with generalities) and experimenting (a practical, experience-based process that is tailored and responsive to the specific circumstances of client, setting, and supervisee). The goal in planning is to translate an abstract model or generic strategy into a specific plan that is adapted to fit the circumstances and preferences of the client within the range of what is possible for the supervisee.

When engaged in experimenting, supervisees have considerable autonomy to make decisions about when and how to implement plans during treatment sessions. Since putting new skills into practice with clients can be anxiety-arousing, supervisees may need encouragement to be successful. Ironically, this may include acknowledgment that they might fail and that is ok, as failure will inevitably accompany growth. Providing such encouragement can help supervisees learn to not catastrophize failures or seek to avoid them through excessive caution, but to see them simply as feedback. In overseeing the experimentation process, supervisors ensure that any potential fallout from supervisee failure will not pose a serious risk of harm to the client. Supervisees can take an active role in this process by identifying techniques they would like to learn and by taking courage in their work with clients to be bold in implementing them. Once experimentation has occurred, this sets the stage for a fresh cycle of learning as the supervisee engages in experiencing and reflecting on the experiment.

In sum, the experiential learning cycle offers several helpful ways of deepening the learning that supervisees gain from their work with clients. Supervisors are encouraged to experiment with incorporating the various facets of the experiential learning cycle into supervision to identify what is most helpful for their supervision.

Feedback: Using Best Practices

Feedback, along with practice and reflection, is one of the most powerful vehicles for promoting learning and professional development in supervision (Wisniewski et al. 2020). However, because constructive feedback can also trigger powerful emotional responses in supervisees, its impact must be monitored, and it must be provided within the context of a safe, supportive supervisory relationship. In this brief overview, I discuss how supervisors can provide feedback in ways that will be most likely to be heard and impactful, and how supervisees can guide requests for feedback.

According to Heckman-Stone's (2004) review of the literature on supervisees' feedback preference and effective feedback methods, the

Table 4.2 Elements of effective feedback

Feedback element	Notes on implementation
Supervisee Preparation	Clear expectations and behaviorally defined performance criteria are specified and agreed upon ahead of time
Observational basis	Supervisors directly observe supervisee's work in sufficient quantity to support reliable feedback
Criteria	Supervisee's performance is compared with specified goals and objectives
Self-evaluation	Supervisees are given the opportunity to self-evaluate prior to receiving evaluative feedback
Valence and sequence	Both positive and constructive feedback should be included, beginning with positive feedback
Timing	Feedback is timely
Frequency	Feedback is frequent
Basis of feedback	Supervisors should identify what the observations the feedback is based on and what skill area is addressed
Clarification	Supervisees should have the opportunity to clarify feedback
Monitor use	Supervisors should monitor supervisees' use of feedback in subsequent work, which permits evaluation of feedback effectiveness

considerations summarized in Table 4.2, should guide supervisors' use of feedback.

A few additional comments about feedback are in order. A common concern among supervisees is that they receive too little constructive feedback (Haft et al. 2024) or that the feedback they receive is too vague, non-specific, or perfunctory to be useful (Westberg and Jason 1993). These concerns are supported by research showing that corrective feedback was provided in less than 10 percent of supervision sessions in an audited sample of 100 sessions of routine supervision (Bailin et al. 2018). Worse still, poor supervisors sometimes respond to requests for feedback by questioning the supervisee's competence: "you seem to need a lot of feedback, I wonder why?" (Ladany 2014). Furthermore, feedback that is not based on direct observation of supervisee's work is perceived as lacking in credibility. Finally, contrary to what some supervisors imagine, supervisees welcome constructive feedback so long as it is observation-based and balanced with positive feedback (Ladany et al. 2013).

Many supervisors struggle with providing constructive feedback, fearing that it may harm the supervisee's confidence or result in a confrontation that may harm the supervisory alliance (Beckman et al. 2017; Borders et al. 2017; Turner et al. 2016). However, research suggests that supervisees who receive constructive feedback in supervision report stronger supervisory alliances and little distress (Beckman et al. 2020). With training and practice, supervisors can learn to give constructive feedback that is clear, concise, and concrete (Borders and Giordano 2016) and do so with confidence (Motley et al. 2014). For more potentially difficult or challenging feedback, supervisors may benefit from advance planning to feel better prepared to deliver such feedback. See Chapter 5 for a more in-depth discussion of how to engage in difficult, confrontative conversations.

Live supervision, which involves having a supervisor provide brief, intermittent feedback to a supervisee during a therapy session (e.g., auditorily through an earpiece, or visually via a direct message during online therapy), can provide a rich learning experience that affords deeper learning than role-play (Räuchle et al. 2025). Live supervision is valued by supervisees and clients and yields comparable client and supervisee outcomes relative to delayed supervision (Maaß et al. 2022). Some of the reasons that feedback provided during live supervision may be effective are that it meets many of the criteria identified above for effective feedback (e.g., is timely, frequent, and observation-based) and is specific to the immediate needs of the clinical context and the supervisee's performance within it. Guidance for using feedback in live supervision can be found in Bernard and Goodyear (2019).

In sum, constructive observation-based feedback is essential to supervisee learning and professional development and a prerequisite for an ethical summative evaluation process. By learning how to give constructive feedback using the evidence-informed methods described above, supervisors can enhance their supervisee's competence and develop greater comfort and confidence in doing so.

Restorative Supervision: Emotional Processing in Supervision

The aim of restorative supervision is to help supervisees learn to process emotionally difficult responses to clinical work to reduce their impact on well-being. Indeed, working as a therapist involves becoming close to clients, and this can result in a variety of emotionally challenging circumstances. Below, I describe some of the different clinical circumstances that more frequently elicit supervisee distress and which may become a focus of restorative supervision. I also describe how both the experiential learning cycle described above, as well as supervisee self-care practices, can be useful in achieving the aims of restorative supervision.

Working with distressed and traumatized clients can elicit feelings of distress and secondary trauma in therapists (Baum and Moyal 2020; Pirelli et al. 2020). Recommended strategies for preventing vicarious trauma include supervision to promote reflection on cases, and engagement in activities designed to promote post-traumatic growth (e.g., gratitude, resilience, and humanity toward others) (Branson 2019; Coleman et al. 2021). Another source of therapist distress occurs when working closely with clients who act in ways that are abrasive, demanding, and difficult. Such behavior frequently arouses negative feelings in therapists, which can cause them to become less empathic and more reactive, putting clients at risk of insensitive or hurtful therapist responses.

Difficult client behavior can sometimes reflect the operation of bias against aspects of the therapist's identity and result in instances of sexual harassment, homophobia, or racial microaggressions toward trainees that can be painful and isolating for supervisees to try to manage without supervisory support (Bautista-Biddle et al. 2021; González Vera et al. 2024). Although many supervisors are aware of these kinds of microaggressions toward trainees, supervisors sometimes struggle with knowing how to assist supervisees in dealing with these experiences (Adams et al. 2022). In preparation for doing such work, it is essential that supervisors have training in multicultural competence that is applicable to supervision (Childs et al. 2024). Additionally, if available, a multicultural peer-consultation team within one's institution, can be a local source of knowledge and awareness by providing "consultation that is multiculturally conscious and integrates front-and-center concepts related to diversity in identities and lived experiences (i.e., multiculturalism), intersectionality, inclusivity, health equity, antiracism, and anti-oppression" (Nagy et al. 2024, p. 314).

When working with supervisees at the outset of supervision, it can help to invite supervisees to bring up hurtful experiences they encounter with clients such as microaggressions and various *isms* in supervision for processing to mitigate the harm and to learn how to respond to or manage such events (D. J. Wheeler et al. 2019). During this initial discussion, it is helpful to explore the supervisee's preferences for the kinds of support they would like to receive when dealing with microaggressions from clients, as preferences vary across trainees (Bullock et al. 2021). In most circumstances, supervisees will be dealing with these encounters on their own and will need support in processing the event subsequently in supervision. Occasionally, however, you may be present with the supervisee (e.g., at an intake, co-therapy, or group therapy session) when a microaggression occurs, and you will need to decide whether and how to intervene in the moment. Understanding how to manage these situations in real time will help you on these occasions and help you advise your supervisee. Research shows that learning strategies to address microaggressions and having the opportunity to practice them and receive feedback on them are effective at enhancing learners' self-efficacy for dealing with microaggressions (Miu et al. 2024). Relevant background knowledge necessary for understanding cultural microaggressions includes cultural competence and cultural humility. Pertinent skills for addressing microaggressions in the moment include safety considerations for both therapist and client, assessing the client's emotional stability, and flexible options for responding to a microaggression, such as clarification, disagreement, sharing the impact of the comment, education, and seeking support after an incident (Miu et al. 2024; D. J. Wheeler et al. 2019).

Finally, some clients may trigger a unique pattern of intense responding, such as attraction or disgust, described by some as countertransference, that also may put both client and therapist at risk (Hayes et al. 2018; Shafranske and Falender 2008).

Regardless of the specific nature of the therapist's reaction, restorative supervision offers a safe place for supervisees to learn how to cope with difficult feelings. Supervisees generally value the opportunity to work through their emotional responses to clinical work in supervision (Spännargård et al. 2025). Supervisors have a responsibility to help supervisees learn to process their emotional responses to clients effectively, so their competence and well-being are not eroded, and client safety is maintained.

Supervisory actions that have been identified as effective in promoting restorative outcomes include offering empathy and praise in response to supervisees' explorations of their emotional responses and efforts to cope with challenging client experiences (Bradley and Becker 2021).

The experiential learning cycle described above can be adapted to help achieve these goals. The most impactful emotional processing occurs through the modes of experiencing and reflecting. With the supervisor's support and encouragement, supervisees are invited to pay close attention to their emotional responses to clients and to put those feelings into words even when, or especially when, they seem improper, taboo, or unprofessional. Of course, this requires supervisees to take a big risk by making themselves vulnerable to supervisors' judgment. Fear of negative evaluation will make such disclosure difficult at best. Supervisors can help make the situation safer by sharing their own experiences of emotional responses to clients and how they dealt with those feelings. Supervisees are more willing to disclose instances of countertransference when there is a positive supervisory alliance (Pakdaman et al. 2015).

Supervisees also need to understand the relationship between their internal reactions and their outward verbal and nonverbal behavior toward the client through reflection. Unfortunately, supervisee feelings toward clients are often not discussed in supervision (Bailin et al. 2018; Novoa-Gómez et al. 2019). Nor do supervisors often invite discussion or exploration of supervisee feelings (McMahon et al. 2023). Supervisees can gain considerable insight into this relationship by studying therapy recordings. One method for doing so, as described by Schneider et al. (2014), involves writing process notes for selected portions of therapy sessions in which the therapist experienced an intense response to the client. Process notes are divided into four columns. In the first column, the supervisee reports the therapeutic dialogue and/or observations of nonverbal communication. The second column is for internal feelings/reactions, including when one was distracted by one's feelings. The third is for strategies or skills used in the session, and the final column is for supervisor notes or comments. Supervisees are invited to note whether, and how, their internal responses affected their ability to remain focused on the client and maintain empathic, therapeutic responding. Although the method is time- and labor-intensive, those who use it argue it is very revealing and worthwhile.

Having reflected on their recording using the method described above, supervisees may have become aware of previously murky feelings, how these affected their stance toward the client, and their own verbal and nonverbal behavior. The next step in the learning cycle is to use theoretically or empirically informed perspectives to broaden supervisees' understanding of their experience. Relevant theoretical perspectives at this stage might include supervision-focused discussions of attachment theory (Fitch et al. 2010) or countertransference (Shafranske and Falender 2008). Ultimately, supervisors will need to help supervisees develop a plan for how to re-engage with the client in a way that permits them an opportunity to try out new ways of responding that align with their empathic, therapeutic goals.

When carrying out this work, supervisors need to be mindful of the line dividing restorative supervision from therapy. Conducting therapy with a supervisee is an unethical boundary violation, something most professionals understand (Schwartz-Mette and Shen-Miller 2017). When the focus of the work is on the supervisee's response to a client with the aim of limiting or undoing the negative impact of a client, or enhancing the supervisee's effectiveness with the client, the work is supervisory rather than therapeutic. If it becomes clear that the supervisee has broader problems or concerns that go beyond the particular client(s) that requires therapeutic work, this is where discussion of the issue in supervision should cease in favor of the supervisee exploring the concerns in outside psychotherapy.

Finally, restorative supervision includes encouraging supervisee self-care as a distinct functional competency. Reviews of the literature reveal that practicing (versus not practicing) self-care among professional psychology and counseling trainees has a variety of psychological benefits (Colman et al. 2016). However, to date, no specific methods of self-care have been adequately validated as superior to others (Callan et al. 2021). What does improve trainee mental health is whether the chosen manner of self-care is aligned with one's top values (Bistricky et al. 2025). Nonetheless, some findings suggest that enhancing self-compassion and mindfulness (Crego et al. 2022; Lyon and Wright 2024), as well as life balance and cognitive awareness of work-related stressors, shows promise as a means of reducing stress and avoiding burnout (Rupert and Dorociak 2019). Supervisors can promote the use of self-care by encouraging their own supervisees' practices, disclosing their own practices, and encouraging a culture of self-care within their institutional setting.

Taken together, restorative supervision is an essential component of clinical supervision. It enables supervisees to process the distress that can accompany clinical work, and to learn competencies that help maintain their well-being and clinical effectiveness.

Planning the Supervision Session

Supervision sessions never seem long enough to deal with all the questions that supervisees bring. To ensure that the most important and urgent matters (not always the same thing!) are discussed, I find it helpful to spend a few minutes at the outset to set an agenda for the meeting so that both members of the dyad have a chance to include items of importance. Shared agenda setting encourages supervisees to take ownership of their learning and professional development and, in cases where agenda setting is a therapy-specific competency, as in cognitive therapy, it provides an opportunity for supervisors to model the skill and provide feedback on supervisee agenda-setting. Supervisors can describe their preferences for how supervision meetings should be organized in their PDS, but will need to help supervisees put this into practice. For instance, in my PDS, I describe an events-based model in which categories of important events in therapy or supervision are listed to consider for discussion. In practice, supervisees often neglect many of these categories unless prompted to review the list when identifying their agenda items.

To ensure that the normative (client welfare), formative (supervisee learning), and restorative (supervisee well-being) goals of supervision are being met, the supervisory dyad can include them as separate columns on the whiteboard or paper used to set the agenda. As items for discussion are added to the agenda, a mark in one or more of the three goal columns provides a quick visual check of whether each supervision goal is being addressed and allows an opportunity for rebalancing if necessary. Alternatively, the dyad might instead consider tracking how much attention is given to each of the three foci described in Bernard's (1997) discrimination model, namely intervention (e.g., therapy techniques), conceptualization, and personalization (i.e., personal responses of supervisee to therapy/supervision).

Supervisees, particularly those at earlier developmental stages, may benefit from some guidance in how to identify and prioritize their learning and clinical guidance needs. Some useful questions for supervisees to consider when identifying their needs/priorities in supervision include:

- What is the biggest challenge I face with each client?
- Is this challenge best understood as a
  - conceptualization problem (e.g., feeling stuck),
  - my emotional response to the client (e.g., feeling afraid), or
  - an intervention problem (e.g., not sure how to intervene)?
- How is my level of presence and responsiveness with each client?
  - Am I able to notice small shifts and respond?
  - Is this something to raise in supervision?

Supervisors may wish to add to the agenda issues and competencies that are often not the focus of attention in supervision and thus risk being overlooked. In my experience, these include

- professional ethics and standards,
- multicultural and diversity issues,
- supervisee distress/reactions to clients,
- issues in the therapeutic or supervisory alliance, and
- parallel process (i.e., when a pattern of interaction between supervisee and client is re-enacted between supervisor and supervisee).

In practice, it often falls to the supervisor to inject these issues into the agenda/discussion during supervision meetings. One way to do so is by asking about hypothetical problems or dilemmas:

- How would you respond if your client asked to be friends on Facebook?

- What cultural differences exist between you and your client, and how might they affect your relationship?
- What feelings does this client elicit in you? How do these feelings affect your relationship?

In sum, collaborating to plan the supervision session agenda allows both supervisor and supervisee to meet their learning or instructional goals, client oversight responsibilities, and address the need for restorative supervision.

Chapter Summary

Supervision meetings offer tremendous scope to meet the normative, formative, and restorative goals of supervision. Meeting normative goals requires the dyad to be aware of the stage of treatment/training and how to avoid harm, provide competent care to clients, and monitor client outcome. Achieving formative goals requires that the supervisor consider and employ a suitable model of supervision to develop supervisee competencies such as the experiential learning model. Regardless of the model chosen, however, frequent, concrete feedback based on direct observation will be essential for supervisee improvement. To carry out restorative supervision to support supervisee well-being, dyads need to be willing to explore supervisees' emotional responses to clients. With multiple goals and diverse strategies available, supervisory dyads are encouraged to consider using an agenda to get the most out of supervisory meetings.

Questions for Review and Reflection

1. The timeline of a typical course of psychotherapy clarifies what to do when. What stands out to you about this timeline and how it might help organize your supervision?
2. The supervisor's greatest ethical responsibility is to ensure client safety. Based on what you have learned about factors that can harm clients, how would you make use of this information as a supervisor, and how would you implement it in supervision?

3. There is a good deal of evidence that experiential methods are the most impactful ways of promoting supervisee learning. What experiential methods do you intend to use in supervision?

4. The goal of restorative supervision is to help supervisees process emotionally charged experiences with clients. Although important and beneficial, restorative supervision is often overlooked in supervision. Why do you think that is? How will you keep a place for it in your supervision?

5. Do you think an agenda is useful for organizing supervision meetings? Why? If you intend to use an agenda, how will that work in your supervision?

CHAPTER 5

Confronting Challenges: Addressing Difficulties in Clinical Supervision

Unfortunately, negative events sometimes occur in supervision and training that damage the supervisory relationship. This harm can be consequential: it can undermine the supervisee's ability to learn and develop, affect the supervisee's work with clients, and interfere with the supervisor's ability to monitor and promote client welfare. In this chapter, I identify challenges that arise from four different sources: (1) supervisors, (2) supervisees, (3) the supervisory relationship, and (4) the training setting (Nelson et al. 2008). The purpose is to raise awareness about common problems, to help prevent them when possible, and to contextualize them if they do occur. I then present ethical principles and conflict resolution strategies that can be used to work through problems and suggest where to turn for help if these do not resolve the difficulties.

Supervisor Behavior Challenges

Power tends to corrupt and absolute power corrupts absolutely.

Acton

Supervision is not a meeting of equals: The supervisor has tremendous power over the supervisee that, if abused, can cause harm. Moreover, supervisors possess both hard and soft power. *Hard power* arises from supervisors' legal and ethical responsibility for client welfare and their role as an evaluator and gatekeeper. These powers enable supervisors to organize and control supervisees' training experiences and, through their evaluations, have an influence on their future training and career opportunities. Conversely, supervisees' power is limited by the fact that supervision is mandatory, they often have no choice over who supervises them, and little opportunity to change supervisors if problems occur. Subjectively, supervisors accrue the *soft power* to persuade from possessing clinical and supervisory expertise and being committed to supervision (De Stefano et al. 2017).

Given the enormous power imbalance in supervision, the potential for abuse certainly exists. Although many supervisors use their power for positive ends and with great restraint (Murphy and Wright 2005), unfortunately this is not universal. As the quote from Acton suggests, unchecked power can lend itself to abuse. Perhaps the most effective check on supervisory power lies in supervisors' awareness of its existence, the ways it may be abused, and their ethical commitment to being transparent about their power and using it responsibly to promote positive outcomes. With that in mind, let us delve into the nature of supervisory power and its abuse.

Empirical research on abusive supervision in the workplace clearly demonstrates that it undermines the performance of individuals, units, and organizations (Tepper et al. 2017). Several qualitative studies have documented instances of supervisory abuse of power and shed light on how it occurs. Supervisees who have experienced negative supervision report power struggles with angry supervisors who used coercive tactics such as threatening to withhold student evaluations (Nelson and Friedlander 2001). For instance, one supervisee reported the following about a supervisor:

> He was super vindictive to the point that at the end of my training year, one of the people I worked with warned the class coming in under us about him, that they should really try to be on his good side. And he then found out, and reached out to the four of us, and basically said, "I don't feel comfortable writing people letters of recommendation if they didn't like the site, so I'd like to know who was talking about the site." (Jackson and Faler 2023, p. 301).

Supervisees have described instances of supervisors' abuse of power that include favoring some supervisees, rigidly imposing a clinical style or orientation, violating supervisee confidentiality (e.g., gossiping about supervisee personal/private information with other supervisors), using power and authority to distance and elevate themselves over supervisees to prevent questioning and assuage their insecurity, and failing to meet their supervisory responsibilities (e.g., to attend scheduled supervision meetings) without needing to acknowledge or apologize for it (Murphy and Wright 2005).

In addition to the above abuses of hard power, supervisors can also damage the relationship by losing soft power in the eyes of their supervisees. Supervisee perceptions of supervisor power are closely connected to their perception of the supervisor's clinical or supervisory expertise. Thus, when supervisors are perceived to be less knowledgeable than the supervisee or make errors, their perceived expertise and the aura of being "all-knowing" are eroded. More significantly, when conflict, disagreement, or a violation of the supervisor's role occurs, this has the effect of making supervisees' implicit awareness of the power differential explicit and can lead to a lessening of trust and confidence in the supervisor (De Stefano et al. 2017).

Although supervisees have less power than supervisors, they still perceive that they have some power, and this perception appears to grow with greater knowledge and understanding of supervision. Thus, doctoral-level supervisees report having greater power than those at the master's level, a difference that may be due to the two groups' different levels of professional development (R. M. Cook et al. 2018). In contrast, group differences such as gender and race, that are not related to knowledge or understanding of supervision, appear to have little impact on supervisee perceptions of power (Wind et al. 2021). Supervisees note that they can exercise their power by sharing feedback to their supervisor, or by withholding information from their supervisor (De Stefano et al. 2017).

Instead of relying on heavy-handed hard power, supervisors can achieve a degree of soft power through demonstrating clinical expertise, exuding warmth, and offering mentorship, all of which create influence through processes of interpersonal attraction rather than coercion (Nye 2004). This soft power to persuade is the basis of positive supervisory relationships and effective supervision. One supervisee described this type of supervisor power in this way:

> I don't view the [supervisor's] power in terms of power differentials, although those are there, but more so the power of having experience. Having experience in things that we're going through for the first time, and the supervisor has not only had that experience themselves countless times, they've had supervisees that had

that experience countless times. And so the power in being able to normalize, the power in being to provide guidance, the power in being able to hold space for somebody's experience, I think is tremendously important. That's how I like to view the lens of power, the power to hold that space, rather than to have power over. (Jackson and Faler 2023, pp. 301–302)

Clearly, this type of soft power can be beneficial. However, if supervisors demonstrate a lack of competence, integrity, or commitment, they may lose the confidence and respect of their supervisees, which is the basis of soft power.

In sum, supervisory power creates the potential for both positive and negative experiences in supervision. The problems associated with power in supervision arise in two distinct ways. When supervisors abuse the hard power that they possess supervisees are vulnerable to coercion and harm. Conversely, supervisors who are disorganized, uncommitted, uninterested, and ineffective do not earn sufficient soft power, as reflected in supervisees' diminished confidence and respect. Together, these two types of *power failure* account for many instances of lousy supervision (Magnuson et al. 2000).

Inadequate and Harmful Supervision

Occurrences of negative supervision can be distinguished according to whether they are simply *inadequate* or are also *harmful* (Ellis et al. 2014). The main types of inadequate supervision involve:

- supervisor neglect, lack of interest, or unawareness (e.g., never observing sessions, disinterest in diversity, uncommitted),
- substandard practice (e.g., not providing evaluative feedback, not using a contract, acting unethically, not discussing client difficulties), and
- global inadequacy (e.g., does not know what to do, incompetent).

Perhaps the most problematic instances of inadequate supervision occur when supervisors either fail to clearly communicate specific performance expectations to supervisees or fail to provide meaningful feedback on their progress relevant to these professional development goals. These lapses set the stage for inevitable conflict as supervisees violate expectations they did not know existed (Nelson et al. 2008) or fail to progress owing to a lack of developmentally relevant feedback (Haft et al. 2024).

Harmful supervision occurs when a supervisee experiences physical, psychological, or emotional harm or trauma because of supervisory practices. Note that harmful supervision does not include instances when supervisees receive constructive feedback about their performance that is upsetting but necessary for their professional development or experience painful struggles with emotionally challenging issues in supervision. Harmful supervisory practices cited by Ellis et al. (2014) include:

- boundary violations (e.g., sexual intimacy with a supervisee),
- aggression (e.g., cruelty, public humiliation, abuse, physical threats),
- exploitation (e.g., exploits dual roles), and
- general harm (e.g., pathologized or traumatized by supervisor).

Unfortunately, both inadequate and harmful supervision appear to be common. In a survey of 363 supervisees, an astonishing 93 percent reported that they had been exposed to at least one instance of inadequate supervision, and 35 percent reported that they had encountered instances of harmful supervision in their training (Ellis et al. 2014). These results are surprising and troubling. Surprising because the high prevalence of inadequate supervision practices and attitudes suggests that, for all the advances we have made in educating supervisors about competent supervisory practice, there is clearly more work to be done. Given that most incidents of inadequate supervision involved either failure to use a contract (54 percent) or observe or monitor supervisee sessions (39.7 percent), supervisor education needs to focus on these areas. A more recent study also found that contract use was absent in about half of the instances of supervision studied, however, where contract use was required, lower occurrences of inadequate supervision were observed (Cook and Ellis 2021). Conceivably, the requirement to complete a supervision contract may serve to promote commitment to fulfilling essential aspects of supervision. Contracts and observation complement each other, insofar as contracts make performance expectations clear, while observation provides the basis for feedback about whether expectations are being met. Together, they make supervision transparent and thereby help protect supervisor and supervisee from misunderstandings and liability concerns. Using a contract and observing supervisee performance through live observation or via electronic recordings (and providing feedback on it) are recommended as best practice by a wide range of organizations and supervisory guidelines (e.g., APA 2014; ASPPB 2015).

The findings of supervisory harm are troubling, because they reveal a dark side to supervision that is deeply incongruent with its ethical and professional aims. The most frequent harms in Ellis et al.'s (2014) study involved exploitation. Over 10 percent of the respondents gave a rating of 0 *not at all* to the items "safe from exploitation" and "[supervisor] avoids exploitative dual roles". These findings strongly suggest that where dual roles exist, supervisory dyads should discuss and implement role separation early on. Other serious instances of harm reported involved being physically threatened and being in a current sexual relationship with a supervisor.

Although these quantitative findings communicate the size of the problem, they do not fully convey the human impact of supervisory harm. The narrative accounts of harmful supervision reported by 11 supervisees presented in Ellis (2017b) reveal a shocking litany of cruelty, racism, indifference, and incompetence. These reports detail unprofessional and disrespectful behaviors that were demeaning, sarcastic, or belittling; incompetent (e.g., criticism without constructive feedback), divisive (e.g., exhibiting favoritism), humiliating, dismissive, or intimidating. Overall, the narratives illustrate a range of harmful practices that negatively impacted the supervisees' experiences and well-being in clinical settings. Supervisors and supervisees should know that all forms of abuse and exploitation are explicitly prohibited by ethical guidelines and professional codes of conduct.

Ineffective and Counterproductive Supervision

Ineffective supervision may be distinguished from inadequate or harmful supervision in that it is not necessarily substandard or damaging (although it could be) but is problematic primarily for failing to achieve the goals of supervision. Using qualitative and quantitative methods, Ladany et al. (2013) found that ineffective supervisor behaviors, as identified by current and former supervisees, consist of a variety of actions that have the net effect of depreciating or devaluing supervision and the supervisory relationship. Examples of devaluing supervision include cutting supervision short to attend to other matters and taking phone calls during supervision. Instances of negative personal and professional qualities include being judgmental and opinionated. Lastly, actions that weakened the supervisory relationship include not respecting boundaries, attacking the supervisee, and treating the supervisee like a servant rather than a trainee. In sum, ineffective supervision occurs when supervisors are uncommitted to supervision or make it a lower priority relative to other commitments, and when the supervisor's attitudes and behavior convey a lack of respect for the supervisee and the supervisory relationship.

Counterproductive supervision events are defined as "any experience that trainees identified as hindering, unhelpful, or harmful in relation to their growth as therapists" (Gray et al. 2001, p. 371). These authors' qualitative analysis of supervisees' experience of such events revealed that trainees identified supervisors dismissing their thoughts and feelings as the primary cause. Following the counterproductive event, all trainees experienced a negative interaction with their supervisor, but most did not believe the supervisor was aware of the event's counterproductive nature. All trainees believed the counterproductive event weakened the supervisory relationship. Counterproductive events generally resulted in trainees changing their approach to their supervisors. Most supervisees became more guarded and less disclosing to their supervisor, including not disclosing their reaction to the counterproductive event to their supervisor.

The Impact of Negative Supervision

Negative supervision, along the lines described above, has several destructive impacts on supervision and supervisees. In the context of workplace supervision, negative supervision has been found to increase symptoms of burnout and intentions to quit among nurses (Kalliath and Beck

2001) and counsellors (Knudsen et al. 2008). Weaker supervisory alliances have been linked to reduced work satisfaction and heightened work stress (Sterner 2009) and with greater perceived stress and reduced control among supervisees (Gnilka et al. 2012). Finally, dissatisfaction with supervision was associated with reduced confidence among professional psychologists (McMahon and Hevey 2017).

These negative outcomes likely come about in part because negative supervision damages the conditions of trust and safety that are essential to supervision performing its restorative function. Indeed, for supervision to support supervisee well-being and be genuinely restorative, supervisees must be willing to share concerns with their supervisor and to process them in supervision. Research suggests that most supervisees withhold information from their supervisor (Yourman and Farber 1996) and that common reasons for nondisclosure include harboring negative feelings toward the supervisor (Ladany et al. 1996) and perceptions of a poor supervisory alliance (Mehr and Daltry 2022). Another reason for nondisclosure of difficulties is its perceived incompatibility with becoming an expert, which is emphasized in fields like clinical psychology (Spence et al. 2014). These findings suggest that negative supervision is damaging both for the direct harms it causes and for undermining the restorative function, thereby cutting off the very process that might help resolve difficulties.

Poor supervision can also have an impact on clients. A study by Callahan et al. (2009) found that a substantial 16 percent of clients' symptom changes during treatment could be attributed to differences in the quality of supervision among supervisors after controlling for differences among therapists. This suggests that, for better or worse, what happens in supervision does not stay in supervision but is transmitted to therapy and is manifested in client outcomes.

One recommendation stemming from the findings of inadequate and harmful supervision is that supervisees be provided with a *supervisee bill of rights* that outlines what they may reasonably expect from their supervisors (and vice versa). One version of such a bill of rights can be found in Ellis (2017a). Among the supervisee's rights is the right to have their concerns about negative supervision addressed. Ideally, the process starts with bringing concerns to the attention of the supervisor. However, this may not be feasible when a supervisor is hostile to such concerns or is threatening. In this case, or when discussion with a supervisor does not resolve the issue to the supervisee's satisfaction, the supervisee may approach the training director (of their program or field site). If this does not yield a satisfactory solution, they may approach an ombudsperson within the university (or training site).

Supervisee Behavior Challenges

Supervisee behavior is also a source of difficulty in supervision. In Nelson et al.'s (2008) interviews with supervisors who were identified as *exceptionally wise* by colleagues, the main supervisee factor identified as contributing to conflict was *supervisee resistance*, defined as "supervisee behaviors that communicate an attitude that supervision is not needed" (p. 178). These difficulties can be manifested in a reluctance or unwillingness to expose one's work to evaluative scrutiny. As an example, I recall supervising an experienced, mature psychology intern whose case reporting in supervision was often vague and short on details. In response to a query about how the most recent session had gone, he would usually say something to the effect of, "Good. You know, the usual things." He seemed to be communicating that supervision was not required. Supervisees may also manifest resistance through nondisclosure of important events in therapy or of emotional responses to clients or the supervisor (Ladany et al. 1996). Finally, resistance may appear in the form of an unwillingness to act on plans or feedback provided in supervision, which, in some cases, may occur in a context of disrespect toward the supervisor.

Supervisees also recognize that their attitudes and behaviors can contribute to difficulties in supervision. Rocha et al. (2025) interviewed masters level supervisees who acknowledged that they sometimes struggled with being passive, unmotivated, or uncommitted to engaging with supervision; failing to be open to discussing problems or clarifying their role and responsibilities, and in not advocating for their needs in supervision.

Other supervisee difficulties mentioned by Nelson et al.'s supervisors included reacting defensively to feedback, not taking responsibility, and being overwhelmed and not managing the demands of fieldwork. Aside from these general themes, specific problems mentioned included supervisees having inadequate skills and ethical or professional violations. When these latter problems are significant, they must be confronted by the supervisor. A strategy for having a difficult conversation about such a serious problem is described further below. Depending on the severity of the problems, the upshot may require the supervisor to advise the training program, require remedial training, or recommend the student be dismissed or counselled out of the profession (see Chapter 6).

When deciding whether the supervisee is the sole locus of supervision problems, supervisors need to remind themselves of the fundamental attribution error (Ross 1977), which is the tendency to underestimate the influence of situational causes and overestimate the role of dispositional causes of behavior. Supervisors need to consider the situational pressures that a struggling supervisee may be experiencing both from within the training context and from outside.

Supervisory Relationship Challenges

The wise supervisors mentioned above identified the evaluative nature of supervision and the associated power differential as the primary relational source of conflict in supervision. Considering that supervision is meant to be simultaneously supportive, nurturing, developmental, and evaluative, it is clearly a challenging balance to achieve. Harmony in the supervision relationship depends on balancing four inherent tensions according to Veilleux et al. (2014):

- promote change versus provide support,
- provide feedback versus sustain relationship,
- provide direction versus accept direction, and
- focus on client versus supervisee development.

Other relational challenges include differences between supervisor and supervisee on dimensions of personality, gender, age, or race, among other intersectional expressions of identity, and how these contribute to misunderstandings or differing views on how to work with clients. To this list, I would add differences in preferred therapeutic orientation, which, if not discussed, may be an ongoing source of tension, if not outright conflict. Taken together, these variables complicate the development and maintenance of an effective supervisory alliance and thus should be monitored for their potential impact and addressed as needed.

Training Site Challenges

Some supervisees receive clinical training in fieldwork sites that have problems that significantly interfere with the quality or quantity of training and supervision provided. Problems may include program instability, concerns related to grievance procedures and the implementation of due process, and problematic supervision policies or practices (Ponce et al. 2021).

An example of a problematic policy is where quality and quantity of service delivery are primary goals, whereas supervision and training are secondary goals. This can lead to conflict when high demands are made on supervisees for service delivery and associated documentation. Supervisees are apt to feel stressed and may resist such demands. These situations may also involve a lack of clarity about what aspects of supervisee performance supervisors are expected to monitor. If the site does not allocate enough time and other supports (e.g., ongoing training in supervision) for supervision and its associated activities, this can create the conditions for supervisor burnout and liability risk for supervisors, supervisees, and the site. Supervisors and supervisees may similarly be at risk of moral injuries when overwork and insufficient support interfere with their ability to fulfill their responsibilities in a manner aligned with their values.

The wise supervisors (Nelson et al. 2008) also noted that dual relationships and conflictual staff dynamics can create problems in supervision. These problems are compounded when supervisors lack trusted colleagues at the site with whom they can consult about managing difficulties in supervision.

Supervisees are encouraged to bring their concerns about the quality or quantity of training at their site to their supervisor. However, when these problems reflect systemic or institutional issues, it may be necessary for the problem-solving process to go beyond the supervisory dyad to engage the site director and the supervisee's training director, who may possibly choose to involve an intermediary agency (e.g., the Informal Problem Consultation Service operated by the Association of Psychology Postdoctoral and Internship Programs, APPIC 2018).

Addressing Challenges in Supervision

An ounce of prevention is worth a pound of cure

Benjamin Franklin

Before we discuss how to address problems in supervision and the essential role that supervisors play in initiating such discussions, it is helpful to first reflect on what both supervisor and supervisee can do to prevent problems. For their part, supervisors can help prevent the occurrence of negative supervisory experiences by attending to the supervisory alliance, clarifying mutual expectations, treating the supervisee with respect and dignity, being committed to supervision, and maintaining strong clinical and supervisory competencies. Ladany et al. (2013) capture the essential practices of the effective supervisor as one who would:

> ...[a] work toward developing a strong supervisory alliance by working toward mutually agreeing with the supervisee on the goals and tasks of supervision...[b] use basic counseling skills such as listening, reflection of feelings, and empathy to facilitate the development of an emotional bond...[c] attend to and offer a balance of attractive or collegial interactions, interpersonal attentiveness, and task-oriented structure...[and, d] attend specifically to the evaluation aspect of supervision by facilitating the setting of supervisory goals and providing both formative and summative feedback. (pp. 42–43).

Conversely, supervisees can help prevent supervision difficulties by demonstrating a commitment to supervision by coming prepared for supervision meetings, participating actively in supervision, completing assigned tasks in a timely fashion, and being open and responsive to supervisory feedback.

Problems in Professionalism

Attitude is a little thing that makes a big difference.

Winston Churchill

The most challenging issues to address in supervision involve problems in professionalism. Professionalism problems, which can affect either the supervisor or supervisee, include difficulties with (Kaslow et al. 2018):

- accountability (e.g., unreliability, being late, or ill-prepared),
- ethical engagement (e.g., dishonesty, boundary violations, violating confidentiality),
- self-reflection (e.g., lack of insight, defensiveness),
- civility (e.g., rudeness, disrespect), and
- cultural humility (e.g., lack of openness, curiosity, superiority).

As professionalism is a foundational attitude for all the functional competencies, a failure of professionalism signals a problem that warrants a serious conversation (see below). Problems of professionalism occur in a small number of professional trainees (Nicholson Perry et al. 2017). Other issues that also should trigger a serious conversation include a failure to achieve expected levels of competence and actions (or a lack of action) that put the client's welfare at risk. When a supervisee's incompetence or unprofessionalism threatens client welfare, supervisors must reassess the degree of clinical autonomy with which they may be entrusted (de Jonge et al. 2022; ten Cate and Schumacher 2022).

The antidote to many professionalism problems is an attitude of openness and humility. Supervisors can usefully model these attitudes with supervisees. A fundamental prerequisite to any concrete problem-solving steps is for supervisors to embrace an attitude of openness within supervision that conveys the message that it is safe and acceptable to bring up any concerns that affect supervision. Achieving a genuinely open atmosphere also requires that supervisors adopt an attitude of humility by acknowledging their own biases and limitations.

The most common limitation facing new supervisors is their lack of supervisory experience. These challenges are compounded when novice supervisors encounter mature supervisees who have more life and clinical experience than they do. Not surprisingly, this inversion of relative experience can elicit threatened responses from supervisors that fuel conflict in supervision (Nelson and Friedlander 2001). Faced with this formidable challenge, novice supervisors may mistakenly assume their options are either to "fake it 'til you make it" by pretending to possess more experience or wisdom than they do and correspondingly belittling or minimizing supervisee skills and knowledge. Or, alternatively, they might assume a "who am I to supervise you?" stance in which they psychologically abdicate their supervisory role by abstaining from providing meaningful formative guidance and evaluation. Novice supervisors can successfully navigate these challenges by threading a middle path between these two extremes. Ideally, the novice supervisor can openly acknowledge their limited experience as well as the supervisee's knowledge and skills, without diminishing the value that supervision offers both parties as a venue for continued professional growth and development. At the outset of supervision, a novice supervisor might find it helpful to say:

> Although I am quite new at this, my own experience of supervision leads me to think that there is always more one can learn from a supervisor who brings a fresh perspective to one's work. As we go forward, I hope we can keep an open dialogue on how supervision is working for both of us so we can adjust as necessary. How does that sound to you?

For supervisees, the attitudes of humility and curiosity are essential to learning and development. During their training, they will work with many different supervisors who will differ in their theoretical orientations, supervisory models and styles, personalities, and on various dimensions of diversity. Maintaining an attitude of openness means assuming that each supervisor has something of value to offer. Humility means appreciating that one can always improve, no matter how much experience or knowledge one has. "What can I learn from this person?" is a question that will serve supervisees (and supervisors!) well. These attitudes can help reduce defensive responding to constructive feedback and thus avoid at least one common source of conflict in supervision. Finally, openness and safety can also permit supervisees to raise concerns in supervision on their own behalf. Doing so in a constructive, mutually respectful way can do much to promote a positive resolution.

Supervisory Ethics: Principles for Managing Difficulties in Supervision

Many of the problems that arise in supervision reflect departures from principles of ethics that govern professional practice and supervision.

Understanding and applying these principles to supervision can prevent difficulties or help manage them when they do occur. The Canadian Psychological Association's *Ethical Guidelines for Supervision in Psychology* (2017b, p. 4) highlights the supervisor's responsibility for resolving conflict in supervision: "The supervisor has a special responsibility to address fluctuations and possible ruptures in the supervisory relationship in ways that are respectful, constructive and open." Indeed, because of the power imbalance, supervisors have the primary responsibility to take the initiative to address problems in supervision, though supervisees should ideally feel safe and empowered to do so. Three guidelines offer general direction to supervisors and supervisees for resolving conflicts within supervision:

> Address professional and interpersonal differences between supervisor and supervisee in as open, amicable, and constructive a way as possible… (I.5)
>
> Be aware of professional and personal limitations that may affect working relationships, be open to and elicit feedback regarding issues, and manage limitations in ways that support a positive supervisory relationship… (II.6)
>
> Identify and address conflict in the supervisory relationship in open, honest, and beneficial ways. (III.1)

These guidelines highlight the general tone desired in these conversations. However, when faced with a difficult problem that is consequential and likely to generate strong emotions, supervisors may benefit from a more specific framework.

The Safety PIN: A Framework for Facilitating Difficult Supervisory Conversations

Difficult conversations, also known as crucial, brave, or courageous conversations, are so named because they address *high-stakes* issues that involve *opposing views* and elicit *strong emotions* (Grenny et al. 2022). Difficult conversations can be daunting. Not surprisingly, many health care professionals report avoiding them, fearing a poor outcome, or from a lack of skill (C. King et al. 2020). When difficult conversations are necessary, as happens when gatekeeping is required, supervisors report finding these discussions emotionally charged and taxing (DeCino et al. 2020). Supervisors can approach difficult conversations with greater confidence and less fear with the aid of a conceptual framework. The *Safety Pin Framework* outlines a method to address a tear in the fabric of supervision or the lack of professionalism in a trainee's work (E. A. Johnson 2025). The PIN acronym stands for how to *Prepare for, Initiate,* and *Navigate* difficult conversations, while *safety* reminds us to seek a beneficial resolution respectfully, constructively, and as amicably as possible, to maintain the supervisory alliance. The framework is offered as a means of aiding supervisors in thinking through a supervision problem and planning how to approach it. It is intended to be used like a workbook. By writing out answers to the question prompts supervisors can build confidence that they can engage in a difficult conversation in a productive way. In developing the *Safety Pin Framework*, I drew on the CPA (2017b) supervision guidelines and other helpful sources (Bernard and Goodyear 2019; Davys 2019; Falender et al. 2009; Friedlander et al. 2024; Grenny et al. 2022; Jacobs et al. 2011; Watkins 2021). The *Safety PIN template* in Appendix A provides a condensed summary of the steps in the approach.

Preparation

Preparing for a difficult conversation involves three steps:

1. detecting the problem,
2. naming and exploring the problem, and
3. identifying conversational goals.

Although problems are sometimes obvious, in other cases it is necessary to be attuned to internal and external problem markers to detect that a problem is present. Internal markers are negative thoughts, feelings, and attitudes toward supervision or a supervisee that indicate that something is off. External markers are observable supervision behaviors that have a negative impact on supervision. They include, reductions in the frequency, duration, or regularity of supervision; superficial depth of discussion, limited engagement, learning, or growth; and insufficient client oversight. To illustrate, many years ago as a new supervisor, I was assigned to supervise a psychology resident's long-term therapy client (the same experienced supervisee I described earlier). Early in our work together, I found the supervisee's dismissive attitude toward supervision left me feeling ineffective in supervision, struggling in ways that left me feeling insecure and apprehensive about supervision meetings.

Had I been able to consider this experience with the aid of the *Safety PIN Framework* I might have more clearly noticed these *internal markers* and reflected on our supervision discussions. This might have allowed me to perceive certain *external problem markers,* principally discussions of the supervisee's therapy client that were limited in detail and lacking any real substance, which had the effect of closing the door to further supervisory discussion.

Looking back, I can more clearly recognize the need for a serious discussion with my supervisee. Using the framework, I would begin by naming the problem to myself and identifying specific examples of behaviors or events that illustrate it. I would then consider how important and severe the problem is. More difficult problems usually are chronic or recurrent and reflect a pattern of concerning behavior. They may involve such things as breaches of ethics or professionalism, deficient competency or effectiveness, a strained supervisory alliance, and problems in the therapeutic alliance or with client safety or well-being. More difficult problems may require consultation with fellow supervisors or the training director.

Looking back, I now would name the problem as a form of supervisee defensiveness that communicates an attitude that supervision is not needed (Nelson et al. 2008). Moreover, the issue had become a pattern that was hollowing out our supervisory work and preventing me from fulfilling my responsibility to oversee the client's welfare and promote my supervisee's professional development. Unless resolved, the problem threatened to increase the risk to client safety and place in doubt the supervisee's entrustability (ten Cate and Chen 2020). Clearly, this issue warranted a serious conversation.

Thus far, the preparation has focused solely on the other person. As supervision is fundamentally a relationship it's helpful to consider whether and how your own attitudes or behavior might be contributing to the problem. One way this can happen is by framing events through unhelpful narratives. Grenny et al. (2022) suggest that three kinds of narratives can blind us to more helpful understandings of the problem. In the *Innocent Victim* story, the narrative frame prevents us from considering our personal contribution to the problem. In the *Villain* story, we fail to consider that the other person might be a reasonable person whose behavior has a rational basis. And in the *Hopeless/Helpless* story, the narrative frame discourages active efforts at problem solving and fails to consider that it might be more solvable than we suppose.

Another personal obstacle to problem solving may reside in your feelings toward the other person and resolving the problem. Are there particular fears you have about confronting the person with this issue? If so, name them. Sometimes what comes between people are the ways that subtle biases can lead us to pick out identity features of the supervisee as the source of the problem. "That fits," we think to ourselves and suddenly a stereotype has turned a unique and complex person into a unidimensional type of person.

Are there connections between your fears and stereotypes with the narratives you have constructed about the problem? How are these affecting how you have been dealing with (or avoiding) the problem, and is there a risk they will negatively affect how you approach the problem now? If so, it may help to take a moment to draw on past positive experiences of problem resolution to establish a more hopeful outlook or consult with a colleague who also knows the supervisee.

Using the framework, my initial preparation for such a discussion might have identified specific examples of the problem and set a conversational goal of naming and exploring the supervisee's lack of openness and detail in our discussions. I might have identified the problem as a failure on the supervisee's part to meet their obligation to be sufficiently forthcoming about their work with their client in supervision. I could have identified specific behaviors to illustrate the problem and conceptualized the problem's importance as linked to it interfering with my responsibility to monitor the client's welfare and to enhance and evaluate the supervisee's work.

This neat picture shifts, however, once I reflect on the narratives I had been using to frame the problem and my feelings about it. In reflecting on the issue, I might realize I had framed the issue in a way that drew on all three problematic narratives as well as stereotyping. In my mind, the supervisee, as an older, experienced clinician was someone who had entrenched habits in how he practiced. The reason, I assumed, that he chose to be so non-disclosing of his work was to shield it from scrutiny and from having to open it up to reflection and change. The problem was him, not me. I feared he would reject my concerns outright or at best play along in a superficially compliant way without making any fundamental change.

With the aid of hindsight and greater understanding of supervision, I can perceive my own role in the problem more clearly. Had I reflected on the problem with the Safety PIN framework I might have realized that I contributed to the problem by not starting supervision on the right footing by clearly establishing my expectations for how he was to engage in supervision. To be honest, I was intimidated by the fact that he was older and had more clinical experience than I did. Moreover, as an inexperienced, untrained supervisor, I harbored feelings of impostor syndrome. All of that likely contributed to my adopting a deferential "who am I to supervise you?" stance, which undercut my supervisory role and my responsibility for establishing the conditions for supervision to be a fruitful exercise. Had I done so, the whole problem might have been avoided or at least rendered more approachable.

The third step in the preparation phase is to reflect on your goals for the conversation. Specifically, what outcome are you seeking for yourself and the other(s) involved? What do you want the impact on the supervisory and therapeutic alliances to be? Regarding process goals, what qualities do you want to model for your supervisee in *how* you have this conversation? Were I to have the conversation with my former supervisee now, my outcome goals would be to name the problem, acknowledge my contribution to it, reset supervision on a proper footing, and to do so in a way that demonstrates my commitment to supervision, to the supervisee's learning, and to the client's well-being. My process goals would be to have an open discussion that avoided blame and promoted mutual understanding.

Initiation

The next phase of the Safety Pin Framework, namely *initiating* the conversation, also has three steps:

1. orienting the other to the need for a serious discussion,
2. identifying your benevolent goals for the conversation, and
3. naming and illustrating the problem with specific behavioral examples.

Returning to the example described above, I might undertake the first step of orienting my supervisee to the need for a serious discussion by saying something like, "I would like to discuss a concern I have about our work together." Now that I have their attention I would continue with, "I'm concerned that this issue is impeding your progress and ability to succeed in this training experience and affecting our work together in supervision".

For the second step, of signaling my benevolent goals for the conversation, I could say, "I am hopeful that by having an open and honest discussion of the issue we can agree on a resolution that will be beneficial to our work together and to your professional development." Although this kind of orienting statement may well temporarily increase the supervisee's anxiety, they won't have to wait long before they know just what the problem is, when you name and describe the problem.

A collaborative and empowering way of undertaking the third step, introducing the problem, is to begin by giving some specific behavioral instances of what you have observed (e.g., "Here are some of the things I have seen that concern me...") and then to invite the supervisee's participation by soliciting their perception (e.g., "Have you also noticed these issues?"), how they would name the problem (e.g., "How would you describe these concerns?"), and their explanation for it ("Why do you think these are a concern?"). This allows the supervisee to get ahead of the discussion and feel a sense of control. If successful, you have not only agreed upon what the problem is, but you have done so with the supervisee's active collaboration. Ideally, this will enhance their openness and engagement throughout the process. In some cases, however, the supervisee may be unable or unwilling to name the problem for what it is, whether from defensiveness or a lack of insight, and you may have to do so explicitly. If so, make sure the supervisee understands why you are framing the problem in this way.

The goal is to identify areas of agreement about the nature of the problem and work toward resolving areas of disagreement to the extent possible. In the example of my experienced supervisee, I could reference the elements of the contract that describe the supervisee's responsibility to keep the supervisor fully informed about their work with their clients. In doing so, I would take responsibility for not having made this expectation clearer at the outset, and indicate my hope that we could have a reset going forward. When this discussion is a more top-down, directive approach, care must be taken that it is not experienced as coercive or as a *fait accompli* and that the supervisee be given ample time and opportunity to respond to the way you have framed the problem. The goal of this stage is to reach a consensus about what the problem is.

Navigation

The final phase of the safety pin framework concerns how to *navigate* the discussion toward understanding *why* the problem occurred and *how* to resolve it. To aid you in working toward these two content goals this phase also involves the use of two process strategies to keep the discussion on track (described below). The first content goal is to explore the problem to achieve a shared understanding of why it happened and what contributed to it. Doing so is necessary to set the stage for problem-solving. Only by coming to a shared understanding of the reasons or causes of the problem can you meaningfully address them. It is crucial to be open to hearing how the supervisee understands why the problem occurs, including any part of the problem that may have to do with your style of supervision or your supervisory relationship. If so, then the solution to the problem may need to focus as much or more on changing your own behavior as the supervisee's. When approaching the supervisee's contribution to the problem, this discussion is more challenging when it involves supervisee lapses in professionalism related to their attitudes and values, or complexities related to subjective cultural and social norms, interpersonal relationships, and degree of remorse experienced (Jha et al. 2016). When these difficulties are present, it is important to calmly take your time in exploring the issues and not feel pressured into a hasty resolution.

Problem exploration may benefit from any or all of the following questions about specific episodes to promote a shared understanding of the reasons for or causes of the problem:

- What was your goal or intention in doing X? Where did that come from?
- How did you understand that doing X would help achieve that goal?
- What feelings or motivations were you experiencing in that moment that might have influenced your decision?
- As you look at it now, can you see how your doing X could be problematic? (e.g., impact on client, supervisor, for violating ethical/professional guidelines, as a clinical error)
- If you were to go back in time to that moment, what would you want to do differently and why?

The goal is to try to achieve a shared understanding of why the problem is occurring.

The second content goal, of seeking a resolution of the problem, builds on the shared understanding of the reasons for the problem to brainstorm potential solutions. By encouraging open discussion and creativity, it may be possible not only to resolve the problem but also to invoke new possibilities that enrich and enliven both the supervisory relationship and the trainee's learning experience. Some potential steps that you may wish to consider as elements of a solution include,

- accepting responsibility [acknowledge harm, apologize],
- correcting a mistake/misunderstanding [repair, reconcile],
- meeting with affected parties,
- considering problem-specific learning strategies, activities, and resources,
- discussing readings (e.g., ethical guidelines, policies/procedures, articles, chapters),

- using modeling and role-play,
- writing about the issue,
- adopting a new plan/strategy/method/goal, or
- exploring additional solutions.

The problem-solving process should conclude with a clear understanding of the responsibilities of both supervisor and supervisee for resolving and monitoring the problem going forward. Ways to do so might include making discussion of the issue a regular item in the supervision agenda and adding monitoring and management of the problem to the contract as a goal. In cases where the supervisee's professionalism or competence problems warrant a remediation plan, the solutions identified may be included in the remediation plan (see Chapter 6 for more about remediation plans).

If the conversation unfolds in an open, non-defensive way, there may be no need to use any special navigational principles or strategies. However, in the spirit of hoping for the best but preparing for the worst, you will want to know them just in case. The primary navigation goal is to keep the conversation on track toward achieving a consensus on the causes of the problem and its solution by *refocusing* the conversation when off-topic issues are raised. For instance, after noticing the emergence of an off-topic issue you might say, "oh, I think we got side-tracked – can we go back to the main issue? You were saying…". The exception to this is when the new issue is more fundamental to the problem, in which case the old issue is *bookmarked* for later discussion (e.g., "this new issue is more important, so let's talk about it now and come back to the other issue later"). Thus, the first navigational principle is to keep the focus of the conversation on the central features of the problem.

The second navigation principle is that whenever a strain or rupture in the alliance occurs, addressing the strain/rupture takes priority. For instance, if the supervisee said "Hearing that feedback makes me feel unsafe – I'm not sure I can work with you if you are going to talk to me like that," it would signal a *confrontation* rupture. Other signs of a confrontation rupture include anger, attacking behavior, manipulation, or a refusal to cooperate. A less obvious but more common type of strain in the alliance occurs in moments of *withdrawal*, when the supervisee falls silent or disengages from active participation in the discussion (Watkins 2021). Supervisee withdrawal, silence, or nondisclosure signals that they may perceive the process to be unsafe, closed, or threatening. Supervisors need to notice and responsively explore these moments, being as open and non-defensive as possible, to repair any strain in the alliance before returning to resolving the original problem (Friedlander 2015). Although it may not be possible to prevent the supervisee from feeling unsafe or threatened during a difficult conversation, your goal should nonetheless be to try to arrange the conditions of the discussion in as open, fair, and transparent way as possible.

Ideally, the process of engaging in a difficult conversation yields agreement on the nature of the problem, its causes, and the supervisee is willing to take the steps that need to be taken to address it during a follow-up phase (see below). Sometimes, however, agreement is not possible because the supervisee lacks insight into their behavior but is nonetheless amenable to making changes. In such cases, the supervisee may benefit from coaching to bring their behavior into line with expectations and requirements if the guidance is made sufficiently clear and tangible. In other cases, supervisees do not have good insight into their difficulties, do not accept supervisory feedback, and are not amenable to making changes. These supervisees are at high risk of performing poorly in training and remediation programs (Mak-van der Vossen et al. 2016). In some of these cases the individual is professionally unsuitable and gatekeeping may be required (see Chapter 6).

When grappling with a significant or difficult-to-resolve conflict, supervisors are strongly encouraged to seek support and guidance from fellow supervisors and/or the program director. Doing so can validate or refine problem-solving strategies, reduce isolation and self-blame, ease the emotional burden, and promote perspective-taking. It can also help determine whether or when third-party mediation or a reassignment of the supervisee to another supervisor in more intractable conflicts should be considered. Conversely, supervisees involved in supervisory conflict may wish to consider consulting not only their peers but also the training director at the fieldwork site or their own program's training director for support and guidance. If this fails to resolve the situation, supervisees should know that most institutions will have additional administrative personnel who may be able to assist (e.g., department heads, deans, equity or human rights officers, and human resources personnel). Also, supervisees should be aware that a complaint may be lodged against an accredited program with its accrediting body, or against a registered supervisor with their regulatory body. Finally, in those rare situations where the dispute is significant and consequential, supervisees may wish to consider retaining legal counsel to advise them, consulting the local human rights office or ombudsperson.

After the Discussion

Follow up. After addressing a conflict, it is essential to have a plan to monitor it going forward and revisit it periodically to assess whether it is fully resolved. In cases where a formal remediation plan is required (see Chapter 6), concrete steps in the plan must be documented and followed closely. Follow-up not only provides the opportunity to address any lingering unresolved issues, but it also reaffirms supervisors' commitment to openness in the supervisory relationship. Supervisees should participate actively in these follow-up discussions.

Chapter Summary

Challenges in supervision commonly arise from one of four sources: (1) the supervisor, (2) the supervisee, (3) the supervisory relationship, and (4) the training site. If not addressed, problems can strain the supervisory relationship, jeopardize client care, and undermine supervisee development. Addressing problems in supervision requires attitudes of humility, openness, and the courage to have uncomfortable conversations. Doing so is prescribed by our ethics and is likely to enhance the supervisory relationship and help achieve the goals of supervision.

Questions for Review and Reflection

1. In thinking about problems in supervision and what contributes to them, what stands out to you as the most problematic factors stemming from supervisors versus from supervisees? What makes these especially difficult to manage?

2. Summarize in one or two sentences the ethical principle(s) that best define how to go about problem-solving in supervision.

3. Many people, including supervisors, will try to avoid addressing a problem they have with another person and the potential conflict that goes with addressing it. How does the Safety PIN framework potentially help people overcome such avoidance? What do you see as most useful about it? What are its limitations?

CHAPTER 6

Concluding Supervision

The concluding phase of supervision requires the dyad to address three key issues: the disposition of the supervisee's clients, the supervisee and supervisor evaluations, and the transition from the end of active supervision to the start of the post-supervision relationship. The chapter provides detailed consideration of how to conduct supervisee evaluations that are fair and accurate. It also discusses how to develop remediation plans for supervisees who are unsuccessful in meeting the goals of their training experience, and the gatekeeping process required when supervisees fail remediation or engage in severe violations of professionalism and ethics.

Ensuring Client Welfare as Supervision Concludes

As the end of the supervisee's training period approaches, the dyad will need to decide the disposition of each of the supervisee's clients. Typically, there are two possibilities. First, and most straightforwardly, therapy with the client is terminated. If, however, the client is not ready for termination and requires continuing treatment, one of several types of transfer may be arranged as discussed below.

Termination

Consistent with evidence-based models of practice, these decisions should be taken in consultation with clients to ensure their needs and preferences are considered (APA Presidential Task Force Evidence-Based Practice 2006). The process of discussing and preparing for the termination of therapy begins at the outset of treatment, when the treatment plan is first proposed and a tentative date for termination or transfer is identified. As treatment continues, the supervisee will need to periodically revisit the issue of termination with the client and supervisor, particularly during the latter stages of the training experience, to help prepare the client and gauge their readiness for termination. Preparing for termination typically includes helping the client to consolidate their gains and anticipate how they will apply their new learning in the future to new or recurrent challenges. It can also include understanding the signs of deterioration that may signal a need to return to therapy.

Decisions about clients' readiness for termination should preferably be based in part on data from outcome monitoring. This information can help evaluate clients' progress across domains such as symptom severity, functioning in work or school, and the social and intimate relationship realms. Other outcomes to consider include gains in coping skills, attitude shifts, or insights. The primary question to consider is whether the client has made sufficient gains in reducing distress, developing coping skills, or achieving stability to go on without the ongoing support of treatment.

Because discussing termination can be anxiety-arousing for both the client and therapist, some supervisees may avoid bringing up the topic with their clients or in supervision. This avoidance, if not addressed in supervision, can result in an unfortunate abruptness to termination that may leave a client unduly distressed and ill-prepared. To help mitigate this tendency, supervisors should periodically explore the termination process in supervision.

When well prepared and effectively carried out, termination can be a therapeutic, empowering process for the client and a source of professional development for the supervisee and supervisor. Clients and supervisees learn that the end of a significant positive relationship can be acknowledged and discussed in a way that enables expression of feelings of warmth, gratitude, and hopefulness, as well as of loss, sadness, and caring. Supervisees can also inquire about what the client found helpful (and not helpful) about treatment. In some ways, these discussions mirror the processing that supervisors and supervisees engage in to conclude the supervisory relationship.

Transfer

Not all clients will be ready for termination at the end of the supervisee's training experience. For these clients, the dyad will need to consider the most appropriate continuing care. If the supervisee will be continuing in the training site with another supervisor, a continuation of the supervisee's treatment of the client under the direction of the new supervisor may be possible, though this should be weighed against the learning benefit the supervisee would gain from working with a new client. Alternatively, the supervisor may transfer the client to a new supervisee, or, personally take over the client's treatment. Finally, if none of these options are deemed possible or suitable, the client may be transferred to the care of another clinician. In no case is it ethically acceptable to simply abandon a client in need of continuing care.

Whatever the nature of the transfer, it needs to involve the full, informed consent of the client ahead of the transfer. This consent is required to allow the new supervisor or therapist access to the treatment plan and session notes. It will also require an update of consent for treatment as the new supervisor or therapist adjusts the treatment plan.

Learning From Client Feedback

Regardless of whether the client is terminated or transferred, supervisees ought to solicit feedback from the client about their experience in treatment. Doing so can be beneficial for the client and the therapist. The key questions to ask focus on the factors that are known to contribute to positive therapy outcomes, such as the core conditions of therapy: therapist warmth, empathy, and acceptance; as well as the client's perception of the therapeutic alliance. Did the client feel understood (empathy) and cared for by the therapist (the bond)? Did the client find that therapy was helpful? Did the way therapy was conducted (the goals and tasks of therapy) align with their preferences, make sense, and feel worthwhile? Did anything detract from the success of therapy? What will the client take away from therapy? This type of inquiry provides an opportunity to gain insight into what was meaningful to the client about therapy and about their relationship to the therapist.

This qualitative feedback complements the quantitative information derived from outcome monitoring. When evaluating outcome monitoring data, consider whether the client showed evidence of reliable change and whether that change was clinically significant (Jacobson and Truax

1991). If so, what outcome domains improved? When this information is combined with the qualitative feedback from the client, what conclusions can be drawn about the success of treatment?

Supervisors can also help supervisees use client feedback to help them become better therapists. Learning from client feedback is a powerful way for therapists to improve. One study demonstrated that tailoring therapy with the aid of client feedback improved outcomes for 9 out of 10 therapists (Anker et al. 2009). While successful outcomes appear to speak for themselves, nonetheless supervisors can help supervisees reflect on what went right and how that came to be. For mixed or frankly unsuccessful outcomes, supervisors can help supervisees derive some useful lessons that may improve the likelihood of obtaining better results in the future.

Closing Files and Dealing With Documentation

Supervisees are responsible for completing all client records prior to concluding supervision and before the final evaluation is undertaken. Supervisors typically must review and sign off on file contents. Client files include notes for all client contacts, intake and/or case conceptualization reports, termination and/or transfer reports, and assessment reports. Also, any substantive client correspondence should be placed in the file, including e-mails. Files should be maintained in the manner and for the length of time prescribed by professional regulations, applicable health information legislation, and the policies of the clinical setting.

Supervisees may find it helpful to create a brief narrative summary of the clients seen under supervision, including their demographics, presenting problems/diagnoses, treatment approach, number of sessions, and outcome, but excluding any identifying information. Supervisees may provide a copy to their supervisor as a basis for future letters of reference. They should also tally the number of client contact hours and supervision hours for each client for future residency and/or licensure applications, a practice facilitated by various software programs designed for this purpose.

Supervisors should ensure their file on the supervisee is complete once the evaluation has been completed to meet practice standards, instructional purposes, and best-practice recommendations (Bernard and Goodyear 2019). Doing so helps with tracking supervisee development (e.g., through noting progress on identified goals and summaries of performance evaluations) and risk management (e.g., by documenting significant clinical or supervisory challenges and associated decisions). Supervision files can include a copy of the supervisee's de-identified description of clients seen under supervision, a copy of the supervision contract and summative evaluations, and documentation of individual supervision meetings, particularly regarding how any situations involving risk or crises were handled (which should also be amply documented in the client record to mitigate liability in the case of adverse events or complaints). Supervisors may also wish to keep copies of letters of reference in the file. As supervision files are not part of clients' official records, they should not include information that could identify clients.

Summative Evaluation

Supervisees' final evaluation involves the summation of all the feedback they have been given on their performance throughout supervision. As this is a critical outcome for the supervisee, it deserves to be undertaken with care and fairness. The following list summarizes recommended final evaluation practices that reflect principles of fairness and supervision guidelines (APA 2014; Bernard and Goodyear 2019; Campbell 2006).

Final evaluations should:

1. Occur within the context of a positive, open supervisory relationship.
2. Be clear, from the beginning, about
    2.1 expectations and the criteria by which supervisees will be judged, and
    2.2 how, and to whom, the evaluation will be disclosed.
3. Use explicit, competency-based performance criteria.
4. Include examples of desired behavior related to goals.

5. Evaluate only those competencies where

    5.1 opportunities have been provided to develop or demonstrate competence, and which have been accompanied by meaningful feedback, and

    5.2 feedback has been regular, timely, and given throughout the training experience on progress toward stated goals.

6. Include supervisee self-assessment as a competency development exercise.

7. Be based on supervisee performances that were

    7.1 observed (live or recorded),

    7.2 representative, and

    7.3 the subject of previous feedback (no new problems or weaknesses should be identified in the final evaluation).

8. Be graded relative to the expected level of performance for the supervisee's stage of development.

Issues to Consider in Evaluation

Final evaluations carry enormous weight. Objectively, they can result in supervisees' requiring remediation or even result in their termination from a training program. Subjectively, they can affect supervisees' self-esteem and self-efficacy, and color the post-supervision relationship. It is therefore concerning to know that final evaluations are prone to supervisor biases and poor practices. In what follows, I describe considerations that are relevant to conducting a fair and accurate evaluation.

Comprehensiveness

The full set of competencies required of practitioners is extensive, if not a little overwhelming. Recall that the cube model portrays competency as the intersection of six functional and six foundational competencies. Furthermore, each of these 36 competency domains includes distinct knowledge, skill, and attitudinal components. Consequently, it is unlikely that any one supervisory experience will comprehensively address all competency domains and elements. Instead, supervisors and supervisees design training experiences to develop a subset of competencies that reflect the best match among the opportunities available within the training site, the supervisor's competencies, and the supervisee's training needs and interests.

Feedback and evaluation should, therefore, focus on the competency domains selected for development. However, because evaluation forms typically present comprehensive lists of competencies, supervisors must identify which competencies were observed, commented on, and developed during practica and limit the evaluation to these. Competencies that were observed, but not the focus of feedback or development, may be evaluated for educational purposes, but should not be included when determining an overall evaluation. This preserves the fairness of the procedure.

The supervisee's developmental level will also be relevant to the decisions taken about the breadth of training supervised and evaluated. Novice supervisees typically require closer supervision and more directive guidance on a more limited range of skills than more advanced supervisees. Thus, the comprehensiveness of evaluation will typically be narrower for less advanced supervisees. For instance, a novice supervisee will be appropriately evaluated against a small set of competency criteria to ensure readiness for the next stage of training. In contrast, a postgraduate supervisee who is being supervised prior to licensure ought to receive a comprehensive evaluation to ensure readiness for independent practice.

Stage of Professional Development and Scaling of Criteria

The criteria used to evaluate supervisees' performance need to be adjusted according to what is reasonable to expect for their level of professional development. To evaluate performance against developmentally appropriate criteria, the scale used to evaluate performance on each of the relevant competencies must offer a suitable method. At present, evaluation forms differ widely in how their scales operationalize evaluation criteria, and there is little agreement or guidance on how best to do so. Differences in scaling can be a source of confusion and frustration to supervisors and supervisees alike. Accordingly, I offer the following comments and recommendations on scaling based on my experience with different scales and evaluation forms.

One approach to developmental scaling involves grading the degree to which the supervisee meets expectations. For example, one scale offers four levels with the following anchors:

1. markedly below expectations
2. below expectations
3. meets expectations
4. exceeds expectations

A strength of this approach is that it permits supervisors to adjust the threshold of meeting expectations up or down, according to the supervisee's developmental level. A limitation is that the threshold depends on the supervisor's judgment. Thus, the same supervisee could receive different evaluations from different supervisors for the same performance. As expectations assume supervisory experience, this type of scale may be challenging for novice supervisors.

Another approach to scaling builds the developmental stages into the scale. One such scale uses five levels:

1. needs remedial work
2. entry level/continued intensive supervision needed
3. intermediate/should remain a focus of supervision
4. high intermediate/occasional supervision needed
5. advanced skills/comparable to autonomous practice at the licensure level.

A strength of this approach is that the various levels of the scale are more objectively operationalized and thus less subject to idiosyncratic definition by supervisors. The major weakness of the scale is that by encompassing the entire range of professional development, the steps of the scale are large and less sensitive to improvement within any given level of development. Thus, novice supervisees are likely, even with excellent performance, restricted to receiving evaluations that place their performance at entry level or intermediate. Not surprisingly, novices often find these evaluations to be uninformative and discouraging. To be fair and informative, an evaluation process must permit a supervisee the possibility of attaining the highest levels of performance available on the scale with sufficient effort and ability.

A blend of the two approaches that preserves the positive elements of each is desirable. Such an approach would begin with identifying the relevant developmental level of the supervisee (e.g., novice, intermediate, etc.). Ideally, each level would include a general description of the degree of competence that can be expected and some competency-specific examples of performance that meet expectations. Having defined the supervisee's developmental level and the appropriate expectations thereof, the four-point expectations scale (markedly below, below, meets, or exceeds) may be used with greater precision.

Validity and Reliability of Supervisor and Self-Evaluations

The summative evaluation process assumes supervisors can objectively appraise their supervisees. However, in light of the emphasis on developing a positive, supportive supervisory relationship, some suggest that supervisor assessments of supervisee performance are positively biased (e.g., Holloway 1984). Consistent with this hypothesis, there is growing evidence that the validity of supervisors' summative evaluations is compromised by *leniency* (a tendency to inflate evaluations relative to actual performance) and *halo* biases (a tendency to use a global impression rather than specific aspects of performance to guide evaluation) (Gonsalvez et al. 2013, 2015, 2021; Gonsalvez and Freestone 2007).

It is possible that supervisors' leniency bias reflects a concern that constructive feedback may undermine the supervisory alliance. Alternatively, supervisors may be rating supervisees' relative progress rather than their demonstrated level of competence. For instance, a supervisee who begins at a low level of competence but progresses to an average level may be rated as highly as one who enters at an average level and progresses to an above-average level. Too great a focus on progress may obscure the degree to which the supervisee is meeting developmental expectations. Halo biases may be more likely to occur when supervisors do not keep sufficiently detailed supervision records about supervisee performance areas that were the subject of positive or constructive feedback.

Considering the intrinsic challenges to objectivity in supervisor evaluations, some propose that they be supplemented by evaluations of supervisee performance by independent assessors. Such evaluations can be conducted in different ways (Kaslow et al. 2009), such as on recorded samples of representative clinical work using objective structured clinical evaluations (Newble 2004) or with standardized patients (Goodie et al. 2022). However, concerns have been raised that supervisees will select a sample of their best work (resulting in an overestimate of the supervisee's typical level of competence) and that the costs and labor-intensive nature of such evaluations are prohibitively expensive (Yap et al. 2021).

Ultimately, supervisor evaluations and independent evaluations provide complementary information. Independent evaluations provide a snapshot of competency at one point in time and thus are most useful for gauging progress toward an objective standard of competence, such as readiness for independent practice. Supervisors, in contrast, are privy to supervisees' efforts and improvements over time. This allows supervisors to evaluate performance in training somewhat independently of competence level attained. Performance in training reflects openness to feedback, commitment to learning and to high standards of ethical and professional practice, and ability to use supervision effectively. Ideally, competency evaluations conducted by supervisors should include two separate categories of evaluation, namely, improvement shown and final level of competence attained. Formally separating evaluations of progress from final standing may help decouple the influence of progress on ratings of final standing, thereby enhancing the reliability and validity of evaluations of final standing.

Recommended Supervisee Evaluation Procedure

The following six-step procedure summarizes the above recommendations for how supervisors can approach evaluation.

Step 1 Formulate the supervisee's present stage of professional development as the context for the evaluation.

Common stages of professional development include: novice, beginner, intermediate learner, advanced learner, and preparing for autonomous practice. To illustrate how these can be operationalized, consider how they are instantiated for trainees within a doctoral professional psychology program: novices have some coursework but no (or little) prior supervised fieldwork experience, beginners have one or two in-house fieldwork experiences, intermediate learners have some extramural fieldwork experience, advanced learners have extensive extramural fieldwork experience, and those preparing for autonomous practice have completed their training (e.g., have their PhD or PsyD) and are completing their supervised practice requirements prior to licensure as an independent practitioner. Keep the trainee's level of professional development in mind as you proceed through the remaining steps of the evaluation.

Step 2 Consider each competency one at a time. Was the specific competency observed to the extent necessary to make a reliable and valid evaluation of it?

- No: Do not evaluate the competency. Instead, mark it as *not observed* and repeat Step 1 for the next competency. Note, some competencies may not have been explicitly observed but may nonetheless be evaluated based on inference (e.g., ethics).
- Yes: Proceed to Step 3

Step 3 Was the specific competency the focus of explicit attention (e.g., was it discussed, addressed with feedback, or taught) within supervision?

- No: Consider whether it would be of value to provide nonevaluative feedback on the degree of improvement and present level of competence. If you think it would be of value to provide these ratings, do so, but do not include them when computing the final evaluation of improvement and present competence.
- Yes: Proceed to Step 4.

Step 4 Evaluate each specific competency distinctly from others (i.e., don't apply an overall halo bias).

For each competency, consider the degree of improvement observed over the period of supervision from baseline or the midway point relative to the end of the training period to inform qualitative comments on the degree of improvement observed.

Rate the present level of competence observed using the scale provided in the evaluation instrument, independent of improvement observed. Qualitative comments on the level of competence demonstrated by the supervisee may be a useful supplement to quantitative ratings. They can provide the context and nuance necessary to explain ratings that deviate noticeably from the trainee's overall level of performance (e.g., problem areas or areas of exceptional skill).

Step 5 Make an overall evaluation.

Use the evaluations of specific competencies made in Step 4 to determine an overall evaluation. The decision on how to summarize the specific evaluations into a global evaluation requires judgment on the part of the assessor. The main decision is whether to weight all items approximately equally and use an average (or median) score, or to weight some competencies more heavily than others. These procedures can produce quite different results. For a student with many ratings of *meets expectations* and one or two ratings of *below expectations* or *requires remedial training*, the use of an average will likely produce an overall score close to *meets expectations*. However, if the competencies on which the supervisee received low ratings are deemed critical to the supervisee's stage of professional development, one could conceivably justify weighting the item very heavily, resulting in an overall evaluation of *below expectations*. Degree of improvement may be incorporated into the overall evaluation, especially for novice supervisees, as the ability to benefit from supervision is a key learning competency that will contribute to success in future fieldwork training.

Typically, overall evaluations are formulated as pass, fail, or in need of remediation (see below). As discussed below, fairness dictates that supervisees receiving a failing grade should have previously received appropriate feedback and opportunities for remediation.

Step 6 Include a recommendation regarding the future training and supervision of the supervisee.

This aspect of the evaluation is not always necessary but can be invaluable. The recommendation should address the question of whether the supervisee is ready to make the transition to a higher level of autonomy in the practice area supervised. If the recommendation is that the supervisee is not yet ready for additional autonomy, it should specify whether the supervisee requires additional supervised practice at the present level of autonomy or remedial supervised experience at a heightened level of supervisory oversight. If the latter, a detailed remediation plan should be drawn up to address competencies that are deemed deficient (see below) and included with the evaluation. If a supervisee's performance is sufficiently incompetent or unethical to warrant removal from the profession, the supervisor should take into account the gatekeeping considerations outlined further below. Finally, the supervisor may also consider making recommendations regarding the potential value of supervised practice in other domains that were not the focus of supervision for the purpose of rounding out the supervisee's competencies or developing a specific practice area of interest.

Supervisee Self-Assessment

Accurate self-assessment is a key competency required for practitioners to practice safely within their areas of competence. Supervisors can facilitate the development of accurate supervisee self-assessment by inviting supervisees to engage in summative self-assessment at the conclusion of their training experience and to calibrate their self-evaluations against the supervisor's evaluation on the same evaluation measure.

Research on self-assessment suggests that novice trainees often underestimate their competence relative to supervisor evaluations (Gonsalvez et al. 2021; Hitzeman et al. 2020). However, with greater clinical experience, the magnitude of underestimation of performance declines (Gonsalvez et al. 2023). These findings are consistent with indications that novice clinicians commonly experience impostor syndrome (Clark et al. 2025) and low levels of professional self-efficacy (Stoltenberg et al. 2014). Conversely, research also suggests that trainees who approach self-evaluation with higher levels of self-compassion tend to report higher levels of counselor self-efficacy and professional competence (Latorre et al. 2023). Supervisors of novice students would do well to be alert for signs that their supervisees are succumbing to an undue tendency toward excessive self-criticism.

Supervisor and supervisee evaluations tend to show more agreement when supervision has included more observation of the supervisee (Hitzeman et al. 2020), which further underscores the value of engaging in regular observation of supervisees. Ultimately, because there are no purely objective methods of evaluation, it is difficult to know with certainty whether the difference between supervisor and supervisee ratings in novices is due to undue self-criticism in trainees, supervisor leniency, or some combination of both.

When comparing the supervisor's evaluation with the supervisee's self-evaluation, the discussion will naturally tend to focus on items where there are divergences in the ratings. Discussion of these will help reveal the different assumptions or contextual information that informed the ratings. Experienced supervisors bring to the evaluation a wealth of experiential data about what is typical or normative for supervisees at a given stage of professional development. Novice supervisors may benefit from consulting with experienced supervisors to clarify what is typical for a given stage of professional development. These norms serve as an implicit criterion for supervisors during evaluation. Because supervisees have less exposure to, and awareness of, such norms, this may be a source of supervisor-supervisee evaluation differences. It can therefore be helpful for supervisors to convey this normative information to supervisees to complement the idiographic portrait of supervisee strengths and areas for growth provided in the evaluation.

Finally, supervisees should be encouraged to reflect on clients' outcome monitoring results to help calibrate their self-assessments. Because these reports may be influenced by many factors beyond the supervisee's control, they should not be used as a criterion for supervisee evaluations, nor should supervisees take too much credit nor blame for them. Rather, they may be useful along with other sources of information to help supervisees self-assess their areas of relative strength and future growth (cf. Waltman et al. 2016).

Evaluations of Supervisors

Supervisors, like supervisees, benefit from formal evaluations to promote their development and gauge their level of competence. One approach to supervisor evaluation is to use a *standardized supervisee*, which is similar to an assessment with a standardized patient (Veilleux et al. 2022). While such procedures are at present in their infancy, they represent a promising method for the future evaluation of supervisors.

More commonly, supervisees provide evaluations of supervisors. Consistent with the emphasis in this book, I recommend supervisees rate the supervisory alliance, for instance, by using the *Brief Supervisory Alliance Scale* (Rønnestad and Lundquist 2009) along with other dimensions of supervision (S. Wheeler and Barkham 2014). Another useful brief instrument is the *Supervision Evaluation and Supervisor Competence Scale-Short Version* (SE-SC-short; Gonsalvez 2021).

However, owing to the power imbalance, special arrangements should be made to ensure that it is safe for the supervisee to evaluate the supervisor honestly, without regard for possible negative repercussions from the supervisor. Research shows that supervisees rate supervisors lower when able to give ratings confidentially rather than to the supervisor directly (O'Donovan and Kavanagh 2014). Factors that can enhance supervisee safety include anonymity and delaying when the feedback is delivered to the supervisor until after the supervisor's evaluation is completed. A further safety step would be to only provide supervisors with summaries of several evaluations once a sufficient number have been collected to ensure the anonymity of the evaluations. Admittedly, this type of delayed feedback is less than optimal for supervisors' learning and development; however, receiving more accurate feedback is some compensation.

To bridge the delay in receiving formal feedback, supervisors may wish to solicit informal, verbal feedback from supervisees about their experience of supervision throughout supervision as well as at the conclusion. Clearly, the non-anonymous nature of such feedback renders its validity uncertain and dependent on the supervisor's ability to create a genuinely safe context for the supervisee to share their experience. Nonetheless, there are several benefits to seeking this type of feedback. Inviting such feedback models a commitment to lifelong learning and development to the supervisee. Such learning will be dependent on supervisors' ability to be open and non-defensive. Finally, the informal evaluation of the supervisor, along with the anonymous formal evaluation, helps to partially equalize the power imbalance in the relationship. This increasing equality marks a step toward supervisor and supervisee becoming colleagues and peers within the profession.

Gatekeeping

No one relishes gatekeeping. Nonetheless, it is an ethical responsibility. The *Ethical Guidelines for Supervision in Psychology* (CPA 2017b) states it clearly:

> With respect to the gatekeeper function … supervisors have an obligation to ensure that successful supervisees meet at least minimal standards of competence for their level of training in their area of activity by the end of supervision; moreover, supervisors assume responsibility for addressing problematic areas of concern identified during the supervisory relationship and for not passing or certifying supervisees who are not meeting developmentally appropriate standards. (p. 6)

The metaphor of supervisor as gatekeeper symbolizes the professional and ethical responsibility that supervisors bear to halt professionally incompetent or unethical supervisees' ongoing progress within the profession to protect the public. We can further distinguish between temporary and terminal gatekeeping. Temporary gatekeeping may involve requiring a trainee to repeat a training experience or successfully complete a defined course of remedial education or training before progress through a training program can be continued. Terminal gatekeeping involves a decision to terminate the trainee's progression toward a degree (i.e., removal from a program) or licensure (i.e., removal from the profession). When problems of professional competency are the reason for gatekeeping, the process ordinarily begins with remediation (Freitag et al. 2023). However, as discussed further below, when problems are considered irremediable, or in instances involving severe breaches of ethics or professional behavior (e.g., sex with a client), supervisors will report this to the supervisee's training program (or licensing board for graduates seeking licensure), who may consider whether immediate dismissal without remediation may be required to fulfill its obligation to protect the public (Schwartz-Mette 2023).

Remediation

According to best practice recommendations (e.g., APA 2014), supervisees are ethically and legally entitled to a fair opportunity to address competence problems that are remediable, i.e., mild to moderate severity competence deficits, or mild problems of professionalism) and, if successful, continue in their program of study (Lease and Grus, 2023). This process ordinarily occurs informally when problems are first identified and discussed in supervision. The need for formal remediation becomes evident when a supervisee exhibits recurrent problems that persist despite feedback and without substantial improvement within a developmentally expected time frame (Schwartz-Mette 2023). Remediation plans are necessary when the severity of the supervisee's problems makes it unlikely that they can function safely and effectively within the next, more autonomous, stage of professional training or development (e.g., going from in-house to external training, from practica to residency, or from residency to readiness for licensure).

When the need for remediation is present, supervisors are obligated to assess and formally document these problems as the basis for developing a formal remediation plan (Renninger and Cavalieri 2023). Documentation, communication, respect, and transparency are essential to the fairness of the process (Veilleux and Scafe 2023). Supervisors need to discuss the need for remediation with the supervisee and the director of training at the site and the supervisee's training program, to collaboratively develop a formal written plan (Lease and Grus 2023). Providing a fair remediation opportunity might involve temporarily reducing other demands on the supervisee, providing additional supervision, guidance, modeling, and feedback, for a reasonable period so they can demonstrate mastery of the specified competencies. In carrying out this work with a supervisee with competence deficits, supervisors need to reflect on how much additional direction and oversight is necessary to provide to ensure client welfare and that appropriate care is delivered. The remediation plan must document the competence areas in which the supervisee is deficient, list performance expectations, and outline steps to be taken to address competence deficits. It should clarify what the responsibilities of each party are, how performance will be monitored and evaluated, the consequences for unsuccessful remediation, and the timelines involved. The supervisor will carry out the plan as documented and will make timely written and oral evaluations of performance according to the specified criteria. Detailed guidance on how to construct and implement a remediation plan is available in Freitag et al. (2023) and Vacha-Haase et al. (2019), and a template for remediation plans can be found in Appendix C of Schwartz-Mette et al. (2023).

When Remediation Fails, Problems Are Severe, and Counseling Out or Dismissal Is Indicated

In cases where the supervisor deems that a supervisee has failed to meet the outcomes required in the remediation plan, the supervisor should consult with other training staff (e.g., other supervisors, the field site's training director, the program's training director) to ensure their judgment is defensible. This consultation is essential because the consequence of failing remediation is typically to counsel the supervisee out of the program (or initiate dismissal procedures) in order to protect the public (Schwartz-Mette 2023). For professionals seeking licensure, failed remediation may lead to professional sanctions, including restrictions on areas of practice, requirements to engage in supervised practice, the revocation of licensure, or loss of employment. These are difficult, highly consequential issues for all involved, and hence consultation with colleagues and the professional literature cited here is essential.

When failed remediation involves a supervisee who requires reasonable accommodations, the final evaluation and subsequent dismissal process should document how, notwithstanding reasonable accommodation, the student failed to meet the minimal standards for essential competencies by referencing the training program's published *Bona Fide Requirements*.

In cases where the trainee is deemed to be *lacking capacity* (Veilleux et al. 2012) the competency deficiency may be judged to be irremediable. Olkin and Gaughen (1991) defined those who are *professionally unsuitable* as "those students whose personal limitations or problem behaviors are of such a nature or severity that they are deemed by educators to impede the students' ability to professional practice" (p. 279). Lease and Grus (2023) noted that some irremediable problems of professional competence occur because of problems in personality or interpersonal functioning:

> The latter may result in trainees who are unable or unwilling to attain accepted minimal levels of competence on designated behaviors, fail to respond to feedback and make progress, lack

self-awareness of their weaknesses, struggle with maintaining professional interactions, have problems with professionalism or interpersonal interactions that they have not addressed, or experience personal or mental health issues that affect their professional functioning (p. 46)

Insofar as professional judgment will be required to make such determinations, it is essential for supervisors to consult widely with fellow supervisors and training directors to ensure they reflect fair and reasonable judgments of when a trainee has been afforded sufficient opportunity to demonstrate competency.

The other, fortunately rare, scenario where dismissal procedures are indicated is when a supervisee commits a severe breach of ethics and professionalism (e.g., having sex with a client, or more generally allowing self-interest to jeopardize their professional judgment). In such cases, the supervisor's role is to inform the relevant program, institutional, and professional authorities about the violation. Typically, this will trigger an investigation to consider the charges of unprofessional conduct or professional unsuitability by a duly appointed committee. The supervisor can anticipate that they will be called upon to provide testimony or evidence relevant to the investigation. Depending on the nature and severity of the breach, the supervisee may face sanctions that include probation (often paired with remediation), or dismissal from the program or profession (L. Forrest et al. 1999).

When dismissal proceedings are initiated, supervisees should be reminded of their due process rights to appeal these decisions. Supervisees must be provided with clear information about the reasons for their dismissal, such as which competencies are deficient, or what ethical or professional violations have occurred. Supervisees should be treated with respect and consideration for the difficulties this decision will create. Supervisors should collaborate with relevant authorities or administrators within the university, training site, or licensing body to ensure that proper, defensible procedures are observed (Shah and Fishel 2023). Having complete documentation of all relevant aspects of the supervisee's training, including supervisory feedback and evaluations, remediation plans and outcomes, and peer consultation is necessary in case of an appeal. Supervisees may wish to consult available supports within their program, institution, or profession, or from a lawyer for guidance on how to respond in these circumstances.

The formal process of dismissing a supervisee from a training program can be sidestepped when supervisees are open to being informally counselled out of the profession (Schwartz-Mette 2023). Typically, this discussion focuses on the poor fit that presumably exists between the supervisee's abilities and those required in the profession, and the likelihood that pursuing a career with a better fit will yield much greater personal and professional satisfaction in the long run.

Transition From Active Supervision to the Post-Supervision Relationship

Once the supervisee's clients are terminated or transferred and the supervisee's formal training period has been successfully concluded, what then? Although active supervision is officially over, an ongoing post-supervision professional relationship remains, which has significant implications for the supervisee's future training trajectory and professional career. Influential roles that (former) supervisors can play during this stage are those of gatekeeper, reference, and mentor.

Progressing Supervisees

In most cases, supervisees succeed in meeting their training goals. Consequently, supervisors may have the opportunity to help further supervisees' progress in the profession through writing letters of reference for advanced training opportunities such as residency or postdoctoral fellowships, for jobs, or for licensure/registration.

Supervisors can mentor supervisees who need letters of reference by having them reflect on the following questions:

- Is the reference current?
  If their experience with a supervisor is from several years ago, chances are they have developed many new skills and interests that their supervisor would not be able to comment on directly.

A supervisory colleague holds a "five-year rule" beyond which he declines to provide a reference unless he has maintained post-supervisory contact and has a continuing perspective (D. Stewart, personal communication, July 22, 2025).

- Is the reference likely to be positive?
  If in doubt, ask whether the supervisor is willing to provide a positive reference. In keeping with the principles of transparency and openness advocated in this book, I prefer to be open about the nature of the letter I would write for the supervisee at the time of the request to allow them to make an informed decision about whether to include me as a referee.

Once a referee has been selected, the referee will require advance notice of when and where the letter(s) is due, along with background information of the position(s) sought (e.g., a copy of the position posting), a copy of the cv, and any other pertinent information (e.g., about other training experiences or interests).

For supervisors who have not written a letter of reference, the following considerations will help you craft a clear, effective letter. The letter should be based primarily on your direct experience with the supervisee and should provide a brief description of that experience, including the length of time you have known and worked with the supervisee and how long ago that was. This information helps the reader evaluate how well you know the supervisee. It should also concisely summarize the number and kinds of clients the supervisee worked with, as well as a brief description of the setting. This sets the stage for you to describe your evaluation of the supervisee's notable strengths and skills as well as any areas for growth and development. Looking ahead, the letter should directly address the supervisee's qualifications for the position, using concrete examples where possible. In sum, a specific letter that details strengths and areas for growth will carry more credibility and weight than a "glowing and global" letter, which is safe but typically unpersuasive. Supervisors may find it helpful to reflect on whether they incline more toward advocacy or accuracy in their letter, and whether that inclination arises from feeling closer to their supervisee or to the individual or program receiving the letter (Hadar and Halevy 2025). Once a draft of the letter is written, you may wish to consider sharing a copy with the supervisee to allow them to correct any factual errors. Finally, supervisors should know that in some jurisdictions or settings, applicants have the right to view their letters of reference.

Informal, post-supervision mentoring may involve assisting former supervisees with developing their professional network through in-person introductions to colleagues at conferences and workshops, or through encouragement to supervisees to become members and active participants in leadership roles in local, regional, or national professional bodies. Over time, former supervisees will transition to becoming colleagues. This transition can take a little getting used to for both parties, but if managed well, can allow for lifelong positive collegial relationships.

Challenges and Opportunities in the Post-Supervision Relationship

The post-supervision relationship includes an ongoing role for the supervisor in advancing the professional progress of the supervisee, as well as the ongoing residue of a close, influential relationship formed during a time of supervisee dependence. Thus the power differential and ongoing influence, although lessened, continue, arguably in perpetuity, or at least during the first years following the end of formal supervision when supervisory power and influence lingers. Accordingly, former supervisees remain vulnerable to subtle influence and outright coercive pressure, and so, intimate sexual relationships between former supervisors and supervisees should remain off-limits (as do intimate relations between former clients and clinicians) according to ethical codes (e.g., APA 2010) and supervision guidelines (APA 2014; ASPPB 2015; CPA 2017b).

Research on intimate sexual relationships between supervisors and supervisees shows that although professionals recognize having sexual relations with supervisees is unethical (Schwartz-Mette and Shen-Miller 2017), experiences of sexual or other forms of harassment do occur during professional training and supervision (Ellis et al. 2014; McAdams 2020; Robinson and Reid 1985). Although actual sexual relationships between current supervisors and supervisees are infrequent, they tend to occur more often after formal supervision ends (Lamb et al. 2003). Thus, the post-supervision period represents a period of vulnerability for supervisors and supervisees (Fox 2018). One reason for this may be the belief that the cessation of formal supervision means that the power differential and supervisor influence have ceased and that the participants are on an equal footing now. Research by Glaser and Thorpe (1986) examining attitudes toward, and experiences of, educator (including supervisor)–student (including supervisee) sexual relationships suggests that such thinking is naïve and/or self-serving.

On a more positive note, the post-supervision relationship can lead to a wide variety of positive working relationships between former supervisors and supervisees. These might include opportunities to pursue mutual professional interests through shared activities such as collaboration on research or program development, or joint participation in professional organizations at the national or state/provincial level. In my own experience, I am grateful to many of my supervisors and mentors who took a kindly interest in my professional progress by writing thoughtful reference letters, introducing and endorsing me to their colleagues when I was on the job market, encouraging me to get involved in professional associations and committees, and by their own examples of dedication and hard work on behalf of the discipline and profession. I have tried to emulate their example with my supervisees.

Looking Ahead

The conclusion of active supervision is not the end of the supervision relationship. In most cases, it continues to be a meaningful and potentially significant relationship. Take this opportunity to consider what you would like your post-supervision relationships to look like. As your relationship transitions in the post-supervision period, how will you move toward a more collegial relationship? How does a relationship with a former supervisee differ from those you might have with other colleagues who were not supervisees?

Chapter Summary

In the concluding phase of supervision, the dyad addresses client needs for termination or transfer, ensures files are complete, and carries out summative evaluations of supervisee and supervisor. The impactful nature of supervisee evaluations dictates that they be conducted as fairly and accurately as possible. In instances of supervisee failure, supervisors collaborate with the supervisee and other colleagues to design a formal remediation plan. In the rare case when a supervisee fails remediation, supervisors need to document the result and the process to support the counseling out or dismissal of the supervisee from the program. Dismissal procedures may also be required for supervisees who have engaged in serious breaches of professional and ethical conduct. In most cases, however, the supervisee is successful, and the final phase of supervision provides a satisfying end to the active portion of the supervision relationship and a helpful transition to the post-supervision phase of the relationship.

Conclusion: The Continuing Supervisory Journey

This brings us to the end of our exploration of supervision together, but I trust this will not be the end of your own supervision journey. Personally, my journey, both as a supervisee and supervisor, has been a story of continual evolution. From my halting, anxious beginning in both roles, I soon began to feel more comfortable as I discovered to my amazement that I had something of value to offer my clients, and later, my supervisees, and had a way of relating to them that worked. Over the years, I have also learned that while there are many commonalities, each supervisory dyad and experience has a unique flavor with distinctive challenges and satisfactions that provide me with opportunities to grow and reflect on my supervisory beliefs and practices.

I hope that reading this book has been helpful in providing you with guidance and tools that you can adapt to your own styles and preferences to find a way—your way—to work together with supervisees effectively and harmoniously. Moving forward, I hope you will find supervision to be an exciting, fulfilling, and meaningful activity that will challenge and inspire you for years to come.

Questions for Review and Reflection

1. What are the key client care considerations when bringing a supervision experience to a close?
2. What makes for a fair and accurate evaluation process?
   - How can you ensure these are included in the evaluations you conduct?
   - What factors might interfere with your ability to carry out evaluations in the way you intend, and how might you avoid or prevent these from affecting your evaluation process?
3. When a supervisee demonstrates problems of professional competence, what are your responsibilities as a supervisor in the evaluation and remediation process? Under what circumstances would a supervisee be dismissed from a training program or the profession? What supports and resources might you need to manage a remediation or dismissal situation?
4. After the formal period of supervision ends, how does the supervisor continue to exert power and influence over supervisees, and what are the implications for the post-supervision relationship?
5. How do you plan to continue learning and developing as a supervisor in the future?

Safety PIN Template for Approaching Difficult Conversations

Step I: Preparation

1. Detect the problem by attending to internal and external markers.
2. Name the problem, evaluate its seriousness, and reflect on your feelings and narrative about it.
3. Identify your goals for the process and outcome of the conversation.

Step II: Initiation

1. Orient the listener to the existence of a critical issue.
2. Describe your benevolent goals/intentions for the conversation.
3. Introduce the problem with clear and specific examples and say why it is a concern.
4. Solicit the supervisee's perception of the examples and how they perceive the problem.
5. Seek consensus on what the problem is.

Step III: Navigation

1. Explore the reasons for the problem.
2. Engage in problem-solving to identify a solution.
3. Agree on how to monitor/manage the problem in the future.
4. Use refocusing to manage off-topic issues.
5. Use bookmarking to temporarily bracket a less important issue.
6. Prioritize attention to strains or ruptures in the supervisory alliance.

References

Aafjes-van Doorn, K., and K. de Jong. 2022. "How to Make the Most of Routine Outcome Monitoring (ROM): A Multitude of Clinical Decisions and Nuances to Consider." *Journal of Clinical Psychology* 78, no. 10, pp. 2054–2065. https://doi.org/10.1002/jclp.23438

Adams, L., G. Gross, J.M. Doran, and M. Stacy. 2022. "Clinical Supervisors' Experiences with and Barriers to Supporting Trainees who have Experienced Identity Based Harassment." *Training and Education in Professional Psychology* 16, no. 4, pp. 403–411. https://doi.org/10.1037/tep0000384

Aguglia, A., M. Belvederi Murri, C. Conigliaro, N. Cipriani, M. Vaggi, G. Di Salvo, G. Maina, V. Cavone, E. Aguglia, G. Serafini, and M. Amore. 2020. "Workplace Violence and Burnout among Mental Health Workers." *Psychiatric Services* 71, no. 3, pp. 284–288. https://doi.org/10.1176/appi.ps.201900161

American Psychological Association. 2010. Ethical Principles of Psychologists and Code of Conduct with the 2010 Amendments. http://www.apa.org/ethics/code/

American Psychological Association. 2014. Guidelines for Clinical Supervision in Health Service Psychology. http://apa.org/about/policy/guidelines-supervision.pdf

American Psychological Association. 2017. Multicultural Guidelines: An Ecological Approach to Context, Identity, and Intersectionality. http://www.apa.org/about/policy/multicultural-guidelines.pdf

American Psychological Association, Commission on Accreditation. 2015. Standards of Accreditation for Health Service Psychology. http://www.apa.org/ed/accreditation/about/policies/standards-of-accreditation.pdf

Ammirati, R.J., and N.J. Kaslow. 2017. "All Supervisors have the Potential to be Harmful." *Clinical Supervisor* 36, no. 1, pp. 116–123. https://doi.org/10.1080/07325223.2017.1298071

Ancis, J.R., and D.S. Marshall. 2010. "Using a Multicultural Framework to Assess Supervisees' Perceptions of Culturally Competent Supervision." *Journal of Counseling and Development* 88, no. 3, pp. 277–284. https://doi.org/10.1002/j.1556-6678.2010.tb00023.x

Anker, M.G., B.L. Duncan, and J.A. Sparks. 2009. "Using Client Feedback to Improve Couple Therapy Outcomes: A Randomized Clinical Trial in a Naturalistic Setting." *Journal of Consulting and Clinical Psychology* 77, no. 4, pp. 693–704. https://doi.org/10.1037/a0016062

APA Presidential Task Force Evidence-Based Practice. 2006. "Evidence-Based Practice in Psychology." *The American Psychologist* 61, no. 4, pp. 271–285. https://doi.org/10.1037/0003-066X.61.4.271

APPIC. 2018. APPIC problem consultation.: www.appic.org/problem-consultation

Association of State and Provincial Psychology Boards. 2015. Supervision Guidelines for Education and Training Leading to Licensure as a Health Service Provider.: www.asppb.net/resource/resmgr/Guidelines/Final _Supervision_Guidelines.pdf

Awa, W.L., M. Plaumann, and U. Walter. 2010. "Burnout Prevention: A Review of Intervention Programs." Patient Education and Counseling 78, no. 2, pp. 184–190. https://doi.org/10.1016/j.pec.2009.04.008

Bailin, A., S.K. Bearman, and R. Sale. 2018. "Clinical Supervision of Mental Health Professionals Serving Youth: Format and Microskills." *Administration and Policy in Mental Health and Mental Health Services Research* 45, no. 5, pp. 800–812. https://doi.org/10.1007/s10488-018-0865-y

Bambling, M., and R. King. 2014. "Supervisor Social Skill and Supervision Outcome." *Counselling and Psychotherapy Research* 14, no. 4, pp. 256–262. https://doi.org/10.1080/14733145.2013.835849

Bambling, M., R. King, P. Raue, R. Schweitzer, and W. Lambert 2006. "Clinical Supervision: Its Influence on Client-Rated Working Alliance and Client Symptom Reduction in the Brief Treatment of Major Depression." *Psychotherapy Research* 16, no. 3, pp. 317–331. https://doi.org /10.1080/10503300500268524

Bandura, A. 1989. "Human agency in Social Cognitive Theory." *The American Psychologist* 44, no. 9, pp. 1175–1184. https://doi.org/10.1037/0003 -066X.44.9.1175

Bandura, A. 1997. *Self-Efficacy: The Exercise of Control.* W. H. Freeman.

Barkham, M., K. De Jong, J. Delgadillo, and W. Lutz. 2023. "Routine Outcome Monitoring Rom and Feedback: Research Review and Recommendations." *Psychotherapy Research* 33, no. 7, pp. 841–855. https://doi.org/10.1080/105 03307.2023.2181114

Barlow, D.H. 2010. "Negative Effects from Psychological Treatments: A Perspective." *The American Psychologist* 65, no. 1, pp. 13–20. https://doi .org/10.1037/a0015643

Barnett, J.E. 2023. "Ethics in Supervision." In *Handbook of Training and Supervision in Cognitive Behavioral Therapy*, eds. M.D. Terjesen, and T. Del Vecchio, 29–45. Springer International Publishing. https://doi .org/10.1007/978-3-031-33735-2_2

Baum, N., and S. Moyal. 2020. "Impact on Therapists Working with Sex Offenders: A Systematic Review of Gender Findings." *Trauma, Violence, and Abuse* 21, no. 1, pp. 193–205. https://doi.org/10.1177/1524838018756120

Bautista-Biddle, M.M., L.M. Pereira, and S.N. Williams. 2021. "The Fallacy of "Good Training Experiences": The Need to Protect Psychology Trainees from Harassment and the Imperative of Multiculturally Competent Supervision." *Training and Education in Professional Psychology* 15, no. 4, pp. 323–330. https://doi.org/10.1037/tep0000353

Beckman, M., B. Bohman, L. Forsberg, F. Rasmussen, and A. Ghaderi. 2017. "Supervision in Motivational Interviewing: An Exploratory Study." *Behavioural and Cognitive Psychotherapy* 45, no. 4, pp. 351–365. https://doi.org/10.1017/S135246581700011X

Beckman, M., L. Forsberg, H. Lindqvist, and A. Ghaderi. 2020. "Providing Objective Feedback in Supervision in Motivational Interviewing: Results from a Randomized Controlled Trial." *Behavioural and Cognitive Psychotherapy* 48, no. 4, pp. 383–394. https://doi.org/10.1017/S1352465819000687

Beinart, H. 2014. "Building and Sustaining the Supervisory Relationship." In *The Wiley International Handbook of Clinical Supervision*, eds. C.E. Watkins, Jr. and D.L. Milne, 255–281. John Wiley and Sons, Ltd. https://doi.org/10.1002/9781118846360.ch11

Benner, A. D., Wang, Y., Shen, Y., Boyle, A. E., Polk, R., and Cheng, Y.-P. 2018. "Racial/Ethnic Discrimination and Well-Being During Adolescence: A Meta-Analytic Review." *American Psychologist* 73, no. 7, pp. 855–883. https://doi.org/10.1037/amp0000204

Bernard, J.M. 1997. "The Discrimination Model." *In Handbook of Psychotherapy Supervision, eds.* C.E. Watkins Jr., 310–327. Wiley.

Bernard, J.M., and R.K. Goodyear. 2019. *Fundamentals of Clinical Supervision,* 6th ed. Pearson.

Bistricky, S.L., Klein, P., Pascuzzi, B., Oliver, S., Gimenez-Zapiola, M., and Schanding, G.T. 2025. "Training and Maintaining Self-Care: Recommendations, Values, and Mental Health." *Training and Education in Professional Psychology.* 19, no. 3, pp. 190–198 https://doi.org/10.1037/tep0000513

Bjornestad, A., V. Johnson, J. Hittner, and K. Paulson. 2014. "Preparing Site Supervisors of Counselor Education Students." *Counselor Education and Supervision* 53, no. 4, pp. 242–253. https://doi.org/10.1002/j.1556-6978.2014.00060.x

Boe, J.L., E. Wieling, and M.O. Caughy. 2024. "Transgender and Gender Diverse Clinical Competency and Affirmative Training in Graduate Education." Training and Education in Professional Psychology 18, no. 2, pp. 117–129. https://doi.org/10.1037/tep0000474

Borders, L.D., and A.L. Giordano. 2016. "Confronting Confrontation in Clinical Supervision: An Analytical Autoethnography." Journal of Counseling and Development 94, no. 4, pp. 454–463. https://doi.org/10.1002/jcad.12104

Borders, L.D., L.E. Welfare, C.R. Sackett, and C. Cashwell. 2017. "New Supervisors' Struggles and Successes with Corrective Feedback." *Counselor Education and Supervision* 56, no. 3, pp. 208–224. https://doi.org/10.1002/ceas.12073

Bordin, E.S. 1983. *"A Working Alliance Model of Supervision." The Counseling Psychologist* 11, pp. 35–42.

Boyd, J.E., A. Zeiss, S. Reddy, and S. Skinner. 2016. "Accomplishments of 77 VA Mental Health Professionals with a Lived Experience of Mental Illness." *American Journal of Orthopsychiatry* 86, no. 6, pp. 610–619. https://doi.org/10.1037/ort0000208

Boyle, S.L., and T.E. Kenny. 2020. "To Disclose or Not to Disclose: Examining Supervisor Actions Related to Self-Disclosure in Supervision." *Journal of Psychotherapy Integration* 30, no. 1, pp. 36–43. https://doi.org/10.1037/int0000181

Bradley, W.J., and K.D. Becker. 2021. "Clinical Supervision of Mental Health Services: A Systematic Review of Supervision Characteristics and Practices Associated with Formative and Restorative Outcomes." *Clinical Supervisor* 40, no. 1, pp. 88–111. https://doi.org/10.1080/07325223.2021.1904312

Branson, D.C. 2019. "Vicarious Trauma, Themes in Research, and Terminology: A Review of Literature." *Traumatology* 25, no. 1, pp. 2–10. https://doi.org/10.1037/trm0000161

Brien, A., C. Bilodeau, R. Savard, and P. Dionne. 2025. "Examining the Associations Between Reflexive Self-Awareness and Self-Compassion on Early Supervisory Alliance Development in Canadian Counseling and Psychotherapy Trainees." *Training and Education in Professional Psychology* 19, pp. 331-338. https://doi.org/10.1037/tep0000521

Bruner, J.S. 1996. *The Culture of Education.* Harvard University Press.

Bullock, J.L., M.T. O'Brien, P.K. Minhas, A. Fernandez, K.L. Lupton, and K.E. Hauer. 2021. "No One Size Fits All: A Qualitative Study of Clerkship Medical Students' Perceptions of Ideal Supervisor Responses to Microaggressions." *Academic Medicine* 96, no. 11S, pp. S71–S80. https://doi.org/10.1097/ACM.0000000000004288

Cairns, L., and Malloch, M. 2024. *Lifelong Learning for Capability.* Springer International Publishing. https://doi.org/10.1007/978-3-031-68240-7

Callahan, J.L., C.M. Almstrom, J.K. Swift, S.E. Borja, and C.J. Heath. 2009. "Exploring the Contribution of Supervisors to Intervention Outcomes." *Training and Education in Professional Psychology* 3, no. 2, pp. 72–77. https://doi.org/10.1037/a0014294

Callahan, J.L., S.A. Gustafson, J.B. Misner, C.M. Paprocki, E.M. Sauer, K.K. Saules, J.L. Schwartz, J.K. Swift, D.M. Whiteside, K.E. Wierda, and E.H. Wise. 2014. "Introducing the Association of Psychology Training Clinics'

Collaborative Research Network: A Study on Client Expectancies." *Training and Education in Professional Psychology* 8, no. 2, pp. 95–104. https://doi .org/10.1037/tep0000047

Callan, S., Schwartz, J., and Arputhan, A. 2021. "Training Future Psychologists to be Competent in Self-Care: A Systematic Review." *Training and Education in Professional Psychology* 15, no. 2, pp. 117–125. https://doi.org/10.1037 /tep0000345

Campbell, J. 2006. *Essentials of Clinical Supervision.* Wiley.

Canadian Psychological Association. 2017a. *Canadian Code of Ethics for Psychologists,* 4th ed. Author.

Canadian Psychological Association. 2017b. *Ethical Guidelines for Supervision in Psychology: Teaching, Research, Practice, and Administration.* Author.

Canadian Psychological Association. 2018. *Psychology's Response to the Truth and Reconciliation Commission of Canada's Report.* https://cpa.ca/docs/File/Task _Forces/TRC%20Task%20Force%20Report_FINAL.pdf

Canadian Psychological Association. 2023a. *Accreditation Standards for Doctoral Programmes and Residency Programs in Professional Psychology,* 6th revision. Author.

Canadian Psychological Association. 2023b. *CPA Guidelines on Telepsychology.* Author.

Caron, E.B., T.A. Lind, and M. Dozier. 2021. "Strategies that Promote Therapist Engagement in Active and Experiential Learning: Micro-Level Sequential Analysis." *The Clinical Supervisor* 40, no. 1, pp. 112–131. https://doi.org/10 .1080/07325223.2020.1870023

Carraccio, C., S.D. Wolfsthal, R. Englander, Ferentz, K., and Martin, C. 2002. "Shifting Paradigms: From Flexner to Competencies." *Academic Medicine* 77, no. 5, pp. 361–367.

Childs, A.W., C.A. Crusto, and R. Miller. 2024. "Getting Racism Out of Our Work GROW: Design, Deployment, and Early Outcomes for a Program to Increase Psychology Supervisor's Multicultural Competence." *Training and Education in Professional Psychology* 18, no. 4, pp. 305–313. https://doi .org/10.1037/tep0000478

Chircop Coleiro, A., M. Creaner, and L. Timulak. 2023. "The Good, the Bad, and the Less than Ideal in Clinical Supervision: A Qualitative Meta-Analysis of Supervisee Experiences." *Counselling Psychology Quarterly* 36, no. 2, pp. 189–210. https://doi.org/10.1080/09515070.2021.2023098

Chong, L.S., A. Scharff, B.A.H. Crawford, S. Aajmain, and J.F. Boswell. 2025. "Prevalence and Navigation of Discrimination and Microaggression Experiences in Psychotherapy and Supervision Processes Among Therapists in Training." *Training and Education in Professional Psychology* 19, no. 1, pp. 69–77. https://doi.org/10.1037/tep0000494

Clark, O.K.T., J.A. Pickard, C.J. Gonsalvez, F.P. Deane, and J. Martin. 2025. "Mindfulness Predicts Impostorism in Trainee Psychologists in Professional Programs." *Clinical Psychologist* 29, no. 1, pp. 82–92. https://doi.org/10.108 0/13284207.2024.2447426

Coleman, A.M., Z. Chouliara, and K. Currie. 2021. "Working in the Field of Complex Psychological Trauma: A Framework for Personal and Professional Growth, Training, and Supervision." *Journal of Interpersonal Violence* 36, no. 5–6, pp. 2791–2815. https://doi.org/10.1177/0886260518759062

Colman, D.E., R. Echon, M.S. Lemay, J. McDonald, K.R. Smith, J. Spencer, and J.K. Swift. 2016. "The Efficacy of Self-Care for Graduate Students in Professional Psychology: A Meta-Analysis." *Training and Education in Professional Psychology* 10, no. 4, pp. 188–197. https://doi.org/10.1037 /tep0000130

Constantine, M.G. 2003. "Multicultural Competence in Supervision: Issues, Processes, and Outcomes." In *Handbook of Multicultural Competencies in Counseling and Psychology,* eds. D.B. Pope-Davis, H.L.K. Coleman, W. Ming Liu, and R.L. Toporek, 383–391. Sage Publications, Inc. https://doi .org/10.4135/9781452231693.n24

Constantino, M.J., J.F. Boswell, and A.E. Coyne. 2021. "Patient, Therapist, and Relational Factors." In *Bergin and Garfield's Handbook of Psychotherapy and Behavior Change* (50th Anniversary ed.), eds. M. Barkham, W. Lutz, and L. G. Castonguay, 225-262. Wiley.

Cook, J.M., P.P. Schnurr, T. Biyanova, and J.C. Coyne. 2009. "Apples don't Fall Far from the Tree: Influences on Psychotherapists' Adoption and Sustained Use of New Therapies." *Psychiatric Services: A Journal of the American Psychiatric Association* 60, no. 5, pp. 671–676. https://doi.org/10.1176 /ps.2009.60.5.671

Cook, R.M., and M.V. Ellis. 2021. "Post-Degree Clinical Supervision for Licensure: Occurrence of Inadequate and Harmful Experiences among Counselors." Clinical Supervisor 40, no. 2, pp. 282–302. https://doi.org/10 .1080/07325223.2021.1887786

Cook, R.M., L.E. Welfare, and D.E. Romero. 2018. "Counselor-in-Training Intentional Nondisclosure in Onsite Supervision: A Content Analysis." *The Professional Counselor* 8, pp. 115–130. https://doi.org/10.15241/rmc.8.2 .115

Cooper, L.D., H.G. Murphy, L.A. Delk, M.G. Fraire, N. Van Kirk, C.P. Sullivan, J.C. Waldron, A.E. Halliburton, F. Schiefelbein, and A. Gatto. 2021. "Implementing Routine Outcome Monitoring in a Psychology Training Clinic: A Case Study of a Process Model." *Training and Education in Professional Psychology* 15, no. 2, pp. 87–96. https://doi.org/10.1037 /tep0000298

Crego, A., J.R. Yela, P. Riesco-Matías, M.-Á. Gómez-Martínez, and A. Vicente-Arruebarrena. 2022. "The Benefits of Self-Compassion in Mental Health Professionals: A Systematic Review of Empirical Research." *Psychology Research and Behavior Management* 15, pp. 2599–2620. https://doi.org/10.2147/PRBM.S359382

Crocker, E.M., and D.M. Sudak. 2017. "Making the Most of Psychotherapy Supervision: A Guide for Psychiatry Residents." *Academic Psychiatry* 41, no. 1, pp. 35–39. https://doi.org/10.1007/s40596-016-0637-5

Crockett, S., and D.G Hays. 2015. "The Influence of Supervisor Multicultural Competence on the Supervisory Working Alliance, Supervisee Counseling Self-Efficacy, and Supervisee Satisfaction with Supervision: A Mediation Model." *Counselor Education and Supervision* 54, no. 4, pp. 258–273. https://doi.org/10.1002/ceas.12025

Cucco, E. 2020. "Who's Afraid of the Big Bad Unconscious: Working with Countertransference in Training." *Journal of Psychotherapy Integration* 30, no. 1, pp. 52–59. http://dx.doi.org/10.1037/int0000163

Cullinan, C.C., R.R. Harrison, and C. Hughes-Reid. 2024. "Meeting the Moment. Centering Cultural Humility and Antiracism in Health Service Psychology Internship Training." *Training and Education in Professional Psychology* 18, no. 3, pp. 213–220. https://doi.org/10.1037/tep0000473

Davis-Wright, J.O., S.D. McMahon, S.A. Miller, and S.N. Vas. 2025. "Exploring the Network Structure of a Measure of Supervision Competence and its Prediction of Trainee Development." *Training and Education in Professional Psychology* 19, no. 2, pp. 106–115. https://doi.org/10.1037/tep0000506

Davys, A. 2019. "Courageous Conversations in Supervision." *Aotearoa New Zealand Social Work* 31, no. 3, pp. 78–86. https://doi.org/10.11157/anzswj-vol31iss3id649

Dawes, R.M. 1994. *House of Cards: Psychology and Psychotherapy Built on Myth.* The Free Press.

Day-Vines, N.L., B. Booker Ammah, S. Steen, and K.M. Arnold. 2018. "Getting Comfortable with Discomfort: Preparing Counselor Trainees to Broach Racial, Ethnic, and Cultural Factors with Clients during Counseling." *International Journal for the Advancement of Counselling* 40, no. 2, pp. 89–104. https://doi.org/10.1007/s10447-017-9308-9

Day-Vines, N.L., S.M. Wood, T. Grothaus, L. Craigen, A. Holman, K. Dotson-Blake, and M.J. Douglass. 2007. "Broaching the Subjects of Race, Ethnicity, and Culture during the Counseling Process." *Journal of Counseling and Development* 85, no. 4, pp. 401–409. https://doi.org/10.1002/j.1556-6678.2007.tb00608.x

DeCino, D.A., P.L. Waalkes, and A. Dalbey. 2020. ""They Stay with You": Counselor Educators' Emotionally Intense Gatekeeping Experiences." *The*

Professional Counselor 10, no. 4, pp. 548–561. https://doi.org/10.15241/dad.10.4.548

de Jonge, L.P.J.W.M., M.J.B. Govaerts, A.A. Timmerman, J.W.M. Muris, A.W.M. Kramer, and C.P.M. Van der Vleuten. 2022. "Supervisors' Approaches to the Early Entrustment of Clinical Tasks: An Observational Study in General Practice." *BMJ Open* 12, no. 8. https://doi.org/10.1136/bmjopen-2021-055471

Delgadillo, J., D. Saxon, and M. Barkham. 2018. "Associations between Therapists' Occupational Burnout and Their Patients' Depression and Anxiety Treatment Outcomes." *Depression and Anxiety* 35, no. 9, pp. 844–850. https://doi.org/10.1002/da.22766

DePue, M.K., R. Liu, G.W. Lambie, and J. Gonzalez. 2022. "Examining the Effects of the Supervisory Relationship and Therapeutic Alliance on Client Outcomes in Novice Therapists." *Training and Education in Professional Psychology* 16, no. 3, pp. 253–262. https://doi.org/10.1037/tep0000320

De Stefano, J., H. Hutman, and N. Gazzola. 2017. "Putting on the Face: A Qualitative Study of Power Dynamics in Clinical Supervision." *Clinical Supervisor* 36, no. 2, pp. 223–240. https://doi.org/10.1080/07325223.2017.1295893

Dorsey, S., S.E.U. Kerns, L. Lucid, M.D. Pullmann, J.P. Harrison, L. Berliner, K. Thompson, and E. Deblinger. 2018. "Objective Coding of Content and Techniques in Workplace-based Supervision of an EBT in Public Mental Health." *Implementation Science* 13, no. 1, Article 19. https://doi.org/10.1186/s13012-017-0708-3

Dreyfus, S.E. 2004. "The Five-Stage Model of Adult Skill Acquisition." *The Bulletin of Science, Technology and Society* 24, no. 3, pp. 177–181. https://doi.org/10.1177/0270467604264992

Duke, É., and C. Montag. 2017. "Smartphone Addiction, Daily Interruptions and Self-Reported Productivity." *Addictive Behaviors Reports* 6, pp. 90–95. https://doi.org/10.1016/j.abrep.2017.07.002

Dunn, R., J.L. Callahan, J.K. Swift, and M. Ivanovic. 2013. "Effects of Pre-Session Centering for Therapists on Session Presence and Effectiveness." *Psychotherapy Research* 23, no. 1, pp. 78–85. https://doi.org/10.1080/10503307.2012.731713

Egan, R., J. Maidment, and M. Connolly. 2017. "Trust, Power and Safety in the Social Work Supervisory Relationship: Results from Australian Research." *Journal of Social Work Practice* 31, no. 3, pp. 307–321. https://doi.org/10.1080/02650533.2016.1261279

Ellis, M.V. 2017a. "Clinical Supervision Contract and Consent Statement and Supervisee Rights and Responsibilities." *Clinical Supervisor* 36, no. 1, pp. 145–159. https://doi.org/10.1080/07325223.2017.1321885

Ellis, M.V. 2017b. "Narratives of Harmful Clinical Supervision." *The Clinical Supervisor* 36, no. 1, pp. 20–87. https://doi.org/10.1080/07325223.2017 .1297752

Ellis, M.V., L. Berger, A.E. Hanus, E.E. Ayala, B.A. Swords, and M. Siembor. 2014. "Inadequate and Harmful Clinical Supervision: Testing a Revised Framework and Assessing Occurrence." *The Counseling Psychologist* 42, no. 4, pp. 434–472. https://doi.org/10.1177/0011000013508656

Ellis, M.V., H. Hutman, and J. Chapin. 2015. "Reducing Supervisee Anxiety: Effects of a Role Induction Intervention for Clinical Supervision." *Journal of Counseling Psychology* 62, no. 4, pp. 608–620. https://doi.org/10.1037 /cou0000099

Ellis, M.V., and N. Ladany. 1997. "Inferences Concerning Supervisees and Clients in Clinical Supervision: An Integrative Review." In *Handbook of Psychotherapy Supervision,* eds. C.E. Watkins, Jr., 467–507. Wiley.

Ellis, M.V., E.J. Taylor, D.A. Corp, H. Hutman, and K.A. Kangos. 2017. "Narratives of Harmful Clinical Supervision: Introduction to the Special Issue." *The Clinical Supervisor* 36, no. 1, pp. 4–19. https://doi.org/10.1080 /07325223.2017.1297753.

Epstein, R.M., and E.M. Hundert. 2002. "Defining and Assessing Professional Competence." JAMA: *The Journal of the American Medical Association* 287, no. 2, pp. 226–235. https://doi.org/10.1001/jama.287.2.226

Eraut, M., and B. du Boulay. 2000. *Developing the Attributes of Medical Professional Judgement and Competence.* University of Sussex.

Ericsson, K.A. 2018. "The Differential Influence of Experience, Practice, and Deliberate Practice on the Development of Superior Individual Performance of Experts." In *The Cambridge Handbook of Expertise and Expert Performance,* eds. K.A. Ericsson, R.R. Hoffman, A. Kozbelt, and A.M. Williams, 745–769. Cambridge University Press. https://doi.org/10.1017/9781316480 748.038

Eubanks, C.F., J.C. Muran, and J.D. Safran. 2018. "Alliance Rupture Repair: A Meta-Analysis." *Psychotherapy* 55, no. 4, pp. 508-519. https://doi. org/10.1037/pst0000185

Faber, S.C., M.T. Williams, I.W. Metzger, M.M. MacIntyre, D. Strauss, C.G. Duniya, K. Sawyer, J.M. Cénat, and V.M. Goghari. 2023. "Lions at the Gate: How Weaponization of Policy Prevents People of Colour from Becoming Professional Psychologists in Canada." *Canadian Psychology / Psychologie Canadienne* 64, no. 4, pp. 335–354. https://doi.org/10.1037/ cap0000352

Falender, C.A. 2016. "Multiple Relationships and Clinical Supervision." In *Multiple Relationships in Therapy and Counseling: Unavoidable, Common, and Mandatory Dual Relations in Therapy,* ed. O. Zur, 209-220. Routledge.

Falender, C.A., C.J. Collins, and E.P. Shafranske. 2009. ""Impairment" and Performance Issues in Clinical Supervision: After the 2008 ADA Amendments Act." *Training and Education in Professional Psychology* 3, no. 4, pp. 240–249. https://doi.org/10.1037/a0017153

Falender, C.A., and E.P. Shafranske. 2012. *Getting the Most Out of Clinical Training and Supervision: A Guide for Practicum Students and Interns.* American Psychological Association.

Falender, C.A., and E.P. Shafranske. 2021. *Clinical Supervision: A Competency-Based Approach,* 2nd ed. American Psychological Association.

Falender, C.A., and E.P. Shafranske. 2023. "Revisiting Competence in Clinical Supervision." *International Journal of Supervision in Psychotherapy* 5, pp. 47–58. https://doi.org/10.47409/ijsp.2023.5.4

Falender, C.A., E.P. Shafranske, and C. Falicov. 2014. "Diversity and Multiculturalism in Supervision." In *Multiculturalism and Diversity in Clinical Supervision: A Competency-based Approach,* eds. C.A. Falender, E.P. Shafranske, and C. Falicov, 3–28. American Psychological Association.

Falender, C.A., E.P. Shafranske, and A. Ofek. 2014. "Competent Clinical Supervision: Emerging Effective Practices." *Counselling Psychology Quarterly* 27, no. 4, pp. 393–408. https://doi.org/10.1080/09515070.2014.934785

Falicov, C.J. 2014. "Psychotherapy and Supervision as Cultural Encounters: The Multidimensional Ecological Comparative Framework." In *Multiculturalism and Diversity in Clinical Supervision: A Competency-based Approach,* eds. C.A. Falender, E.P. Shafranske, C. Falicov, 29–58. American Psychological Association.

Farber, B.A., J.Y. Suzuki, and D.A. Lynch. 2019. "Positive Regard and Affirmation." In *Psychotherapy Relationships that Work: Vol. 1. Evidence-based Therapist Contributions*, eds. J.C. Norcross and M.J. Lambert, 3rd ed., 288–322. Oxford. doi:10.1093/med-psych/9780190843953.001.0001

Feldman, B., H. Levenson, and L. Angus. 2024. "An Empirical Analysis of Corrective Experiences in Psychotherapy Supervision." *Journal of Psychotherapy Integration* 34, no. 4, pp. 502–514. https://doi.org/10.1037/int0000329

Fitch, J.C., M.C. Pistole, and J.E. Gunn. 2010. "The Bonds of Development: An Attachment-Caregiving Model of Supervision." *The Clinical Supervisor* 29, no. 1, pp. 20–34. https://doi.org/10.1080/07325221003730319

Flückiger, C., A.C. Del Re, B.E. Wampold, and A.O. Horvath. 2018. "The Alliance in Adult Psychotherapy: A Meta-Analytic Synthesis." *Psychotherapy* 55, pp. 316–340. http://dx.doi.org/10.1037/pst0000172

Forrest, L., N. Elman, S. Gizara, and T. Vacha-Haase. 1999. "Trainee Impairment: A Review of Identification, Remediation, Dismissal, and Legal Issues." *The Counseling Psychologist* 27, no. 5, pp. 627–686. https://doi.org/10.1177/0011000099275001

Forrest, L., N.S. Elman, K.E. Bodner, and N.J. Kaslow. 2022. "Trainee Confidentiality: Confusions, Complexities, Consequences, and Possibilities." *Training and Education in Professional Psychology* 16, no. 3, pp. 306–314. https://doi.org/10.1037/tep0000364

Forrest, L.M., and N.S. Elman. 2023. "Trainee Confidentiality: The Hidden Challenge of Competence Problems." In *Supporting Trainees with Competence Problems: A Practical Guide for Psychology Trainers,* eds. R.A. Schwartz-Mette, E.A. Hunter, and N.J. Kaslow, 125–147. American Psychological Association. https://doi.org/10.1037/0000340-008

Forshammar Geisler, C., M. Geisler, and S. Buratti. 2025. "The Moderating Role of Clinical Supervision on the Relationship Between Emotional Demands and Exhaustion Among Clinical Psychologists in Sweden." *The Clinical Supervisor* 44, no. 1, pp. 77–98. https://doi.org/10.1080/07325223.2024.2442986

Foskett, A.J., and K.J. Van Vliet. 2021. "Understanding Supervisee Nondisclosures in Supervision with Videorecording Review and Interpersonal Process Recall." *Counselling and Psychotherapy Research* 21, no. 1, pp. 188–197. https://doi.org/10.1002/capr.12306

Fouad, N.A., C.L. Grus, R.L. Hatcher, N.J. Kaslow, P.S. Hutchings, M.B. Madson, F.L. Collins, and R.E. Crossman. 2009. "Competency Benchmarks: A Model for Understanding and Measuring Competence in Professional Psychology Across Training Levels." *Training and Education in Professional Psychology* 3, no. 4S, pp. S5–S26. https://doi.org/10.1037/a0015832

Fox, G.S. 2018. "We Didn't See it Coming, and You Should have Thought Twice: Sexual Advances from Our Former Teachers." *Academic Psychiatry* 42, no. 4, pp. 555–558. https://doi.org/10.1007/s40596-018-0905-7

Freitag, S.L., E.D. Marshall-Lee, S. Zhang, S.R. Seitz, and N.J. Kaslow. 2023. "Remediation Processes for Health Service Psychology Trainees with Problems of Professional Competence." In *Handbook of Training and Supervision in Cognitive Behavioral Therapy,* eds. M.D. Terjesen, and T. Del Vecchio, 273–290. Springer. https://doi-org.uml.idm.oclc.org/10.1007/978-3-031-33735-2_16

Friedlander, M.L. 2015. "Use of Relational Strategies to Repair Alliance Ruptures: How Responsive Supervisors Train Responsive Psychotherapists." *Psychotherapy* 52, no. 2, pp. 174–179. https://doi.org/10.1037/a0037044

Friedlander, M.L., M. Herman, M. Potel, and J. Bate. 2024. "Supervisor Responsiveness from the Inside Out." *The Clinical Supervisor* 44, no. 1, pp. 215–241. https://doi.org/10.1080/07325223.2024.2437368

Gaete, J., and T. Strong. 2017. "Facilitating Supervisees' Developing Competence Through Supervisory Conversation." *Counselling Psychology Quarterly* 30, no. 2, pp. 166–187. https://doi.org/10.1080/09515070.2016.1167013

Galán, C.A., C.L. Boness, I. Tung, M.A. Bowdring, S.L. Sequeira, C.C. Call, S.M. Savell, and J.B. Northrup. 2024. "Clinical Psychology Graduate Programs: Falling Short in Cultural Humility Training." *Training and Education in Professional Psychology* 18, no. 3, pp. 265–278. https://doi.org/10.1037/tep0000443

Garfield, S. 1994. "Research on Client Variables in Psychotherapy." In *Handbook of Psychotherapy and Behavior Change*, eds. A.E. Bergin and S.L. Garfield, 4th ed., 190–228. Wiley.

Gazzola, N., and S. Iwakabe. 2022. "Psychotherapy Failures: To Err is Human." *Counselling Psychology Quarterly* 35, no. 4, pp. 719–723. https://doi.org/10.1080/09515070.2022.2142383

Geller, J.D., B.A. Farber, and C.E. Schaffer. 2010. "Representations of the Supervisory Dialogue and the Development of Psychotherapists." *Psychotherapy* 47, pp. 211–220. https://doi.org/10.1037/a0019785

Gibson, A.S., M.V. Ellis, and M.L. Friedlander. 2019. "Toward a Nuanced Understanding of Nondisclosure in Psychotherapy Supervision." *Journal of Counseling Psychology* 66, no. 1, pp. 114–121. https://doi.org/10.1037/cou0000295

Glaser, R.D., and J.S. Thorpe. 1986. "Unethical Intimacy: A Survey of Sexual Contact and Advances Between Psychology Educators and Female Graduate Students." *The American Psychologist* 41, no. 1, pp. 43–51. https://doi.org/10.1037/0003-066X.41.1.43

Gnilka, P.B., C.Y. Chang, and B.J. Dew. 2012. "The Relationship Between Supervisee Stress, Coping Resources, the Working Alliance, and the Supervisory Working Alliance." *Journal of Counseling and Development* 90, pp. 63–70. https://doi.org/10.1111/j.1556-6676.2012.00009.x

Gonsalvez, C.J. 2021. "A Short Scale to Evaluate Supervision and Supervisor Competence—The SE-SC8." *Clinical Psychology and Psychotherapy* 28, no. 2, pp. 452–461. https://doi.org/10.1002/cpp.2510

Gonsalvez, C.J., J. Bushnell, R. Blackman, F. Deane, V. Bliokas, K. Nicholson Perry, A. Shires, Y. Nasstasia, C. Allan, and R. Knight. 2013. "Assessment of Psychology Competencies in Field Placements: Standardized Vignettes Reduce Rater Bias." *Training and Education in Professional Psychology*, 7, no. 2, pp. 99–111. https://doi.org/10.1037/a0031617

Gonsalvez, C.J., and F.L. Calvert. 2014. "Competency-Based Models of Supervision: Principles and Applications, Promises and Challenges." *Australian Psychologist* 49, no. 4, pp. 200–208. https://doi.org/10.1111/ap.12055

Gonsalvez, C.J., F.P. Deane, R. Blackman, M. Matthias, R. Knight, Y. Nasstasia, and V. Bliokas. 2015. "The Hierarchical Clustering of Clinical Psychology Practicum Competencies: A Multisite Study of Supervisor Ratings."

Clinical Psychology: Science and Practice 22, no. 4, pp. 390–403. https://doi .org/10.1111/cpsp.12123

Gonsalvez, C.J., and J. Freestone. 2007. "Field Supervisors' Assessments of Trainee Performance: Are They Reliable and Valid?" *Australian Psychologist* 42, no. 1, pp. 23–32. https://doi.org/10.1080/00050060600827615

Gonsalvez, C.J., T. Riebel, L.J. Nolan, S. Pohlman, and W. Bartik. 2023. "Supervisor versus Self-Assessment of Trainee Competence: Differences Across Developmental Stages and Competency Domains." *Journal of Clinical Psychology* 79, no. 12, pp. 2959–2973. https://doi.org/10.1002/jclp.23590

Gonsalvez, C.J., J. Terry, F.P. Deane, Y. Nasstasia, R. Knight, and C.H. Gooi. 2021. "End-of-Placement Failure Rates among Clinical Psychology Trainees: Exceptional Training and Outstanding Trainees or Poor Gate-Keeping?" *Clinical Psychologist* 25, no. 3, pp. 294–305. https://doi.org/10.1080/1328 4207.2021.1927692

González Vera, J.M., M.M. Domenech Rodríguez, C.M. Navarro Flores, A.L. Vázquez, G.G. San Miguel, M. Phan, E.G. Wong, K.S. Klimczak, J. Bera, L. Papa, and J. Estrada. 2024. "Invisible Wounds: Testimony of Microaggressions from the Experiences of Clinicians of Color in Training." *Training and Education in Professional Psychology* 18, no. 4, pp. 331–339. https://doi.org/10.1037/tep0000489

Goodie, J.L., L.D. Bennion, N.A. Schvey, D.S. Riggs, M. Montgomery, and R.M. Dorsey. 2022. "Development and Implementation of an Objective Structured Clinical Examination for Evaluating Clinical Psychology Graduate Students." *Training and Education in Professional Psychology* 16, no. 3, pp. 287–298. https://doi.org/10.1037/tep0000356

Goodyear, R.K. 2014. "Supervision as Pedagogy: Attending to its Essential Instructional and Learning Processes." *The Clinical Supervisor* 33, no. 1, pp. 82–99. https://doi.org/10.1080/07325223.2014.918914

Gray, L.A., N. Ladany, J.A. Walker, and J.R. Ancis. 2001. "Psychotherapy Trainees' Experience of Counterproductive Events in Supervision." *Journal of Counseling Psychology* 48, no. 4, pp. 371–383. https://doi.org/10.1037/0022 -0167.48.4.371

Greene, J.H., and P.S. Flasch. 2019. "Integrating Intersectionality into Clinical Supervision: A Developmental Model Addressing Broader Definitions of Multicultural Competence." *Journal of Counselor Preparation and Supervision* 12, no. 4, Article 14. https://research.library.kutztown.edu/jcps/vol12/iss4/14

Grenny, J., K. Patterson, R. McMillan, A. Switzler, and E. Gregory. 2022. *Crucial Conversations: Tools for Talking When Stakes are High,* 3rd ed. McGraw-Hill.

Hadar, B., and N. Halevy. 2025. "Letters of Recommendation as Institutionalized Gossip: Tie Strength and the Advocacy-Accuracy Tradeoff in Brokering." *Journal of Experimental Social Psychology* 116. https://doi.org/10.1016/j.jesp.2024.104685

Haft, S.L., C.A. Callaway, and N.H. Liu. 2024. "Managing Clinical Supervision Dilemmas: A Mixed-Methods Vignette Study." *Training and Education in Professional Psychology* 18, no. 4, pp. 399–412. https://doi.org/10.1037/tep0000483

Hamza, D.M., K.E. Hauer, A. Oswald, E. van Melle, Z. Ladak, I. Zuna, M.E. Assefa, G.N. Pelletier, M. Sebastianski, D. Keto-Lambert, and S. Ross. 2023. "Making Sense of Competency-based Medical Education CBME Literary Conversations: A BEME Scoping Review: BEME Guide No. 78." *Medical Teacher* 45, no. 8, pp. 802–815. https://doi.org/10.1080/0142159X.2023.2168525

Hannan, C., M.J. Lambert, C. Harmon, S.L. Nielsen, D.W. Smart, K. Shimokawa, and S.W. Sutton. 2005. "A Lab Test and Algorithms for Identifying Clients at Risk for Treatment Failure." *Journal of Clinical Psychology* 61, no. 2, pp. 155–163. https://doi.org/10.1002/jclp.20108

Hatcher, R.L. 2021. "Responsiveness, the Relationship, and the Working Alliance in Psychotherapy." In *The Responsive Psychotherapist: Attuning to Clients in the Moment,* eds. J.C. Watson and H. Wiseman, 37–58. American Psychological Association.

Hatcher, R.L., N.A. Fouad, C.L. Grus, L.F. Campbell, S.R. McCutcheon, and K.L. Leahy. 2013. "Competency Benchmarks: Practical Steps Toward a Culture of Competence." *Training and Education in Professional Psychology* 7, no. 2, pp. 84–91. https://doi.org/10.1037/a0029401

Hayes, J.A., C.C. Cartwright, and F. Zhao. 2023. "Training Therapists to Manage Countertransference via Reflective Practice." In *Becoming Better Psychotherapists: Advancing Training and Supervision,* eds. L.G. Castonguay and C.E. Hill, 127–147. https://doi.org/10.1037/0000364-007

Hayes, J.A., C.J. Gelso, S. Goldberg, and D.M. Kivlighan. 2018. "Countertransference Management and Effective Psychotherapy: Meta-Analytic Findings." *Psychotherapy* 55, no. 4, pp. 496–507. https://doi.org/10.1037/pst0000189

Hays, D.G., H.B. Bayne, J.L. Gay, Z.P. McNiece, and C. Park. 2023. "A Systematic Review of Whiteness Assessment Properties and Assumptions: Implications for Counselor Training and Research." *Counseling Outcome Research and Evaluation* 14, no. 1, pp. 58–76. https://doi.org/10.1080/21501378.2021.1891877

Heckman-Stone, C. 2004. "Trainee Preferences for Feedback and Evaluation in Clinical Supervision." *The Clinical Supervisor* 22, no. 1, pp. 21–33. https://doi.org/10.1300/J001v22n01_03

Hill, H.R.M., T.P. Crowe, and C.J. Gonsalvez. 2016. "Reflective Dialogue in Clinical Supervision: A Pilot Study Involving Collaborative Review of Supervision Videos." *Psychotherapy Research* 26, no. 3, pp. 263–278. https://doi.org/10.1080/10503307.2014.996795

Hitzeman, C., C.J. Gonsalvez, E. Britt, and K. Moses. 2020. "Clinical Psychology Trainees' Self versus Supervisor Assessments of Practitioner Competencies." *Clinical Psychologist* 24, no. 1, pp. 18–29. https://doi.org /10.1111/cp.12183

Holloway, E.L. 1984. "Outcome Evaluation in Supervision Research." *The Counseling Psychologist* 12, no. 4, pp. 167–174. https://doi.org/10.1177 /0011000084124014

Hook, J. N., D.E. Davis, J. Owen, E.L. Worthington, and S.O. Utsey. 2013. "Cultural Humility: Measuring Openness to Culturally Diverse Clients." *Journal of Counseling Psychology* 60, no. 3, pp. 353–366. https://doi.org /10.1037/a0032595

Huang, C. 2022. "A Meta-Analysis of the Problematic Social Media Use and Mental Health." *International Journal of Social Psychiatry* 68, no. 1, pp. 12–33. https://doi.org/10.1177/0020764020978434

Huddle, T.S., and G.R. Heudebert. 2007. "Viewpoint: Taking Apart the Art: The Risk of Anatomizing Clinical Competence." *Academic Medicine* 82, no. 6, pp. 536–541. https://doi.org/10.1097/ACM.0b013e3180555935

Humphreys, L., R. Crino, and I. Wilson. 2018. "The Competencies Movement: Origins, Limitations, and Future Directions." *Clinical Psychologist* 22, no. 3, pp. 290–299. https://doi.org/10.1111/cp.12143

Hunt, M.G., P. Aggarwal, K. Bootes, J. Cummings, K.E. Daniel, J. Davila, E.A. Kapoulea, C.L. Larson, and K.A. Maranzan. 2025. "Report of the Council of University Directors of Clinical Psychology CUDCP Burnout Task Force: Workload, Burnout, and Emotional Health in Clinical Psychological Trainees." *Training and Education in Professional Psychology* 19, no. 2, pp. 85–96. https://doi.org/10.1037/tep0000496

International Standards Organisation ISO. 2012. *International Standard ISO/ IEC 17024: Conformity Assessment – General Requirements for Bodies Operating Certification of Persons.* ISO.

Ivers, N.N., J.L. Rogers, L.D. Borders, and A. Turner. 2017. "Using Interpersonal Process Recall in Clinical Supervision to Enhance Supervisees' Multicultural Awareness." *Clinical Supervisor* 36, no. 2, pp. 282–303. https://doi.org/10.1 080/07325223.2017.1320253

Jackson, S.T., and A. Faler. 2023. "Supervision from the Perspective of the Supervisee." In *Handbook of Training and Supervision in Cognitive Behavioral Therapy*, eds. M.D. Terjesen, and T. Del Vecchio, 293–305. Springer. https:// doi.org/10.1007/978-3-031-33735-2_17

Jacobs, S.C., S.K. Huprich, C.L. Grus, E.A. Cage, N.S. Elman, L. Forrest, R. Schwartz-Mette, D.S. Shen-Miller, K.S. Van Sickle, and N.J. Kaslow. 2011. "Trainees with Professional Competency Problems: Preparing Trainers for Difficult but Necessary Conversations." *Training and Education in Professional Psychology* 5, no. 3, pp. 175–184. https://doi.org/10.1037/a0024656

Jacobson, N.S., and P. Truax. 1991. "Clinical Significance: A Statistical Approach to Defining Meaningful Change in Psychotherapy Research." *Journal of Consulting and Clinical Psychology* 59, no. 1, pp. 12–19. https://doi.org/10.1037/0022-006X.59.1.12

Jacquart, J., S. Wardle-Pinkston, J. Ziegler, D. Sbarra, and M.F. O'Connor. 2024. "Improving Culturally Responsive Clinical Training: Exploring the Acceptability and Feasibility of an Exposure-based Strategy." *Training and Education in Professional Psychology* 18, no. 1, pp. 87–97. https://doi.org/10.1037/tep0000462

Jha, V., S. Brockbank, and T. Roberts. 2016. "A Framework for Understanding Lapses in Professionalism among Medical Students: Applying the Theory of Planned Behavior to Fitness to Practice Cases." *Academic Medicine* 91, no. 12, pp. 1622–1627. https://doi.org/10.1097/ACM.0000000000001287

Jin, J., M. Lagunas, M. Foster, E. Mateer, E. Ichimura, C. Duffield, and T. Taone. 2024. "Deliberate Practice in Anti-racist Psychology." *Training and Education in Professional Psychology* 18, no. 3, pp. 248–255. https://doi.org/10.1037/tep0000447

Johnson, E.A. 2017. *Working Together in Clinical Supervision: A Guide for Supervisors and Supervisees.* Momentum Press.

Johnson, E.A. 2019. "Recommendations to Enhance Psychotherapy Supervision in Psychology." *Canadian Psychology - Psychologie Canadienne* 60, no. 4, pp. 290–301. https://doi.org/10.1037/cap0000188

Johnson, E.A. 2025, April 8. *Using the Safety PIN Framework to Facilitate Difficult Conversations in Clinical Supervision.* Workshop presentation to The Saskatoon and Area Clinical Psychology Residency Program and The University of Saskatchewan Clinical Psychology Program faculty at the University of Saskatchewan, Saskatoon, SK, Canada.

Johnson, E.A., and Stewart, D.W. 2000. "Clinical Supervision in Canadian Academic and Service Settings: The Importance of Education, Training, and Workplace Support for Supervisor Development." *Canadian Psychology* 41, pp. 124–130. https://doi.org/10.1037/h0086862

Johnson, E.A., and D.W. Stewart. 2008. "Perceived Competence in Supervisory Roles: A Social Cognitive Analysis." *Training and Education in Professional Psychology* 2, pp. 229–236. https://doi.org/10.1037/1931-3918.2.4.229

Johnson, J., C. Corker, and D.B. O'Connor. 2020. "Burnout in Psychological Therapists: A Cross-Sectional Study Investigating the role of Supervisory Relationship Quality." *Clinical Psychologist* 24, no. 3, pp. 223–235. https://doi.org/10.1111/cp.12206

Johnson, W.B., J.E. Barnett, N.S. Elman, L. Forrest, and N.J. Kaslow. 2012. "The Competent Community: Toward a Vital Reformulation of Professional Ethics." *The American Psychologist* 67, no. 7, pp. 557–569. https://doi.org/10.1037/a0027206

Johnson, W.B., and K.A. Griffin. 2025. *On Being a Mentor: A Guide for Higher Education Faculty,* 3rd ed. Routledge. https://doi.org/10.4324/9781003195825

Jones, C.T., and S.F. Branco. 2020. "The Interconnectedness between Cultural Humility and Broaching in Clinical Supervision: Working from the Multicultural Orientation Framework." *The Clinical Supervisor* 39, no. 2, pp. 198–209. https://doi.org/10.1080/07325223.2020.1830327

Jones, C.T., L.E. Welfare, S. Melchior, and R.M. Cash. 2019. "Broaching as a Strategy for Intercultural Understanding in Clinical Supervision." *The Clinical Supervisor* 38, no. 1, pp. 1–16. https://doi.org/10.1080/07325223.2018.1560384

Kaeding, A., C. Sougleris, C. Reid, M.F. van Vreeswijk, C. Hayes, J. Dorrian, and S. Simpson. 2017. "Professional Burnout, Early Maladaptive Schemas, and Physical Health in Clinical and Counselling Psychology Trainees." *Journal of Clinical Psychology* 73, no. 12, pp. 1782–1796. https://doi.org/10.1002/jclp.22485

Kagan, H., and N. Kagan. 1997. "Interpersonal Process Recall: Influencing Human Interaction." In *Handbook of Psychotherapy Supervision,* ed. C.E. Watkins Jr., 296–309. Wiley.

Kagan, N.I., and H. Kagan. 1990. "IPR -A Validated Model for the 1990s and Beyond." *The Counseling Psychologist* 18, no. 3, pp. 436–440. https://doi.org/10.1177/0011000090183004

Kahn, J.H. 2011. "Multilevel Modeling: Overview and Applications to Research in Counseling Psychology." *Journal of Counseling Psychology* 58, no. 2, pp. 257–271. https://doi.org/10.1037/a0022680

Kalliath, T.J., and A. Beck. 2001. "Is the Path to Burnout and Turnover Paved by a Lack of Supervisory Support? A Structural Equations Test." *New Zealand Journal of Psychology* 30, pp. 72–78.

Kaslow, N.J., E.W. Farber, C.J. Ammons, C.C. Graves, J.N. Hampton-Anderson, D.E. Lewis, N. Lim, B.G. McKenna, S. Penna, and J.E. Cattie. 2022. "Capability-Informed Competency Approach to Lifelong Professional Development." *Training and Education in Professional Psychology* 16, pp. 182–189. https://doi.org/10.1037/tep0000392

Kaslow, N.J., C.L. Grus, L.J. Allbaugh, D. Shen-Miller, K.E. Bodner, J. Veilleux, and K. Van Sickle. 2018. "Trainees with Competence Problems in the Professionalism Domain." *Ethics and Behavior* 28, no. 6, pp. 429–449. https://doi.org/10.1080/10508422.2018.1438897

Kaslow, N.J., C.L. Grus, L.F. Campbell, N.A. Fouad, R.L. Hatcher, and E.R. Rodolfa. 2009. "Competency Assessment Toolkit for Professional Psychology." *Training and Education in Professional Psychology* 3, no. 4S, pp. S27–S45. https://doi.org/10.1037/a0015833

Kennedy, A., K. McGowan, and M. El-Hussein. 2023. "Indigenous Elders' wisdom and Dominionization in Higher Education: Barriers and Facilitators to Decolonisation and Reconciliation." *International Journal of Inclusive Education* 27 no. 1, pp. 89–106. https://doi.org/10.1080/13603116.2020.1829108

Keum, B.T., and L. Wang. 2021. "Supervision and Psychotherapy Process and Outcome: A Meta-Analytic Review." *Translational issues in Psychological Science* 7, 89–108. http://dx.doi.org/10.1037/tps0000272

King, C., T. Edlington, and B. Williams. 2020. "*Avoiding Difficult Conversations in the Australian Health Sector.*" *SAGE Open Nursing* 6. https://doi.org/10.1177/2377960820941978

King, K.M., and L.D. Borders. 2019. "An experimental Investigation of White Counselors Broaching Race and Racism." *Journal of Counseling and Development* 97, no. 4, pp. 341–351. https://doi.org/10.1002/jcad.12283

Knox, S. 2015. "Disclosure—and Lack Thereof—in Individual Supervision." *The Clinical Supervisor* 34, no. 2, pp. 151–163. https://doi.org/10.1080/07325223.2015.1086462

Knox, S., A.W. Burkard, L.M. Edwards, J.J. Smith, and L.Z. Schlosser. 2008. "Supervisors' Reports of the Effects of Supervisor Self-Disclosure on Supervisees." *Psychotherapy Research* 18, no. 5, pp. 543–559. https://doi.org/10.1080/10503300801982781

Knox, S., W. Caperton, D. Phelps, and N. Pruitt. 2014. "A Qualitative Study of Supervisees' Internal Representations of Supervisors." *Counselling Psychology Quarterly* 27, no. 4, pp. 334–352. https://doi.org/10.1080/09515070.2014.886999

Knudsen, H.K., L.J. Ducharme, and P.M. Roman. 2008. "Clinical Supervision, Emotional Exhaustion, and Turnover Intention: A Study of Substance Abuse Treatment Counselors in the Clinical Trials Network of the National Institute of Drug Abuse." *Journal of Substance Abuse Treatment* 35, pp. 387–395. https://doi.org/10.1016/j.jsat.2008.02.003

Kolb, D.A. 1984. *Experiential Learning: Experience as the Source of Learning and Development.* Prentice Hall.

Kühne, F., Maas, J., Wiesenthal, S., and Weck, F. 2019. "Empirical Research in Clinical Supervision: A Systematic Review and Suggestions for Future studies." *BMC Psychology,* 7, no. 1, pp. 54–54. https://doi.org/10.1186/s40359-019-0327-7

Ladany, N. 2014. "The Ingredients of Supervisor Failure." *Journal of Clinical Psychology* 70, no. 11, pp. 1094–1103. https://doi.org/10.1002/jclp.22130

Ladany, N., and M.L. Friedlander. 1995. "The Relationship between the Supervisory Working Alliance and Trainees' Experience of Role Conflict and Role Ambiguity." *Counselor Education and Supervision* 34, pp. 220–231. https://doi.org/10.1002/j.1556-6978.1995.tb00244.x

Ladany, N., M.L. Friedlander, and M.L. Nelson. 2005. *Critical Events in Psychotherapy Supervision: An Interpersonal Approach.* American Psychological Association.

Ladany, N., C.E. Hill, M.M. Corbett, and E.A. Nutt. 1996. "Nature, Extent, and Importance of What Psychotherapy Trainees do not Disclose to Their Supervisors." *Journal of Counseling Psychology* 43, pp. 10–24. https://doi .org/10.1037/0022-0167.43.1.10

Ladany, N., M. Mori, and K.E. Mehr. 2013. "Effective and Ineffective Supervision." *The Counseling Psychologist* 41, pp. 28–47. https://doi .org/10.1177/0011000012442648

Lamb, D.H., S.J. Catanzaro, and A.S. Moorman. 2003. "Psychologists Reflect on Their Sexual Relationships with Clients, Supervisees, and Students: Occurrence, Impact, Rationales, and Collegial Intervention." *Professional Psychology, Research and Practice* 34, no. 1, pp. 102–107. https://doi .org/10.1037/0735-7028.34.1.102

Lambert, M.J. 2015. "Progress Feedback and the OQ-System: The Past and the Future." *Psychotherapy* 52, pp. 381–390. https://doi.org/10.1037/pst0000027

Lambert, M.J., and A.E. Bergin. 1994. "The Effectiveness of Psychotherapy." In *Handbook of Psychotherapy and Behavior Change*, eds. A.E. Bergin and S.L. Garfield, 4th ed., pp. 141–189. Wiley.

Lambert, M.J., and E.J. Hawkins. 2001a. "Psychological Treatment, Effectiveness of." *International Encyclopedia of the Social and Behavioral Sciences,* 12372–12377. Elsevier Science.

Lambert, M.J., and E.J. Hawkins. 2001b. "Using Information about Patient Progress in Supervision: Are Outcomes Enhanced?" *Australian Psychologist* 36, pp. 131–138. https://doi.org/10.1080/00050060108259645

Lambert, M.J., and B.M. Ogles. 2014. "Common Factors: Post-Hoc Explanation or Empirically-based Therapy Approach." *Psychotherapy* 51, pp. 500–504. https://doi.org/10.1037/a0036580

Lambert, M.J., J.L. Whipple, and M. Kleinstäuber. 2018. "Collecting and Delivering Progress Feedback: A Meta-Analysis of Routine Outcome Monitoring." *Psychotherapy* 55, no. 4, pp. 520–537. https://doi.org/10.1037 /pst0000167

Latorre, C., M. Leppma, L.F. Platt, N. Shook, and J. Daniels. 2023. "The Relationship between Mindfulness and Self-Compassion for Self-Assessed Competency and Self-Efficacy of Psychologists-in-Training." *Training and Education in Professional Psychology* 17, no. 2, pp. 213–220. https://doi .org/10.1037/tep0000395

Lavik, K.O., H. Froysa, K.F. Brattebo, J. McLeod, and C. Moltu. 2018. "The First Sessions of Psychotherapy: A Qualitative Meta-Analysis of Alliance Formation Processes." *Journal of Psychotherapy Integration* 28, pp. 348–366. http://dx.doi.org/10.1037/int0000101

Lease, S.H., and C.L. Grus. 2023. "Problems of Professional Competence." In *Supporting Trainees with Competence Problems: A Practical Guide for Psychology Trainers,* eds. R.A. Schwartz-Mette, E.A. Hunter, and N.J. Kaslow, 43–60. American Psychological Association. https://doi.org/10.1037/0000340-004

Lester, S. 2014. "Professional Standards, Competence and Capability." *Higher Education, Skills and Work-Based Learning* 4, no. 1, pp. 31–43. https://doi.org/10.1108/HESWBL-04-2013-0005

Li, X., C. Lin, M. Wu, and F. Li. 2022. "Supervisory Working Alliance Trajectories and Client Outcome in Chinese Trainees." *The Clinical Supervisor* 41, no. 2, pp. 187–209. https://doi.org/10.1080/07325223.2022.2114968

Liao, T., E. Quinlan, and S. Mohi. 2022. "Factors Influencing the Theoretical Orientations of Early Career Psychologists." *Clinical Psychologist* 26, no. 1, pp. 23–33. https://doi.org/10.1080/13284207.2021.2022434

Lo, L.Y., and N. Thompson. 2025. "A Study on Varying Impact of Supervisory Relationships on Counselling Trainees' Self-Perceived Performance." *International Journal for the Advancement of Counselling* 47, no. 2, pp. 418–438. https://doi.org/10.1007/s10447-025-09596-1

Lohani, G., and P. Sharma. 2023. "Effect of Clinical Supervision on Self-Awareness and Self-Efficacy of Psychotherapists and Counselors: A Systematic Review." *Psychological Services* 20, pp. 291–299. https://doi.org/10.1037/ser0000693

Lozano, J.F., A. Boni, J. Peris, and A. Hueso. 2012. "Competencies in Higher Education: A Critical Analysis from the Capabilities Approach." *Journal of Philosophy of Education* 46, no. 1, pp. 132–147. https://doi.org/10.1111/j.1467-9752.2011.00839.x

Lucock, M.P., P. Hall, and R. Noble. 2006. "A Survey of Influences on the Practice of Psychotherapists and Clinical Psychologists in Training in the UK." *Clinical Psychology and Psychotherapy* 13, pp. 123–130. https://doi.org/10.1002/cpp.483

Luke, C., C. Bravo, H. Payne, and S. Kazanas. 2020. "Female Counselors-in-Training Self-Advocate when they Disclose Inappropriate Client Sexualized Behaviors." *Journal of Counselor Leadership and Advocacy* 7, no. 1, pp. 15–29. https://doi.org/10.1080/2326716X.2020.1729278

Lund, E.M., R.C. Wilbur, and A.M. Kuemmel. 2020. "Beyond Legal Obligation: The Role and Necessity of the Supervisor-Advocate in Creating a Socially just, Disability-Affirmative Training Environment." *Training and Education in Professional Psychology* 14, no. 2, pp. 92–99. https://doi.org/10.1037/tep0000277

Lutz, W., A.-K. Deisenhofer, J. Rubel, B. Bennemann, J. Giesemann, K. Poster, and B. Schwartz. 2022. "Prospective Evaluation of a Clinical Decision Support System in Psychological Therapy." *Journal of Consulting and Clinical Psychology* 90, no. 1, pp. 90–106. https://doi.org/10.1037/ccp0000642

Lyon, A.R., and Wright, S.L. 2024. "Mindfulness, Self-Compassion, Gratitude, and Burnout in Health Service Psychology Trainees." *Training and Education in Professional Psychology* 18, no. 4, pp. 340–349. https://doi.org/10.1037/tep0000479

Maas, C.J.M., and J.J. Hox. 2005. "Sufficient Sample Sizes for Multilevel Modeling." *Methodology: European Journal of Research Methods for the Behavioral and Social Sciences* 1, pp. 85–92. https://doi.org/10.1027/1614-2241.1.3.86

Maaß, U., F. Kühne, N. Poltz, A. Lorenz, D.S. Ay-Bryson, and F. Weck. 2022. "Live Supervision in Psychotherapy Training—A Systematic Review." *Training and Education in Professional Psychology* 16, no. 2, pp. 130–142. https://doi.org/10.1037/tep0000390

Madsen, J.W., V. Markova, L. Hernández, L.M. Tomfohr-Madsen, and S.D. Miller. 2023. "Training Practices in Routine Outcome Monitoring among Accredited Psychology Doctoral Programs in Canada." *Training and Education in Professional Psychology* 17, no. 1, pp. 98–105. https://doi.org/10.1037/tep0000389

Magnuson, S., S. Wilcoxon, and K. Norem. 2000. "A Profile of Lousy Supervision: Experienced Counselors' Perspectives." *Counselor Education and Supervision* 39, pp. 189–202. https://doi.org/10.1002/j.1556-6978.2000.tb01231.x

Mak-van der Vossen, M.C., W.N.K.A. van Mook, J.M. Kors, W.N. van Wieringen, S.M. Peerdeman, G. Croiset, and R.A. Kusurkar. 2016. "Distinguishing Three Unprofessional Behavior Profiles of Medical Students Using Latent Class Analysis." *Academic Medicine* 91, no. 9, pp. 1276–1283. https://doi.org/10.1097/ACM.0000000000001206

Manathunga, C. 2007. "Supervision as Mentoring: The Role of Power and Boundary Crossing." *Studies in Continuing Education* 29, no. 2, pp. 207–221. https://doi.org/10.1080/01580370701424650

Mandel, S. 2015. "Exploring the Differences in Expectations between Supervisors and Supervisees during the Initial Clinical Experience." *Perspectives on Administration and Supervision* 25, no. 1, pp. 4–30. https://doi.org/10.1044/aas25.

Mann, S.T., and M. Merced. 2018. "Preparing for Entry-Level Practice in Supervision." *Professional Psychology, Research and Practice* 49, no. 1, pp. 98–106. https://doi.org/10.1037/pro0000171

Marsh, T., D. Coholic, S. Cote-Meek, and L. Najavits. 2015. "Blending Aboriginal and Western Healing Methods to Treat Intergenerational Trauma with Substance Use Disorder in Aboriginal Peoples who Live in Northeastern Ontario, Canada." *Harm Reduction Journal* 12, no. 14, pp. 1-12. https://doi.org/10.1186/s12954-015-0046-1

Martin, D.G., and E.A. Johnson. 2024. *Counseling and Therapy Skills,* 5th ed. Waveland Press.

Martin, P., L. Lizarondo, S. Kumar, D. Snowdon, and S. Patman. 2021. "Impact of Clinical Supervision on Healthcare Organisational Outcomes: A Mixed Methods Systematic Review." *PLoS One* 16, no. 11. https://doi.org/10.1371/journal.pone.0260156

Martinez, M., C. Miranda, A. Lonikar, R. Cesar, K. Reed, J. Krizizke, and J. Bergkamp. 2024. "When Voices are Left Unheard: BIPOC Doctoral Student Feedback Toward a Decolonized Curriculum." *Training and Education in Professional Psychology* 18, no. 2, pp. 105–116. https://doi.org/10.1037/tep0000468

Maslach, C., W.B. Schaufeli, and M.P. Leiter. 2001. "Job Burnout." *Annual Review of Psychology* 52, no. 2001, pp. 397–422. https://doi.org/10.1146/annurev.psych.52.1.397

Maurya, R.K., and A.C. DeDiego. 2025. "Artificial Intelligence Integration in Counsellor Education and Supervision: A Roadmap for Future Directions and Research Inquiries." *Counselling and Psychotherapy Research* 25, no. 1. https://doi.org/10.1002/capr.12727

McAdams, C.J. 2020. "Perspectives on Sexual Power, #MeToo." *Academic Psychiatry* 44, no. 1, pp. 26–28. https://doi.org/10.1007/s40596-019-01146-3

McAleavey, A.A., K. de Jong, H.A. Nissen-Lie, J.F. Boswell, C. Moltu, and W. Lutz. 2024. "Routine Outcome Monitoring and Clinical Feedback in Psychotherapy: Recent Advances and Future Directions." *Administration and Policy in Mental Health* 51, no. 3, pp. 291–305. https://doi.org/10.1007/s10488-024-01351-9

McIntosh, P. 2015. "Extending the Knapsack: Using the White Privilege Analysis to Examine Conferred Advantage and Disadvantage." *Women and Therapy* 38, no. 3–4, pp. 232–245. https://doi.org/10.1080/02703149.2015.1059195 Reprinted from "White Privilege: Unpacking the Invisible Knapsack," 1989, *Peace and Freedom Magazine, July/August*, pp. 10–12.

McMahon, A. 2020. "Five Reflective Touchstones to Foster Supervisor Humility." *The Clinical Supervisor* 39, no. 2, pp. 178–197. https://doi.org/10.1080/07325223.2020.1827332

McMahon, A., and D. Hevey. 2017. ""It has Taken me a Long Time to Get to This Point of Quiet Confidence": What Contributes to Therapeutic Confidence for Clinical Psychologists?" *Clinical Psychologist Australian Psychological Society* 21, no. 3, pp. 195–205. https://doi.org/10.1111/cp.12077

McMahon, A., C. Seery, S. Moorhead, and G. O'Brien. 2023. "Analysis of Supervisory Interventions in a Transdisciplinary Youth Mental Health Service." *Psychological Services* 20, no. 2, pp. 256–266. https://doi.org/10.1037/ser0000695

McMillan, T. 2023. "Anishinaabe Values and Servant Leadership: A Two-Eyed Seeing Approach." *The Journal of Values Based Leadership* 16, no. 1. https://doi.org/10.22543/1948-0733.1428

McNamara, M.L., K.A. Kangos, D.A. Corp, M.V. Ellis, and E.J. Taylor. 2017. "Narratives of Harmful Clinical Supervision: Synthesis and Recommendations." *Clinical Supervisor* 36, no. 1, pp. 124–144. https://doi .org/10.1080/07325223.2017.1298488

Mehr, K.E., and R.M. Daltry. 2022. "Supervisor Self-Disclosure, the Supervisory Alliance, and Trainee Willingness to Disclose." *Professional Psychology, Research and Practice* 53, no. 3, pp. 313–317. https://doi .org/10.1037/pro0000424

Mehr, K.E., N. Ladany, and G.I.L. Caskie. 2010. "Trainee Nondisclosure in Supervision: What are They not Telling You?" *Counselling and Psychotherapy Research* 10, pp. 103–113. https://doi.org/10.1080/14733141003712301

Milne, D.L. 2007. "An Empirical Definition of Clinical Supervision." *British Journal of Clinical Psychology* 46, no. 4, pp. 437–447. https://doi.org/10.1348 /014466507X197415

Milne, D.L. 2009. *Evidence-based Clinical Supervision: Principles and Practice.* Wiley.

Milne, D.L. 2014. "Beyond the "Acid Test": A Conceptual Review and Reformulation of Outcome Evaluation in Clinical Supervision." *American Journal of Psychotherapy* 68, no. 2, pp. 213–230. https://doi.org/10.1176 /appi.psychotherapy.2014.68.2.213

Milne, D.L., and C.E. Watkins, Jr. 2014. "Defining and Understanding Clinical Supervision: A Functional Approach." In *The Wiley International Handbook of Clinical Supervision,* eds. C.E. Watkins, Jr. and D.L. Milne, 3–19. Wiley. https://doi.org/10.1002/9781118846360.ch1

Min, Y., and K.-E. Kim. 2024. "Supervisee Nondisclosures in Clinical Supervision: A Meta-Analysis." *Clinical Psychologist 28*, no. 2, pp. 94–110. https://doi.org/10.1080/13284207.2024.2353243

Mitchell, M.D., and S.K. Butler. 2021. "Acknowledging Intersectional Identity in Supervision: The Multicultural Integrated Supervision Model." *Journal of Multicultural Counseling and Development* 49, no. 2, pp. 101–115. https:// doi.org/10.1002/jmcd.12209

Miu, A.S., L.S. Howe-Martin, A.A. Palomin, and A. Mercado. 2024. "What do I say now?": Using a Multicultural Deliberate Practice Workshop to Improve Mental Health Providers' Responses to Microaggressions." *Training and Education in Professional Psychology* 18, no. 3, pp. 256–264. https://doi .org/10.1037/tep0000453

Moral, M., and E. Turner. 2019. "Supervision of Supervision." In *Coaching Supervision: Advancing Practice, Changing Landscapes,* eds. J. Birch and P. Welch, 188-199. Routledge.

Motley, V., M.K. Reese, and P. Campos. 2014. "Evaluating Corrective Feedback Self-Efficacy Changes among Counselor Educators and Site Supervisors."

Counselor Education and Supervision 53, no. 1, pp. 34–46. https://doi .org/10.1002/j.1556-6978.2014.00047.x

Muran, J.C., C.F. Eubanks, and L.W. Samstag. 2021. "One More Time with Less Jargon: An Introduction 'Rupture Repair in Practice.'." *Journal of Clinical Psychology* 77, pp. 361-368. https://doi.org/10.1002/jclp.23105

Murphy, M.J., and D.W. Wright. 2005. "Supervisees' Perspectives of Power use in Supervision." *Journal of Marital and Family Therapy* 31, no. 3, pp. 283–295. https://doi.org/10.1111/j.1752-0606.2005.tb01569.x

Nagy, G.A., Z. Smith, S.K. Pardej, R. Zelkowitz, B.W. Katz, B. Young, C. Sloan, J. Carpenter, A. Saulson, and C. Larson. 2024. "Development, Implementation, and Sustainment of Multicultural Peer-Consultation Teams in Distinct Mental Health Settings: An Implementation-Focused Comparative Case Study." *Training and Education in Professional Psychology* 18, no. 4, pp. 314–322. https://doi.org/10.1037/tep0000480

Nelson, M.L., K.L. Barnes, A.L. Evans, and P.J. Triggiano. 2008. "Working with Conflict in Clinical Supervision: Wise Supervisors' Perspectives." *Journal of Counseling Psychology* 55, pp. 172–184. https://doi.org/10.1037/0022-0167.55.2.172

Nelson, M.L., and M.L. Friedlander. 2001. "A Close Look at Conflictual Supervisory Relationships: The Trainee's Perspective." *Journal of Counseling Psychology* 48, pp. 384–395. https://doi.org/10.1037/0022-0167.48.4.384

Newble, D. 2004. "Techniques for Measuring Clinical Competence: Objective Structured Clinical Examinations." *Medical Education* 38, pp. 199–203. https://doi.org/10.1111/j.1365-2923.2004.01755.x

Newton, C., J.M. Steele, N. Jaber, and A. Pace. 2025. "The Cross-Racial Training Approach: A Practical Training Framework." *Training and Education in Professional Psychology* 19, no. 1, pp. 37–50. https://doi.org/10.1037/tep 0000497

Ngo, H., N. Sokolovic, A. Coleman, and J.M. Jenkins. 2022. "Teaching Empathy to Mental Health Practitioners and Trainees: Pairwise and Network Meta-Analyses." *Journal of Consulting and Clinical Psychology* 90, no. 11, pp. 851–860. https://doi.org/10.1037/ccp0000773

Nicholson Perry, K., M. Donovan, R. Knight, and A. Shires. 2017. "Addressing Professional Competency Problems in Clinical Psychology Trainees." *Australian Psychologist* 52, no. 2, pp. 121–129. https://doi.org/10.1111 /ap.12268

Norcross, J.C., and M.J. Lambert. 2018. "Psychotherapy Relationships that Work III." *Psychotherapy* 55, no. 4, pp. 303–315. https://doi.org/10.1037 /pst0000193

Norcross, J.C., and G.C. VandenBos. 2018. *Leaving it at the Office, Second Edition: A Guide to Psychotherapist Self-Care.* Guilford, ProQuest Ebook

Central. https://ebookcentral.proquest.com/lib/umanitoba/detail.action?doc ID=5401080.

Novoa-Gómez, M., O. Córdoba-Salgado, N. Rojas, L. Sosa, D. Cifuentes, and S. Robayo. 2019. "A Descriptive Analysis of the Interactions during Clinical Supervision." *Frontiers in Psychology* 10, Article 669. https://doi.org/10.3389/fpsyg.2019.00669

Nye, J., Jr. 2004. *Soft Power: The Means to Success in World Politics.* Public Affairs.

O'Donovan, A., W.K. Halford, and B. Walters. 2011. "Towards Best Practice Supervision of Clinical Psychology Trainees." *Australian Psychologist* 46, pp. 101–112. https://doi.org/10.1111/j.1742-9544.2011.00033.x

O'Donovan, A., and D.J. Kavanagh. 2014. "Measuring Competence in Supervisees and Supervisors." In *The Wiley International Handbook of Clinical Supervision,* eds. C.E. Watkins, Jr. and D.L. Milne, 458–467. Wiley.

Olk, M.E., and M.L. Friedlander. 1992. "Trainees' Experiences of Role Conflict and Role Ambiguity in Supervisory Relationships." *Journal of Counseling Psychology* 39, no. 3, pp. 389–397. https://doi.org/10.1037/0022-0167.39.3.389

Olkin, R. 2009. "The Three Rs of Supervising Graduate Psychology Students with Disabilities: Reading, Writing, and Reasonable Accommodations." *Women and Therapy* 33, no. 1–2, pp. 73–84. https://doi.org/10.1080/02703140903404788

Orlinsky, D.E., and M.H. Rønnestad. 2005. *How Psychotherapists Develop: A Study of Therapeutic Work and Professional Growth,* 1st ed. American Psychological Association.

Owen, J. 2013. "Early Career Perspectives on Psychotherapy Research and Practice: Psychotherapist Effects, Multicultural Orientation, and Couple Interventions." *Psychotherapy* 50, no. 4, pp. 496–502. https://doi.org/10.1037/a0034617

Pakdaman, S., E. Shafranske, and C. Falender. 2015. "Ethics in Supervision: Consideration of the Supervisory Alliance and Countertransference Management of Psychology Doctoral Students." *Ethics and Behavior* 25, pp. 427–441. https://doi.org/10.1080/10508422.2014.947415

Panahi, S., and A. Tremblay. 2018. "Sedentariness and Health: Is Sedentary Behavior more than just Physical Inactivity?" *Frontiers of Public Health* 6, Article 258. https://doi.org/10.3389/fpubh.2018.00258

Park, E.H., G. Ha, S. Lee, Y.Y. Lee, and S.M. Lee. 2019. "Relationship between the Supervisory Working Alliance and Outcomes: A Meta-Analysis." *Journal of Counseling and Development* 97, no. 4, pp. 437–446. https://doi.org/10.1002/jcad.12292

Pearlstein, J.G., A.T. Schmidt, E.M. Lund, L.R. Khazem, and N.H. Liu. 2022. "Guidelines to Address Barriers in Clinical Training for Trainees with Sensory

Disabilities." *Training and Education in Professional Psychology* 16, no. 3, pp. 220–228. https://doi.org/10.1037/tep0000367

Pearlstein, J.G., and P.D. Soyster. 2019. "Supervisory Experiences of Trainees with Disabilities: The Good, the Bad, and the Realistic." *Training and Education in Professional Psychology* 13, no. 3, pp. 194–199. https://doi.org/10.1037/tep0000240

Pelling, N. 2021. "Singaporean Supervisory Identity Development and its Relationship to Supervisory Experience, Counselling Experience, and Training in Supervision." *Asia Pacific Journal of Counselling and Psychotherapy* 12, no. 2, pp. 186–204. https://doi.org/10.1080/21507686.2021.1960400

Peters, H.C., S. Bruner, M. Luke, K. Dipre, and K. Goodrich. 2022. "Integrated Supervision Framework: A Multicultural, Social Justice, and Ecological Approach." *Canadian Psychology : Psychologie Canadienne* 63, no. 4, pp. 511–522. https://doi.org/10.1037/cap0000342

Phillips, J. C., M.C. Parent, V.C. Dozier, and P.L. Jackson. 2017. "Depth of Discussion of Multicultural Identities in Supervision and Supervisory Outcomes." *Counselling Psychology Quarterly* 30, no. 2, pp. 188–210. https://doi.org/10.1080/09515070.2016.1169995

Pilling, S., and A.D. Roth. 2014. "The Competent Clinical Supervisor." In *The Wiley International Handbook of Clinical Supervision*, eds. C.E. Watkins, Jr. and D.L. Milne, pp. 20–37. Wiley.

Pirelli, G., D.L. Formon, and K. Maloney. 2020. "Preventing Vicarious Trauma (VT), Compassion Fatigue (CF), and Burnout (BO) in Forensic Mental Health: Forensic Psychology as Exemplar." *Professional Psychology: Research and Practice* 51, no. 5, pp. 454–466. http://dx.doi.org/10.1037/pro0000293

Ponce, A.N., A.C. Aosved, and K. Hill. 2021. "Facilitation of Consultation and Communication between Psychology Doctoral Programs and Internships." *Training and Education in Professional Psychology* 15, no. 3, pp. 189–194. https://doi.org/10.1037/tep0000313

Proctor, B. 1986. "A Cooperative Exercise in Accountability." In *Enabling and Ensuring*, eds. M. Marken and M. Payne, 21–34. Leicester National Youth Bureau and Council for Education and Training in Youth and Community Work.

Råbu, M., C. Moltu, P.-E. Binder, and J. McLeod. 2016. "How does Practicing Psychotherapy Affect the Personal Life of the Therapist? A Qualitative Inquiry of Senior Therapists' Experiences." *Psychotherapy Research* 26, no. 6, pp. 737–749. https://doi.org/10.1080/10503307.2015.1065354

Rajesh, A., K.A. Zhang, C. Kelly, Y. Aguilar Silvan, C.K. Diehl, A.F. Obee, M.K. Wilson, V. Perez, E. Howard, S. Kang, J.B. Duong, H. Weiss, P. Sayegh, S.C. South, E.M. Manczak, J.T. Merchant, B.M. Merrill, and N.R. Eaton. 2024. "Diversity, Equity, Inclusion, Justice, and Antiracism Statements by Clinical

Psychological Science Programs." *Training and Education in Professional Psychology* 18, no. 3, pp. 183–193. https://doi.org/10.1037/tep0000452

Ranihusna, D. 2025. "The Virtual Supervision Revolution: Enhancing Counselor Competency in Tele-Mental Health Through AI-Enhanced Feedback Systems". *International Journal of Research in Counseling* 4 (1):1-11. https://doi.org/10.70363/ijrc.v4i1.277.

Räuchle, J., F. Kühne, A. Zacharias, G. Große, F. Weck, and U. Maaß. 2025. "Insights from Roleplays with Standardised Patients and Live Supervision for Psychotherapy and Counselling Training—A Qualitative Study." *Counselling and Psychotherapy Research* 25, no. 2. https://doi.org/10.1002/capr.70018

Reese, R.J., E.L. Usher, D.C. Bowman, L.A. Norsworthy, J.L. Halstead, S.R. Rowlands, and R.R. Chisholm. 2009. "Using Client Feedback in Psychotherapy Training: An Analysis of its Influence on Supervision and Counselor Self-Efficacy." *Training and Education in Professional Psychology,* 3, pp. 157–168. https://doi.org/10.1037/a0015673

Reid, L.E., H.C. Lee, M.T. Morrow, A.R. Gillem, and E. Bartoli. 2024. "Evaluation of a Multicultural Competence Curriculum in a Psychology-based Counseling Program." *Training and Education in Professional Psychology* 18, no. 3, pp. 204–212. https://doi.org/10.1037/tep0000460

Renninger, S.M., and C.E. Cavalieri. 2023. "Identification and Assessment of Problems of Professional Competence." In *Supporting Trainees with Competence Problems: A Practical Guide for Psychology Trainers,* eds. R.A. Schwartz-Mette, E.A. Hunter, and N.J. Kaslow, 79–98. American Psychological Association. https://doi.org/10.1037/0000340-006

Roberts, B.L. 2012. "Beyond Psychometric Evaluation of the Student—Task Determinants of Accommodation." *Canadian Journal of School Psychology* 27, no. 1, pp. 72–80. https://doi.org/10.1177/0829573512437171

Roberts, B., C.E. Mohler, D. Levy-Pinto, C. Nieder, E.M. Duffett, and M.A. Sukhai. 2014. "Defining a New Culture: Creative Examination of Essential Requirements in Academic Disciplines and Graduate Programs." *National Educational Association of Disabled Students.* https://www.Cags.ca/documents/publications/3rdparty/Discussion%20paper%20Essential%20Requirements%20FINAL 202014-09.

Robinson, W.L., and P.T. Reid. 1985. "Sexual Intimacies in Psychology Revisited." *Professional Psychology: Research and Practice* 16, pp. 512–520. https://doi.org/10.1037/0735-7028.16.4.512

Rocha, J., P.A. Carrola, Y. Giresunlu, and S.M. Shin. 2025. "Counseling Supervisees Perspectives of Supervisee Behaviors that Hinder the Supervision Process: A Mixed-Methods Approach." *The Clinical Supervisor* 44, no. 2, pp. 374–394. https://doi.org/10.1080/07325223.2025.2506394

Rocha, J., and G. Kemer. 2022. "What must Supervisees do to Promote Supervision? An Exploratory Sequential Mixed Methods Approach." *Clinical Supervisor* 41, no. 1, pp. 70–87. https://doi.org/10.1080/07325223.2022.2045526

Rodolfa, E., R. Bent, E. Eisman, R. Nelson, L. Rehm, and P. Ritchie. 2005. "A Cube Model for Competency Development: Implications for Psychology Educators and Regulators." *Professional Psychology: Research and Practice* 36, pp. 347–354. https://doi.org/10.1037/0735-7028.36.4.347

Rodriguez Espinosa, P., Y. Johnson-Esparza, G. López, J. Benson, N.C. Moss, R. Avila-Rieger, K.L. Venner, and S.P. Verney. 2024. "The Development and Current Directions of a Diversity Specialty Clinic: Implications for Multicultural Training in Psychology." *Training and Education in Professional Psychology* 18, no. 3, pp. 221–229. https://doi.org/10.1037/tep0000465

Rogers, B., K. Swift, K. van der Woerd, M. Auger, R. Halseth, D. Atkinson, S. Vitalis, S. Wood, and A. Bedard. 2019. "At the Interface: Indigenous Health Practitioners and Evidence-Based Practice." *National Collaborating Centre for Aboriginal Health.* Retrieved from: https://www.nccih.ca/docs/context/RPT-At-the-Interface-Halseth-EN.pdf

Rognstad, K., T. Wentzel-Larsen, S.-P. Neumer, and J. Kjøbli. 2023. "A Systematic Review and Meta-Analysis of Measurement Feedback Systems in Treatment for Common Mental Health Disorders." *Administration and Policy in Mental Health and Mental Health Services Research* 50, no. 2, pp. 269–282. https://doi.org/10.1007/s10488-022-01236-9

Rønnestad, M.H., and K. Lundquist. 2009. *Brief Supervisory Alliance Questionnaire.* Department of Psychology, University of Oslo.

Ross, L. 1977. "The Intuitive Psychologist and his Shortcomings: Distortions in the Attribution Process." *Advances in Experimental Social Psychology* 10, pp. 173–220. https://doi.org/10.1016/s0065-2601(08)60357-3

Rousmaniere, T.G., R.K. Goodyear, S.D. Miller, and B.E. Wampold, eds. 2017. *The Cycle of Excellence: Using Deliberate Practice to Improve Supervision and Training.* John Wiley and Sons, Incorporated.

Rousmaniere, T.G., J.K. Swift, R. Babins-Wagner, J.L. Whipple, and S. Berezins. 2016. "Supervisor Variance in Psychotherapy Outcome in Routine Practice." *Psychotherapy Research* 26, no. 2, pp. 196–205. https://doi.org/10.1080/10503307.2014.963730

Ruiz, F.J., I. Dereix-Calonge, and M.A. Sierra. 2019. "The Increase in Emotional Symptoms of Novice Clinical Psychology Trainees Compared with a Control Cohort." *Revista Latinoamericana de Psicología* 51, no. 3. https://doi.org/10.14349/rlp.2019.v51.n3.6

Rupert, P.A., and K.E. Dorociak. 2019. "Self-Care, Stress, and Well-Being among Practicing Psychologists." *Professional Psychology, Research and Practice* 50, no. 5, pp. 343–350. https://doi.org/10.1037/pro0000251

Safran, J.D., I. Abreu, J. Ogilvie, and A. DeMaria. 2011. "Does Psychotherapy Research Influence the Clinical Practice of Researcher–Clinicians?" *Clinical Psychology: A Publication of the Division of Clinical Psychology of the American Psychological Association* 18, no. 4, pp. 357–371. https://doi.org/10.1111 /j.1468-2850.2011.01267.x

Safran, J.D., P. Crocker, S. McMain, and P. Murray. 1990. "Therapeutic Alliance Rupture as a Therapy Event for Empirical Investigation." *Psychotherapy* 27, pp. 154–165. https://doi.org/10.1037/0033-3204.27.2.154

Safran, J. D., Muran, J. C., and Eubanks-Carter, C. 2011. "Repairing Alliance Ruptures." *Psychotherapy* 48, pp. 80–87. https://doi.org/10.1037/a0022140

Schiefele, A.-K., W. Lutz, M. Barkham, J. Rubel, J. Böhnke, J. Delgadillo, M. Kopta, D. Schulte, D. Saxon, S.L. Nielsen, and M.J. Lambert. 2017. "Reliability of Therapist Effects in Practice-based Psychotherapy Research: A Guide for the Planning of Future Studies." *Administration and Policy in Mental Health and Mental Health Services Research* 44, no. 5, pp. 598–613. https://doi.org/10.1007/s10488-016-0736-3

Schneider, D.A., E. Rodriguez-Keyes, and E.K. Keenan. 2014. "Seeing Through the Eyes of the Other Using Process Recordings." In *Clinical Supervision Activities for Increasing Competence and Self-Awareness,* eds. R.A. Bean, S.D. Davis, and M.P. Davey, 21–26. Wiley.

Schwartz-Mette, R.A. 2023. "Remediation, Counseling Out, and Dismissal." In *Supporting Trainees with Competence Problems: A Practical Guide for Psychology Trainers,* eds. R.A. Schwartz-Mette, E.A. Hunter, and N.J. Kaslow, 99–123. American Psychological Association. https://doi.org/10.1037/0000340-007

Schwartz-Mette, R.A., E.A. Hunter, and N.J. Kaslow. 2023. "Appendix C Competency Remediation Plan." In *Supporting Trainees with Competence Problems: A Practical Guide for Psychology Trainers,* eds. R.A. Schwartz-Mette, E.A. Hunter, and N.J. Kaslow, 239–242. American Psychological Association.

Schwartz-Mette, R.A., and D.S. Shen-Miller. 2017. "Ships in the Rising Sea? Changes Over Time in Psychologists' Ethical Beliefs and Behaviors." *Ethics and Behavior* 28, no. 3, pp. 176–198. https://doi-org.uml.idm.oclc.org/10.1 080/10508422.2017.1308253

Seabrook, M. 2022. ""The Golden Question". Addressing Supervisee Self-Care in Clinical Supervision." *Counselling and Psychotherapy Research* 22, pp. 1041–1055. https://doi.org/10.1002/capr.12543

Shafranske, E.P., and C.A. Falender. 2008. "Supervision Addressing Personal Factors and Countertransference." In *Casebook for Clinical Supervision: A Competency-based Approach,* eds. C.A. Falender and E.P. Shafranske, 97–120. American Psychological Association.

Shah, S., and S.R. Fishel. 2023. "Legal Issues in Working with Trainees with Problems of Professional Competence." In *Supporting Trainees with Competence*

Problems: A Practical Guide for Psychology Trainers, eds. R.A. Schwartz-Mette, E.A. Hunter, and N.J. Kaslow, 171–191. American Psychological Association. https://doi.org/10.1037/0000340-010

Shulman, L.S. 2005. "Signature Pedagogies in the Professions." *Daedalus* 134, no. 3, pp. 52–59. https://doi.org/10.1162/0011526054622015

Simionato, G., S. Simpson, and C. Reid. 2019. "Burnout as an Ethical Issue in Psychotherapy." *Psychotherapy* 56, no. 4, pp. 470–482. https://doi.org/10.1037/pst0000261

Sisko, S., and M. Rosenfield. 2025. "Cultural Responsiveness in Clinical Supervision." In *Culturally Responsive Psychotherapy, Counselling and Psychology: Practices for Inclusion and Accountability,* eds. S. Sisko, 73–94. Palgrave Texts in Counselling and Psychotherapy. Palgrave Macmillan, Cham. https://doi.org/10.1007/978-3-031-81831-8_4

Small, G.W., J. Lee, A. Kaufman, J. Jalil, P. Siddarth, H. Gaddipati, T.D. Moody, and S.Y. Bookheimer. 2020. "Brain Health Consequences of Digital Technology Use." *Dialogues in Clinical Neuroscience* 22, no. 2, pp. 179–187. https://doi.org/10.31887/DCNS.2020.22.2/gsmall

Soheilian, S.S., A.G. Inman, R.S. Klinger, D.S. Isenberg, and L.E. Kulp. 2014. "Multicultural Supervision: Supervisees' Reflections on Culturally Competent Supervision." *Counselling Psychology Quarterly* 27, no. 4, pp. 379–392. https://doi.org/10.1080/09515070.2014.961408

Spännargård, Å., S. Fagernäs, and S. Alfonsson. 2025. "Discrepancies between Guidelines, Preferences and Actual Activities in Psychotherapy Supervision." *Counselling and Psychotherapy Research* 25, no. 1. https://doi.org/10.1002/capr.12824

Spence, N., J.R.E. Fox, L. Golding, and A. Daiches. 2014. "Supervisee Self-Disclosure: A Clinical Psychology Perspective." *Clinical Psychology and Psychotherapy* 21, pp. 178–192. https://doi.org/10.1002/cpp.1829

Sterner, W.R. 2009. "Influence of the Supervisory Working Alliance on Supervisee Work Satisfaction and Work-Related Stress." *Journal of Mental Health Counseling* 31, pp. 249–263. https://doi.org/10.17744/mehc.31.3.f3544l502401831g

Stewart, D.W., and Johnson, E.A. 2023. "The Relational-Expressive Dual-Continuum Model of Clinical Supervisor Training." *Training and Education in Professional Psychology* 17, no. 2, pp. 142–148. https://doi.org/10.1037/tep0000393

Stewart, D.W., Shields, R.E., and Sinclair, C. 2025. "Application of the Canadian Code of Ethics for Psychologists to Telepsychology." *Canadian Psychology / Psychologie Canadienne.* https://doi.org/10.1037/cap0000416

Stiles, W.B. 2021. "Responsiveness in Psychotherapy Research: Problems and Ways Forward." In *The responsive Psychotherapist: Attuning to Clients in the Moment,* eds. J.C. Watson and H. Wiseman, 15–36. American Psychological Association.

Stoltenberg, C.D., K.C. Bailey, C.B. Cruzan, J.T. Hart, and U. Ukuku. 2014. "The Integrative Developmental Model of supervision." In *The Wiley International Handbook of Clinical Supervision,* eds. C.E. Watkins, Jr. and D.L. Milne, 576–597. Wiley. https://doi.org/10.1002/9781118846360.ch28

Sue, D.W., D. Sue, H.A. Neville, and L. Smith. 2022. *Counseling the Culturally Diverse: Theory and Practice,* 9th ed. Wiley.

Sukumaran, N., J. Nilsson, and A. Kim. 2025. "Racial Microaggressions in Cross-Racial Supervision: Counseling and Multicultural Self-Efficacy, Supervisory Working Alliance, and Supervisor Multicultural Competency." *Clinical Supervisor* 44, no. 2, pp. 294–311. https://doi.org/10.1080/07325 223.2025.2506392

Swift, J.K., J.L. Callahan, T.G. Rousmaniere, J.L. Whipple, K. Dexter, and E.R. Wrape. 2015. "Using Client Outcome Monitoring as a Tool for Supervision." *Psychotherapy* 52, pp. 180–184. https://doi.org/10.1037/a0037659

Tasca, G.A., L. Angus, R. Bonli, M. Drapeau, M. Fitzpatrick, J. Hunsley, and M. Knoll. 2019. "Outcome and Progress Monitoring in Psychotherapy: Report of a Canadian Psychological Association Task Force." *Canadian Psychology = Psychologie Canadienne* 60, no. 3, pp. 165–177. https://doi.org/10.1037 /cap0000181

Taylor, J.M., and G.J. Neimeyer. 2022. "The Development of the Professional Competencies Scale: Foundational, Functional, and Continuing Competencies." *Training and Education in Professional Psychology* 16, no. 2, pp. 112–120. https://doi.org/10.1037/tep0000383

Teichman, Y., E. Berant, G. Shenkman, and G. Ramot. 2023. "Supervisees' Perspectives on the Contribution of Supervision to Psychotherapy Outcomes." *Counselling and Psychotherapy Research* 23, no. 2, pp. 516–529. https://doi .org/10.1002/capr.12540

ten Cate, O., and H.C. Chen. 2020. "The Ingredients of a Rich Entrustment Decision." *Medical Teacher* 42, no. 12, pp. 1413–1420. https://doi.org/10.10 80/0142159X.2020.1817348

ten Cate, O., and D.J. Schumacher. 2022. "Entrustable Professional Activities Versus Competencies and Skills: Exploring why Different Concepts are Often Conflated." *Advances in Health Sciences Education: Theory and Practice* 27, no. 2, pp. 491–499. https://doi.org/10.1007/s10459-022-10098-7

Tepper, B.J., L. Simon, and H.M. Park. 2017. "Abusive Supervision." *Annual Review of Organizational Psychology and Organizational Behavior* 4, no. 1, pp. 123–152. https://doi.org/10.1146/annurev-orgpsych-041015-062539

Thériault, A., and N. Gazzola. 2018. "Dilemmas that Undermine Supervisor Confidence." *Counselling and Psychotherapy Research* 18, no. 1, pp. 14–25. https://doi.org/10.1002/capr.12153

Thériault, A., and N. Gazzola. 2019. "Becoming a Counselling Supervisor in Canada: Key Elements from the Perspective of Supervisors." *International*

Journal for the Advancement of Counselling 41, no. 1, pp. 155–173. https://doi.org/10.1007/s10447-018-9351-1

Thomas, J.T. 2007. "Informed Consent Through Contracting for Supervision: Minimizing Risks, Enhancing Benefits." *Professional Psychology: Research and Practice* 38, pp. 221–231. https://doi.org/10.1037/0735-7028.38.3.221

Thomas, J.T. 2014. "International Ethics for Psychotherapy Supervisors: Principles, Practices, and Future Directions." In *The Wiley International Handbook of Clinical Supervision,* eds. C.E. Watkins, Jr. and D.L. Milne, 131–154. Wiley.

Tiet, Q.Q., J. Brooks, C. Patton, B. Brownstein, and T.J. Mixon. 2024. "Specific Stressors Linked to Functional Outcomes in Psychology Doctoral Students." *Training and Education in Professional Psychology* 18, no. 4, pp. 350–358. https://doi.org/10.1037/tep0000481

Turner, L.B., A.J. Fischer, and J.K. Luiselli. 2016. "Towards a Competency-based, Ethical, and Socially Valid Approach to the Supervision of Applied Behavior Analytic Trainees." *Behavior Analysis in Practice* 9, pp. 287–298. https://doi.org/10.1007/s40617-016-0121-4

Vacha-Haase, T., N.S. Elman, L. Forrest, J. Kallaugher, S.H. Lease, J.C. Veilleux, and N.J. Kaslow. 2019. "Remediation Plans for Trainees with Problems of Professional Competence." *Training and Education in Professional Psychology* 13, no. 4, pp. 239–246. https://doi.org/10.1037/tep0000221

Valdiviezo-Oña, J., N. Ortiz-Mancheno, and C. Paz. 2025. "Clinical Supervisors' Expectations and Experiences with a Routine Outcome Monitoring System in a Psychotherapy Training Service." *Counselling and Psychotherapy Research* 25, no. 1, p. e12826. https://doi.org/10.1002/capr.12826

Vandament, M.L., C. Duan, and S. Li. 2022. "Relationships among Supervisee Perceived Supervisor Cultural Humility, Working Alliance, and Supervisee Self-Efficacy among White Supervisor and Supervisee of Color Dyads." *Training and Education in Professional Psychology* 16, no. 3, pp. 244–252. https://doi.org/10.1037/tep0000370

Van der Hallen, R. 2023. "Suicide Exposure and the Impact of Client Suicide: A Structural Equation Modeling Approach." *Archives of Suicide Research* 27, no. 2, pp. 426–438. https://doi.org/10.1080/13811118.2021.2020190

Vandette, M.-P., G. Jones, J. Gosselin, and C.S. Kogan. 2021. "The Role of the Supervisory Working Alliance in Experiential Supervision-of-Supervision Training: A Mixed Design and Multiple Perspective Study." *Journal of Psychotherapy Integration* 31, no. 4, pp. 435–451. https://doi.org/10.1037/int0000269

Van Hoy, A., and M. Rzeszutek. 2022. "Burnout and Psychological Wellbeing among Psychotherapists: A Systematic Review." *Frontiers in Psychology* 13. https://doi.org/10.3389/fpsyg.2022.928191

van Leeuwen, M.E., and J.M. Harte. 2017. "Violence Against Mental Health Care Professionals: Prevalence, Nature and Consequences." *The Journal of*

Forensic Psychiatry and Psychology 28, no. 5, pp. 581–598. https://doi.org/10 .1080/14789949.2015.1012533

Veilleux, J.C., E. Sandeen, and E. Levensky. 2014. "Dialectical Tensions, Supervisor Attitudes, and Contextual Influences in Psychotherapy Supervision." *Journal of Contemporary Psychotherapy* 44, pp. 31–41. https:// doi.org/10.1007/s10879-013-9245-9

Veilleux, J.C., and M. Scafe. 2023. "Building Program Policies in a Communitarian and Multiculturally Sensitive Training Culture." In *Supporting Trainees with Competence Problems: A Practical Guide for Psychology Trainers*, eds. R.A. Schwartz-Mette, E.A. Hunter, and N.J. Kaslow, 193–212. American Psychological Association.

Veilleux, J.C., R.A. Schwartz-Mette, and S.J. Gregus. 2022. "Development of the Standardized Supervisee Framework as a Novel Approach to Supervision Training." *Training and Education in Professional Psychology* 16, no. 4, pp. 341–353. https://doi.org/10.1037/tep0000373

Vekaria, B., T. Thomas, P. Phiri, and M. Ononaiye. 2023. "Exploring the Supervisory Relationship in the Context of Culturally Responsive Supervision: A Supervisee's Perspective." *Cognitive Behaviour Therapist* 16. https://doi .org/10.1017/S1754470X23000168

Vertue, F.M., and B.D. Haig. 2008. "An Abductive Perspective on Clinical Reasoning and Case Formulation." *Journal of Clinical Psychology* 64, pp. 1046–1068. https://doi.org/10.1007/978-3-030-01051-5_6

Volpe, U., M. Luciano, C. Palumbo, G. Sampogna, V. Del Vecchio, and A. Fiorillo. 2014. "Risk of Burnout among Early Career Mental Health Professionals." *Journal of Psychiatric and Mental Health Nursing* 21, pp. 774–781. https:// doi.org/10.1111/jpm.12137

Waltman, S.H., S.A. Frankel, and M.A. Williston. 2016. "Improving Clinician Self-Awareness and Increasing Accurate Representation of Clinical Competencies." *Practice Innovations* 1, no. 3, pp. 178–188. https://doi.org/10.1037/pri0000026

Wampold, B.E. 2015. "How Important are the Common Factors in Psychotherapy? An Update." *World Psychiatry* 14, no. 3, pp. 270–277. https:// doi.org/10.10002/wps.20238

Wampold, B.E., and E.L. Holloway. 1997. "Methodology, Design, and Evaluation in Psychotherapy Supervision Research." In *Handbook of Psychotherapy Supervision,* ed. C.E. Watkins, 11–27. Wiley.

Warlick, C.A., M. Narayan, R. Standridge Fletcher, T.P. Patterson, A. Armstrong Gala, A. Van Gorp, and N.M. Farmer. 2025. "Comparing Burnout between Licensed Professional Clinicians and Trainees." *Training and Education in Professional Psychology* 19, no. 2, pp. 97–105. https://doi.org/10.1037 /tep0000504

Watkins, C.E., Jr. 2012. "Development of the Psychotherapy Supervisor: Review of and Reflections on 30 Years of Theory and Research." *American*

Journal of Psychotherapy 66, no. 1, pp. 45–83. https://doi.org/10.1176/appi
.psychotherapy.2012.66.1.45

Watkins, C.E., Jr. 2018. "The Supervisee's Internal Supervisor Representations:
Their Role in Stimulating Psychotherapist Development." *International
Journal of Psychotherapy* 22, no. 3, pp. 63–73.

Watkins, C.E., Jr. 2020a. "The Psychotherapy Supervisor as an Agent of
Transformation: To Anchor and Educate, Facilitate and Emancipate."
American Journal of Psychotherapy 73, pp. 57–62. https://doi.org/10.1176
/appi.psychotherapy.20190016

Watkins, C.E., Jr. 2020b. "What do Clinical Supervision Research Reviews Tell
Us? Surveying the Last 25 Years." *Counselling and Psychotherapy Research* 20,
no. 2, pp. 190–208. https://doi.org/10.1002/capr.12287

Watkins, C.E., Jr. 2021. "Rupture and Rupture Repair in Clinical Supervision:
Some Thoughts and Steps Along the Way." *The Clinical Supervisor* 40, no. 2,
pp. 321–344. https://doi.org/10.1080/07325223.2021.1890657

Watkins, C.E., Jr., I.E. Cădariu, and L.I. Vîşcu. 2024a. "Extending Hoggan's
Taxonomy of Transformative Learning Outcomes to Psychotherapy
Supervisor Development." *International Journal of Supervision in Psychotherapy*
6, pp. 7–21.

Watkins, C.E., Jr., I.-E. Cădariu, and L.-I. Vîşcu. 2024b. ""Let Us begin Well
Together": A Preparation-Positivity-Purpose Checklist for Helping Beginning
Supervisors Optimize the Start of Supervision." *Journal of Contemporary
Psychotherapy* 54, no. 4, pp. 363–372. https://doi.org/10.1007/s10879-024
-09631-z

Watkins, C.E., I.-E. Cădariu, L.-I. Vîşcu, and R. Viliūnienė. 2024.
"Psychotherapy Supervision: An Invitational, Clarifying, Educational,
Empowering, and Transparent (ICEE-T) Written Agreement." *American
Journal of Psychotherapy* 77, no. 4, pp. 195–199. https://doi.org/10.1176
/appi.psychotherapy.20230048

Watkins, C.E., Jr., and J.N. Hook. 2016. "On a Culturally Humble Psychoanalytic
Supervision Perspective: Creating the Cultural Third." *Psychoanalytic
Psychology* 33, pp. 487–517. https://doi.org/10.1037/pap0000044

Watkins, C.E., Jr., J.N. Hook, J. Owen, C. DeBlaere, D.E. Davis, and D.R. Van
Tongeren. 2019. "Multicultural Orientation in Psychotherapy Supervision:
Cultural Humility, Cultural Comfort, and Cultural Opportunities." *American
Journal of Psychotherapy* 72, no. 2, pp. 38–46. https://doi.org/10.1176/appi
.psychotherapy.20180040

Watkins, C.E., Jr., J.N. Hook, H. Zhang, M.M. Wilcox, S. Winkeljohn Black, C.
DeBlaere, D.E. Davis, and J. Owen. 2025. "Revisiting Cultural Humility in
Psychotherapy Supervision: A Descriptive Status Report." *American Journal*

of Psychotherapy 78, no. 2, pp. 103–113. https://doi.org/10.1176/appi
.psychotherapy.20240008

Watkins, C.E., Jr., L.-I. Vîşcu, and I.-E. Cadariu. 2021. "Psychotherapy
Supervision Research: On Roadblocks, Remedies, and Recommendations."
European Journal of Psychotherapy, Counselling, and Health 23, no. 1, pp.
8–25. https://doi.org/10.1080/13642537.2021.1881139

Westberg, J., and H. Jason. 1993. "Providing Constructive Feedback." In
Collaborative Clinical Education: The Foundation of Effective Health Care, eds.
J. Westberg and H. Jason, 297–318. Springer.

Westwood, S., L. Morison, J. Allt, and N. Holmes. 2017. "Predictors of Emotional
Exhaustion, Disengagement and Burnout among Improving Access to
Psychological Therapies IAPT Practitioners." *Journal of Mental Health* 26, no.
2, pp. 172–179. https://doi.org/10.1080/09638237.2016.1276540

Wheeler, D.J., J. Zapata, D. Davis, and C. Chou. 2019. "Twelve Tips for
Responding to Microaggressions and Overt Discrimination: When the
Patient Offends the Learner." *Medical Teacher* 41, no. 10, pp. 1112–1117.
https://doi.org/10.1080/0142159X.2018.1506097

Wheeler, S., and M. Barkham. 2014. "A Core Evaluation Battery for Supervision."
In *The Wiley International Handbook of Clinical Supervision,* eds. C.E.
Watkins, Jr. and D.L. Milne, 367–385. Wiley.

Whipple, J., T. Hoyt, T. Rousmaniere, J. Swift, T. Pedersen, and V. Worthen.
2020. "Supervisor Variance in Psychotherapy Outcome in Routine
Practice: A Replication." *Sage Open* 1, no. 1, pp. 1–11. https://doi.org
/10.1177/2158244019899047

Wilbur, R.C., A.M. Kuemmel, and R.J. Lackner. 2019. "Who's on First?
Supervising Psychology Trainees with Disabilities and Establishing
Accommodations." *Training and Education in Professional Psychology* 13,
no. 2, pp. 111–118. https://doi.org/10.1037/tep0000231

Wilcox, M.M., A. Farra, S. Winkeljohn Black, E. Pollard, J.M. Drinane, K.W.
Tao, C. DeBlaere, J.N. Hook, D.E. Davis, C.E. Watkins, and J. Owen.
2024. "Cultural Humility and Racial Microaggressions in Cross-Racial
Clinical Supervision: A Moderated Mediation Model." *Journal of Counseling
Psychology* 71, no. 4, pp. 304–314. https://doi.org/10.1037/cou0000732

Wilcox, M.M., D.N. Franks, T.O. Taylor, C.P. Monceaux, and K. Harris. 2020.
"Who's Multiculturally Competent? Everybody and Nobody: A Multimethod
Examination." *The Counseling Psychologist* 48, no. 4, pp. 466–497. https://
doi.org/10.1177/0011000020904709

Wilcox, M.M., S. Winklejohn Black, A. Farra, D. Zimmerman, J.M. Drinane,
K.W. Tao, C. DeBlaere, J.N. Hook, D.E. Davis, C.E. Watkins, Jr., and J.
Owen. 2023. "Cultural Humility, Cultural Comfort, and Supervision

Processes and Outcomes for BIPOC Supervisees." *The Counseling Psychologist* 51, no. 7, pp. 1037–1058. https://doi.org/10.1177/00110000231188337

Williams, D.R., J.A. Lawrence, B.A. Davis, and C. Vu. 2019. "Understanding How Discrimination can Affect Health." *Health Services Research* 54, no. S2, pp. 1374–1388. https://doi.org/10.1111/1475-6773.13222

Williams, M.T., McWilliams, J., and Abdulrehman, R. 2023. "Antiracist Supervision and Training: Bringing Change to Mental Health Care." *The Clinical Supervisor* 42, no. 2, pp. 237–247. https://doi.org/10.1080/07325 223.2023.2249464

Wind, S.A., R.M. Cook, and W.B. McKibben. 2021. "Supervisees' of Differing Genders and Races Perceptions of Power in Supervision." *Counselling Psychology Quarterly* 34, no. 2, pp. 275–297. https://doi.org/10.1080/09515 070.2020.1731791

Winkeljohn Black, S., M.M. Wilcox, A.E. Pérez-Rojas, and L. West. 2025. "Identifying and Enhancing the Necessary Ingredients for Cultural Humility in Supervisory Relationships." *Psychotherapy* 62, no. 1, pp. 55–62. https:// doi.org/10.1037/pst0000538

Wisniewski, B., K. Zierer, and J. Hattie. 2020. "The Power of Feedback Revisited: A Meta-Analysis of Educational Feedback Research." *Frontiers in Psychology* 10. https://doi.org/10.3389/fpsyg.2019.03087

Wong, L.C.J., P.T.P. Wong, and F.I. Ishiyama. 2012. "What Helps and What Hinders in Cross-Cultural Clinical Supervision: A Critical Incident Survey." *The Counseling Psychologist* 41, pp. 66–88. https://doi .org/10.1177/0011000012442652

Wood, H. 2007. "Boundaries and Confidentiality in Supervision." In *On Supervision: Psychoanalytic and Jungian Analytic Perspectives,* eds. A. Petts, and B. Shapley, 23–44. Karnac. https://doi.org/10.4324/9780429478055-2

Worthen, V.E., and M.J. Lambert. 2007. "Outcome Oriented Supervision: Advantages of Adding Systematic Client Tracking to Supportive Consultations." *Counseling and Psychotherapy Research* 7, pp. 48–53. https:// doi.org/10.1080/14733140601140873

Worthington, E.L., Jr. 1987. "Changes in Supervision as Counsellors and Supervisors Gain Experience: A Review." *Professional Psychology: Research and Practice* 18, pp. 189–208. https://doi.org/10.1037/0735-7028.18.3.189

Wrape, E.R., J.L. Callahan, C.J. Ruggero, and C.E. Watkins, Jr. 2015. "An Exploration of Faculty Supervisor Variables and Their Impact on Client Outcomes." *Training and Education in Professional Psychology* 9, no. 1, pp. 35–43. https://doi.org/10.1037/tep0000014

Wright, C.V., C. Goodheart, D. Bard, B.L. Bobbitt, Z. Butt, K. Lysell, D. McKay, and K. Stephens. 2020. "Promoting Measurement-based Care and Quality Measure Development: The APA Mental and Behavioral Health

Registry Initiative." *Psychological Services* 17, no. 3, pp. 262–270. https://doi .org/10.1037/ser0000347

Xu, M., M.L. Friedlander, V. Konatakos, and K. Shaffer. 2021. "Relational Discussions in Theoretically Diverse Models of Psychotherapy Supervision: How Common are They?" *The Clinical Supervisor* 40, no. 2, pp. 303–320. https://doi.org/10.1080/07325223.2020.1861572

Yang, Y., and J.A. Hayes. 2020. "Causes and Consequences of Burnout among Mental Health Professionals: A Practice-Oriented Review of Recent Empirical Literature." *Psychotherapy* 57, no. 3, pp. 426–436. https://doi.org/10.1037 /pst0000317

Yap, K., J. Sheen, M. Nedeljkovic, L. Milne, K. Lawrence, and M. Hay. 2021. "Assessing Clinical Competencies using the Objective Structured Clinical Examination OSCE in Psychology Training." *Clinical Psychologist* 25, no. 3, pp. 260–270. https://doi.org/10.1080/13284207.2021.1932452

Yourman, D.B., and B.A. Farber. 1996. "Nondisclosure and Distortion in Psychotherapy Supervision." *Psychotherapy* 33, pp. 567–575. https://doi .org/10.1037/0033-3204.33.4.567

Zhu, P., D.T. Isawi, and M.M. Luke. 2023. "A Discourse Analysis of Cultural Humility within Counseling Dyads." *Journal of Counseling and Development* 101, no. 2, pp. 167–179. https://doi.org/10.1002/jcad.12457

About the Author

Dr. Edward Johnson, C. Psych., is an award-winning professor of clinical psychology at the University of Manitoba. He has taught courses on clinical supervision, psychotherapy, clinical research, and professional ethics. Dr. Johnson is a recognized expert in clinical supervision, who has published articles and a textbook on supervision. He regularly gives invited workshops on supervision to professional training bodies. He has served as the President of the Canadian Council of Professional Psychology Programs and as a member of the Canadian Psychological Association's Accreditation Panel.

Index

www.ingramcontent.com/pod-product-compliance
Lightning Source LLC
Chambersburg PA
CBHW071012200526
45171CB00007B/58